T0300319

ROUTLEDGE LIBRARY EDITIONS:
WORK & SOCIETY

Volume 19

THE CONCEPT AND MEASUREMENT OF INVOLUNTARY UNEMPLOYMENT

THE CONCEPT AND MEASUREMENT OF INVOLUNTARY UNEMPLOYMENT

Edited by
G. D. N. WORSWICK

Routledge
Taylor & Francis Group

LONDON AND NEW YORK

First published in 1976 by George Allen & Unwin Ltd.

This edition first published in 2024
by Routledge
4 Park Square, Milton Park, Abingdon, Oxon OX14 4RN

and by Routledge
605 Third Avenue, New York, NY 10158

Routledge is an imprint of the Taylor & Francis Group, an informa business

British Library Cataloguing in Publication Data
A catalogue record for this book is available from the British Library

ISBN: 978-1-032-80236-7 (Set)
ISBN: 978-1-032-82415-4 (Volume 19) (hbk)
ISBN: 978-1-032-82427-7 (Volume 19) (pbk)
ISBN: 978-1-003-50444-3 (Volume 19) (ebk)

DOI: 10.4324/9781003504443

Publisher's Note
The publisher has gone to great lengths to ensure the quality of this reprint but points out that some imperfections in the original copies may be apparent.

Disclaimer
The publisher has made every effort to trace copyright holders and would welcome correspondence from those they have been unable to trace.

The Concept and Measurement of Involuntary Unemployment

edited by

G. D. N. WORSWICK

for the
Royal Economic Society

London
GEORGE ALLEN & UNWIN LTD
Ruskin House · Museum Street

© George Allen & Unwin Ltd 1976

ISBN 0 04 331065 6

Preface

The papers reproduced in this collection were first presented at a conference of the Royal Economic Society on the concept and measurement of involuntary unemployment held at Durham in March 1974. Some latitude has been allowed to authors in preparing their papers for publication, but there have been no substantial departures from the original texts. The discussion at each session was opened by discussants selected from among the members of the conference. Although there is not space to reproduce the contributions here, their value to the conference as a whole should not go without recognition. Miss G. I. Little undertook the considerable task of preparing the papers for publication, for which I am very grateful; thanks also are due to Miss S. Colwell for re-typing many of the papers.

N.I.E.S.R.   G.D.N.W.

June 1975

Contents

Contributors

F. T. BLACKABY is Deputy Director of the National Institute of Economic and Social Research; he is working on a study of British economic policy 1960–74.

J. K. BOWERS is a Lecturer in Economics at Leeds University. He was previously a Research Officer at the National Institute of Economic and Social Research. His main research interest is in aspects of the British labour market, particularly labour supply and he has written a number of articles on unemployment and activity rates.

S. BRITTAN is principal economic commentator of the *Financial Times* and a Visiting Fellow of Nuffield College, Oxford. Apart from macro-economic and employment policy, he is interested in the border areas between political philosophy and political economy. His publications include *Capitalism and the Permissive Society* and *Second Thoughts on Full Employment Policy*.

A. J. BROWN is Professor of Economics at Leeds University. From 1966–73 he directed a project on U.K. regional economics at the National Institute of Economic and Social Research. He is the author of *The Framework of Regional Economics in the United Kingdom* and *The Great Inflation, 1939–51*.

M. R. FISHER is a Fellow of Downing College and a University Lecturer in Economics at Cambridge University. His previous work includes *The Economic Analysis of Labour* and *Measurement of Labour Disputes and Their Economic Effects*.

D. HARRIS has been Director of the Directorate for Social and Demographic Statistics at the Commission of the European Communities since 1973. He was previously Statistician at the Board of Trade and Statistician and Chief Statistician at H.M. Treasury and at the Central Statistical Office.

M. J. HILL is Deputy Director of a study of field social work which is being carried out in the Department of Social and Administrative Studies of Oxford University. He was previously engaged in a survey of the characteristics of unemployed men, and was senior author of *Men Out of Work*.

A. G. HINES is Head of the Department of Economics, Birkbeck College, and has been Professor of Economics in the University of London since 1972. His publications include a book *On the Reappraisal of Keynesian Economics* and numerous articles in economics and statistics journals.

RICHARD KAHN is a Fellow of King's College and Emeritus Professor of Economics at Cambridge University. He is the author of numerous articles on economic subjects, several of which have been collected into a book: *Selected Essays on Employment and Growth*.

COLIN LEICESTER is a Senior Fellow of the Institute of Manpower Studies and Editor of its quarterly review of the British labour market, *I.M.S. Monitor*. He was the author of a report, *Britain 2001 AD*, commissioned by the Post Office and containing forecasts of the British labour market in 30 years' time.

DAVID METCALF is Reader in Economics at Reading University. He has written extensively on labour issues and is particularly interested in urban labour-market problems.

RAY RICHARDSON is a lecturer at the London School of Economics. He has done research in a number of areas, including medical manpower shortages, the problems of declining urban labour markets, labour turnover, the industrial wage structure and some aspects of unemployment.

ADRIAN SINFIELD is Senior Lecturer in Sociology at Essex University. He has carried out studies of unemployment on Tyneside and in New York State. He has also been consultant on the long-term unemployed to O.E.C.D.

JIM TAYLOR is Senior Lecturer in Economics at Lancaster University. His research interests are primarily in labour economics and regional economics, and his recent publications include a book entitled *Unemployment and Wage Inflation*.

A. R. THATCHER has been Director of Statistics at the Department of Employment since 1968. He introduced the New Earnings Survey and has been responsible for many official publications, including *British Labour Statistics: Historical Abstract, 1886–1968*.

Introduction

G. D. N. WORSWICK

In October 1972 the number of registered unemployed in Great Britain recorded by the Department of Employment was 807,000; excluding the 'temporarily stopped' it was 792,000. In November, in a 'Memorial to the Prime Minister', the Economic Radicals, a group including a number of well-known academic economists, stated that the unemployment statistics were 'unreliable and even specious' and ventured the opinion that 'real unemployment' amounted to perhaps 300,000 people – half a million less than the official figure of wholly unemployed. A few weeks later the analysis of the 1971 Census of Population was published; it stated that in April 1971 there were some 1,366,000 persons who were 'economically active' but 'out of employment', a figure over half a million greater than the registered unemployed recorded by the Department of Employment at that time. Thus, within a few weeks, we had two statements which might be construed as indicating that the registered unemployment figures were in error by half a million, but unfortunately the direction of the implied error was not the same in the two cases. Meanwhile a Working Party of officials had been set up as a result of a request from the Prime Minister for an inquiry into the nature of the unemployment statistics and this Working Party duly reported in November 1972. Its principal conclusions were that the *temporarily stopped* are different from the main body of unemployed and their numbers should be presented quite separately, a practice which was immediately adopted. The Working Party, however, concluded that it was not possible to isolate a group of *short-term unemployed* or to identify categories of those alleged to be *not genuinely seeking work* or who were *unemployable*. The report argued that earlier estimates of the numbers who are seeking work but are not registered as unemployed had been greatly exaggerated in some quarters. It did not deal directly with the allegation of the Economic Radicals that over half of the registered unemployed were in some sense not really unemployed. Since no reasons had been given for this assertion, however, there was not much for the Working Party to come to grips with.

Mr Samuel Brittan's suggestion of a Royal Economic Society conference on the concept and measurement of involuntary unemployment was thus a timely one. The President of the Society, Sir Donald MacDougall, invited me to act as convener of the conference and in this task I was assisted by a committee, consisting of Mr Roger Thatcher, C.B.E., of the Department of Employment, Dr Malcolm Fisher of Downing College, Cambridge, and Mr Samuel Brittan of the *Financial Times*. Dr Howard Thomas of the London Graduate School of Business Studies acted as organising secretary. The papers which are published here were commissioned as a result of our deliberations and were presented at St Aidan's College at the University of Durham in March 1974.

The simplest way to arrange a conference of this kind is to make a list of persons known or believed to be engaged in research in the field concerned and to invite them to submit papers. We did in fact take this step of listing potential contributors, keeping in mind the Society's desire to encourage especially younger economists, but we took a further step of drawing up a plan for the conference which enabled us to indicate to various contributors where we thought their contribution might fit in most appropriately. The plan consisted of three questions and an afterthought.

Question 1: What is it that we ought to measure? Does economic theory provide any guide? Keynes had introduced the concept of involuntary unemployment (or so we thought until we saw Richard Kahn's paper). Was this attempt to distinguish involuntary and voluntary unemployment merely technical, or was it intended to raise issues of personal and social responsibility? When a man loses a job and cannot obtain another it may be his own fault; it is not difficult to recognise such cases. Equally it is not difficult to find instances where there is nothing the individual could do to prevent the loss of a job; we then say it was the fault of the economic or social system. The importance of the distinction is obvious. If the responsibility lies with the individual, social action to help him find another job may be desirable, but it is certainly not necessary. But if the loss of the job lies outside his own control, then only social action can provide any remedy. Was this what Keynes was after

with his distinction? We thought it would make a good start to invite
one of those who was associated with Maynard Keynes at the time
of writing the *General Theory* and ask him how it looked at the time
and how the concept stood up to the subsequent experience of full
or near-full employment, and who better than Lord Kahn? Clearly
we needed an account of the recent development of the theory of
job search and we were grateful to Dr Malcom Fisher for under-
taking such a survey. Those two papers were, we thought, sufficient
to open a discussion of the first question, but then we had a stroke of
luck in an offer from Professor Hines to submit a paper which, in
part, was a critique of the new job-search theory and thus fitted
neatly into the opening session.

Question 2: What is it that we do measure? Different countries use
different methods for estimating the numbers unemployed. In Britain
the main source of statistics has always been the unemployment register held in the offices of the Department of Employment. There are
other sources of information, such as the Census of Population already mentioned, and in 1973 we had the first results from the
General Household Survey, which is a continuous interview survey
covering about 15,000 households in the course of a year.

It is important for any discussion of the significance of unemploy-
ment statistics to know precisely what they do measure and for
Britain we were very fortunate to have a paper from the Chief
Statistician of the Department of Employment, Mr Roger Thatcher.
In addition, we invited Mr Harris, Head of the Statistics Division of
the E.E.C., to explain the activities of the Statistical Office of the
Commission as regards unemployment. We also invited Professor
Wiles of the London School of Economics to say something about
how the measurement of unemployment was tackled in communist
countries. He reproduced for us calculations he had already made
for the Soviet Union and added new calculations for Yugoslavia.
Since the former had already been published in a 'Note on Soviet
Unemployment by US Definitions', *Soviet Studies*, April 1972,
Professor Wiles' paper is not reprinted here.

*Question 3: Does what we measure match up to what we ought to
measure?* Unemployment statistics are needed as 'economic indicators' and as 'social indicators'. In the former aspect they are needed

by those concerned with the overall management of the economy. But they can also be used, as the Working Party put it, as a measure of 'social distress'. It would seem that we needed one paper on the suitability or otherwise of the present unemployment statistics in the context of overall economic management and another on their value as social indicators. In particular, was it the case that the pain or distress of unemployment in the 1970s was, as was widely believed, much less than it had been, for example, in the 1930s, on the grounds that the duration of unemployment was shorter and that if unemployment did occur the income support was much better than it used to be?

The afterthought was to cover the eventuality that the answer to Question 3 might be negative. To take one specific instance, we already knew that the unemployment figures had been subject to attack in their role as 'economic indicators'. Specifically, it had been suggested that as a measure of the pressure of demand for labour the figures for unfilled vacancies were more suitable than the unemployment figures. It would be worth seeking a report on research which had been done in this area.

In the event we adhered to this broad framework, with some alterations in the second part of the programme. Sessions 1 and 2 turned out as has already been described. In the third session we had three papers dealing with various aspects of unemployment, mainly as economic indicators. Mr Bowers and Professor Brown dealt especially with the relations between unemployment and vacancies. Mr Taylor presented a paper on unemployment and labour hoarding. In the fourth session we concentrated on the social aspects of unemployment, taking papers from Mr Hill, Mr Sinfield, and Messrs Metcalf and Richardson, as well as a paper by Mr Leicester on duration. The final session returned to the economic problem with a long paper by Mr Brittan, dealing both with economic theory and with the management of the British economy, and with another paper by Mr Blackaby dealing, among other things, with the changing attitudes towards the unemployment indicator as a trigger for expansionist policies.

Part I

WHAT IS IT THAT
WE OUGHT TO MEASURE?

Chapter 1

Unemployment as seen by the Keynesians[1]

RICHARD KAHN

There can be no doubt that Keynes' distinction between 'involuntary' and 'voluntary' unemployment presented in his *General Theory*[2] was the basis for his analysis of the causes of unemployment and for his formulation of the remedies. The unemployment in question was 'involuntary'. Keynes' concept of 'involuntary unemployment' constituted a resounding challenge to the established school of thought. Keynes was entitled to regard Pigou's *Theory of Unemployment*[3] as representative of the classical (now often called 'neo-classical') school.

But here I am confronted by a difficulty. The first use of the term 'involuntary unemployment' of which I am aware occurs in Pigou's popular little book, *Unemployment*, published in the Home University Library series in 1914: 'Unemployment clearly does not include all the idleness of wage earners, *but only that part of it which is, from their point of view and, in their existing conditions at the time, involuntary.*' [4] A few pages further on Pigou wrote: 'The amount of unemployment . . . in any industry is measured by the number of hours' work . . . by which the employment of the persons attached to or occupied in that industry falls short of the number of hours' work that these persons would have been willing to provide at the current rate of wages under current conditions of employment.'[5] Pigou proceeded to base his definition on the drafting of the National Insurance Act. A man is not disqualified from being treated as unemployed because 'in the district where he was last ordinarily employed' he refuses work offered 'at a rate lower, or on conditions less favourable, than those which he habitually obtained in his usual employment in that district, or would have obtained had he continued to be so employed', or if he cannot find work 'in any other district, otherwise than at a rate of wage lower, or on conditions less favourable, than those generally obtained in such district by agreement between associations of employers and of workmen, or, failing any such agreement, then those generally recognised in such district by good employers'.[6]

Excluded under this definition of unemployment are the incapacitated, the old, those who are idle from choice, including vagrants, and those on strike.

Dennis Robertson also used the term 'involuntary unemployment' in his early book.[7] To me it was a shock when, in the course of preparing this paper, I discovered that the term 'involuntary unemployment' was already in use in 1914, and that of all possible people it was used by Pigou, whom in 1936 Keynes was going rightly to denounce for publishing a book (in 1933) which was exclusively concerned with unemployment which was not involuntary.

I suffered another shock when I reread the first few pages of Pigou's 1933 book. Although Keynes was right in maintaining that the subject of Pigou's book was 'voluntary unemployment', in these opening pages Pigou implicitly denied this. Without actually using the term 'involuntary unemployment', Pigou wrote: 'A man is only unemployed when he is *both* not employed and *also* desires to be employed. . . . The desire to be employed must be taken to mean desire to be employed at current rates of wages. . . . A man is not unemployed because he would like to work if the current wage were £1,000 a day but does not so like when the current wage is 5s a day.'[8]

By taking the ridiculous figure of £1,000 a day, Pigou seriously obscured the argument. What about a man who would like to work if the current wage were 6s a day but does not so like when the current wage is 5s a day?

Pigou's book is, in fact, largely devoted to unemployment of that kind of man. Apart from frictional and cyclical unemployment, unemployment is due to the real wage being maintained – usually through collective bargaining or State action – at a level above that at which everybody would be employed.[9] As Keynes pointed out, the title of Pigou's book was ' something of a misnomer'. The book is not really concerned with unemployment but with the question of 'how much employment there will be . . . when the conditions of full employment are satisfied'.[10]

Pigou appears to have been unaware of the inconsistency between his definition of unemployment in the first few pages of his book and the subject-matter of his book. Keynes appears to have overlooked the first few pages. And even if Pigou became aware of his inconsistency after reading Keynes' criticism of his book, he did not draw attention to it in his review of the *General Theory*.[11]

I come now to Keynes' own treatment in his *General Theory*. Coming back to it after a period of 38 years, I feel that Keynes made unnecessarily heavy weather of the concepts involved. He had said about as much as needed to be said in explanation of the idea of 'involuntary unemployment' in the statement that 'the population generally is seldom doing as much work as it would like to do on the basis of the current wages. . . . More labour would, as a rule, be forthcoming at the existing money-wage if it were demanded.'[12] But Keynes' formal definition of 'involuntary unemployment' ran as follows:

'Men are involuntarily unemployed if, in the event of a small rise in the price of wage-goods relatively to the money-wage, both the aggregate supply of labour willing to work for the current money-wage and the aggregate demand for it at that wage would be greater than the existing volume of employment.'[13]

I am today unable to see why it was necessary to be so complicated. The quotation which I have given from page 7 of the *General Theory* seems perfectly adequate. Or, in slightly different words, there is involuntary unemployment to the extent that, at the current money-wage and with the current price-level, the number of men desiring to work exceeds the number of men for whose labour there is a demand.

There seems to be no need to introduce into the argument the effect of a small fall in the real wage on the supply of labour. (The effect is in either direction according as the supply curve of labour is forward or backward rising.) And the fact that a fall in the real wage is associated with an increase in employment resulting from an increase in demand does not seem to be particularly relevant.[14]

I deliberately concluded my last paragraph but one with the words 'the number of men for whose labour there is a demand' rather than with the words 'the number of men employed'. The reason is that apart from 'involuntary unemployment' there is 'voluntary unemployment'. Furthermore, Keynes excluded 'frictional unemployment' – due to 'temporary loss of work of the "between jobs" type' – from his definition of 'involuntary unemployment'.[15] He also excluded the effect of 'intermittent demand for highly specialised resources', and, I suppose, 'seasonal unemployment'.

Keynes did not, in so many words, refer to 'structural unemployment', but clearly he would have included it in 'involuntary unemployment'.

'Full employment' means the absence of 'involuntary unemployment', but not of 'voluntary', 'frictional', or presumably 'seasonal' unemployment. This leads to a simpler definition of 'involuntary unemployment'. It is the kind of unemployment which is non-existent when the situation is such that an increase in effective demand will fail to bring about an increase of output because it will fail to result in additional employment.[16]

'Cyclical unemployment' is, of course, included in 'involuntary unemployment'. Keynes did not use the term; in a letter to Beveridge he referred to it as 'so-called', and pointed out that 'I am mainly concerned with what you call cyclical unemployment.'[17]

In the same letter to Beveridge, Keynes referred to a kind of unemployment which is not, I think, mentioned in the *General Theory* – 'unemployment due to a lack of homogeneity in the units of labour'. Clearly he had in mind the 'unemployability' which arises when an inefficient man is either unable to accept a wage at which it would be worthwhile employing him because the wage system does not permit it, or is unwilling to accept such a wage, possibly because he fares better as an unemployed man. This kind of unemployment is also, of course, excluded from 'involuntary unemployment'. It is, in a sense, part of 'voluntary unemployment'.

Keynes' treatment of 'voluntary unemployment' also seems to me unsatisfactory. It is 'due to the refusal or inability of a unit of labour, as a result of legislation or social practice or of combination for collective bargaining or of slow response to change or of mere human obstinacy, to accept a reward corresponding to the value of the product attributable to its marginal productivity'.[18] That seems reasonably straightforward.

But Keynes seems to me to place too much weight on the idea that a reduction of money-wages 'would lead, through strikes or otherwise, to a withdrawal from the labour market of labour which is now employed'.[19] In criticising Pigou's *Theory of Unemployment*, Keynes stated that 'the whole of Pigou's book is written on the assumption *that any rise in the cost of living, however moderate, relatively to the money-wage will cause the withdrawal from the labour market of a number of workers greater than that of all the existing unemployed.*'[20] It is not clear why it matters whether the withdrawal would be greater or less than the number of existing unemployed. Presumably it would depend on the magnitude of the rise in the cost of living.

But the real obscurity lies in the concept of withdrawal. Presumably Keynes did not mean the withdrawal which is the manifestation of a strike. What he should have said is that the repercussions of a rise in the cost of living would result in a reduction in the demand for labour to the point at which the supply price of the amount of labour demanded is equal to the new real wage. The repercussions would take the form of a wage–price vicious spiral, which brings restraints on demand into operation, monetary and possibly fiscal, automatic as well as possibly discretionary. Keynes emphasised that organised labour is normally unwilling to accept a cut in the money-wage, whereas it often does tacitly accept a moderate fall in the real wage. This after all is the normal procedure between wage settlements, when the cost of living is constantly rising, in all those industries in which wages are governed exclusively by national settlements. But this fact does not need to be cited in order to define voluntary unemployment.

At this point I have to make an apology. It was only in the process of preparing this paper that I discovered – too late for remedial action – that it is not I who should be presenting this paper. Referring to Keynes' new concept of involuntary unemployment, presented in his *General Theory*, David Worswick, in his letter of invitation to me, expressed the hope that I would give an account of how Keynes and my colleagues and I 'saw things at the time and how far this has been borne out by subsequent experience'.

As I have been asked to be personal, I am bound to say – partly in a self-defensive, and partly in a shame-faced, attitude – that the concept of 'voluntary unemployment' left me very cold and that I took no interest in the wording of Chapter 2 of the *General Theory* which I have been criticising. I began the study of economics in June 1927. Between then and the date of publication of the *General Theory* (February 1936), unemployment was always over 10 per cent (the number unemployed was always over 1,200,000) and in the early 1930s rose above 20 per cent (in 1932 unemployment was about 22 per cent – a total of 2,700,000).[21] To my young mind the important thing was to demonstrate analytically the hollowness of the arguments that were used against the adoption of the obvious remedies. I recollect feeling particularly incensed by a talk to the Marshall Society by Sir Horace Wilson, Permanent Secretary of the Ministry of Labour until 1930 and then official Industrial Adviser to the government, in which he purported to show that real unemployment did not amount to much, after you had deducted those whose names appeared on the register only because they had staked out a precautionary claim to unemployment benefit but became absorbed again into industry within a day or two, after you had deducted those changing from one job to another or suffering seasonal or cyclical unemployment, those attached to industries in which 5 per cent or less were unemployed, the 'temporarily stopped' and the 'casuals', after you had deducted those who were of doubtful employment value and were unable or unwilling to accept any alternative employment on offer, and after you had deducted women and juveniles and men over 50 years of age. I was still more incensed by the notorious White Paper of 1929.[22] The contribution of the Ministry of Labour was based on the assumption that the only persons who could benefit from State-aided works were those fitted for heavy manual work, excluding those highly skilled men whose skill would deteriorate as a result of being employed on heavy manual work. In the Memorandum by the Ministry of Labour it was stated that, although the total number unemployed amounted to slightly over one million, in each year the total number who had registered as unemployed was 3 to 4 million. The White Paper also included the Treasury Memorandum in which the notorious Treasury view was expounded.

It seemed clear that, however successfully the problem of unemployment was tackled, there would still remain a considerable amount of 'involuntary unemployment'. It seemed to me unimportant exactly how 'involuntary' and 'voluntary' employment were defined.

Fortunately, Roy Harrod took the matter seriously and, although he did not receive the galley proofs of the *General Theory* until June 1935, his criticisms did result in considerable improvement.[23]

In the course of his friendly review of the *General Theory* published in November 1936,[24] Jacob Viner commented on Keynes' definition and treatment of involuntary unemployment.[25] In his reply Keynes wrote that 'this part of my book is particularly open to criticism. I already feel myself in a position to make improvements.'[26]

Beveridge, in the middle of 1936, read a highly critical paper about the *General Theory* at the London School of Economics.[27] At a time when there were $1\frac{3}{4}$ million unemployed, he completely denied that there was any evidence for the existence of 'involuntary unemployment'. He did, of course, admit the existence of 'cyclical unemployment', but had failed to realise that Keynes included this in 'involuntary unemployment' and that, though he did not use the phrase, it was the main subject of Keynes' book. Beveridge would have preferred to call 'voluntary unemployment' 'wage unemployment'. He utterly rejected Keynes' analysis and conclusions.[28] In 1944 Beveridge published his *Full Employment in a Free Society*, with a motto on the title page – 'Misery generates hate.' He wrote that: 'A new era of economic theorising about employment and unemployment was inaugurated by the publication in 1936 of the *General Theory* – by J. M. Keynes.' And later on: 'There may be unemployment through chronic deficiency of demand for labour, as well as unemployment through fluctuation of demand and through friction.'[29]

While the *General Theory* was going through the press, Joan Robinson wrote her *Essays in the Theory of Employment*, published in 1937. In her first essay, entitled 'Full Employment',[30] she completely broke away from Keynes' definitions and classifications. Keynes read the draft and, as Joan Robinson wrote in 1972, 'it can be taken that he accepted my amendment to his definition of full employment'.[31] Keynes had written to her: 'I like very much indeed the section on full employment and I think your treatment is a considerable improvement.'[32] On the assumption of perfect mobility of labour, Joan Robinson thought it 'plausible to say, in a general way, that in any given conditions of the labour market there is a certain more or less definite level of employment at which money wages will rise, and a lower level of employment at which money wages fall.

Between the two critical levels there will be a neutral range within which wages are constant.' 'The point of full employment is the point at which every impediment on the side of labour to a rise in money wages finally gives way.'[33] In her 1972 comment Joan Robinson wrote that, at the time when the essay was written, 'there had been no experience of continuous near-full employment. I certainly would not want to maintain now that there is some particular level of unemployment (say, a statistical record of 3 per cent) at which money-wage rates will remain constant.'[34]

The second essay in Joan Robinson's book was on 'Mobility of Labour'. She wrote: 'No precise meaning can be given to the notion of full employment for a system within which mobility of labour is imperfect, unless it is taken to imply a state of affairs in which there is complete full employment all round, that is to say, in which no available labour is unemployed in any district or in any occupations.'[35] In the course of correspondence with Keynes about a draft of this essay, she wrote: 'I am more doubtful about the idea that the amount of employment which is full employment is increased. This seems to reintroduce the idea of voluntary unemployment, which I tried to get rid of in my other essay (on "Full Employment"). *Individuals* may be voluntarily unemployed if they are holding out for a wage, but it is very hard to make sense of the idea of net voluntary unemployment.'[36]

Joan Robinson was doubtful also about the concept of 'frictional unemployment'. 'It is impossible to . . . give precision to the concept of specifically "frictional" unemployment, because it is impossible to make a hard-and-fast distinction between unemployment which is due to frictions and unemployment which is due to a deficiency of effective demand. . . . It seems preferable to say that full employment, in a precise sense, can never be attained so long as frictions exist, rather than to use "full employment" in an imprecise sense in which it can be said to be attainable, such unemployment as remains being vaguely attributable to frictions.'[37] Keynes did not entirely agree. 'I have found what you have to say about this is very helpful and stimulating, but I still consider that it is a necessary concept to which it is possible to give a useful interpretation.'[38]

David Worswick, in his letter of invitation, asked me to state whether it was conceived at the time that Keynes' new concept of involuntary unemployment 'constituted a step forward in positive economics. Or was the main implication a moral shift, in the sense that an implication of the concept is that, however much he may try, the individual unemployed man can do little to help himself?' My answer is that the concept of involuntary unemployment provided part of the basis of the Keynesian analysis of the causes of unemployment and of his exposition of the remedies. There was very little moral shift. This was partly because even a classical or 'neo-classical' economist could scarcely attach much, if any, blame to the normal unemployed individual for being unemployed.

But on the effect of an all-round rise in money-wages in a closed system Keynes did make an extremely important break-through. . . . He was the first to demonstrate that, apart from the effect of a tightening of the state of credit resulting from the quantity of money being held constant, prices would rise in the same proportion, and neither the real wage nor the levels of output and employment would be altered, except in so far as the rise created an expectation of a further rise, in which case investment would be stimulated and, therefore, output and employment would rise.

The final question which David Worswick addressed to me was how far our feelings at the time about Keynes' concepts 'had been borne out by subsequent experience'. My own answer is that the distinction between 'voluntary' and 'involuntary' unemployment, while important conceptually as a basis for the Keynesian system of analysis, has not proved to have any practical significance, either in terms of statistical measurement or in terms of targets or objectives.

In his own popular writings, such as *Can Lloyd George Do It?*, published in 1929, and *The Means to Prosperity*, published in 1933, Keynes had not found it necessary to make the distinction. In the course of *The Means to Prosperity*, Keynes did, however, comment that 'many people are trying to solve the problem of unemployment with a theory which is based on the assumption that there is no unemployment'. In *How to Pay for the War*,[39] published in *The Times* in November 1939 and in book form in February 1940, Keynes simply stated that output could be increased by absorbing a 'considerable proportion of the 12¾ per cent of insured workers who were unemployed (in the fiscal year 1938-9), by bringing into employment . . . boys, women and retired or unoccupied persons, and by more intensive work and overtime'.

In 1937 unemployment was still 1·5 million (over 10 per cent).

Nevertheless, in three articles published in *The Times* on the 12th, 13th and 14th January 1937, under the title 'How to Avoid a Slump,'[40] Keynes sounded a note of caution:

'It is widely agreed that it is more important to avoid a descent into another slump than to stimulate . . . still greater activity than we have. . . . It is natural to interject that it is premature to abate our efforts to increase employment so long as the figures of unemployment remain so high. . . . I believe that we are approaching, or have approached, the point where there is not much advantage in applying a further general stimulus at the centre. . . . The economic structure is unfortunately rigid. . . . The later stages of recovery require a different technique. To remedy the condition of the distressed areas, *ad hoc* measures are necessary.'

Keynes was relying, not on the distinction between 'involuntary' and 'voluntary' unemployment, but – in effect, though he did not use the term – on the concept of 'regional unemployment', which had not figured in the *General Theory*. 'We are in more need today of a rightly distributed demand than a greater aggregate demand.'

Keynes' attitude, displayed in these articles, is summarised in the following sentences: 'Three years ago it was important to use public policy to increase investment. It may soon be equally important to retard certain types of investment, so as to keep our most easily available ammunition in hand for when it is more required.'[41]

In September 1930 unemployment amounted to about 2,300,000 – above 19 per cent. In a memorandum addressed to a Committee of Economists of the Economic Advisory Council, Keynes replied to a questionnaire which had been issued to the members. In answering the question 'how much too high are (a) real wages, (b) money wages?' Keynes wrote:

'If we put our present abnormal unemployment at 1,500,000, I should estimate (in order of magnitude) that one third of this is due to the world slump, five-ninths to the emergence of a transfer problem and one-ninth to excessive real wages. . . .'

Thus, in the language of the *General Theory*, 'voluntary unemployment' amounted to about 165,000. Including this 'voluntary unemployment', 'normal', as opposed to 'abnormal', unemployment amounted to about 800,000 (about 6½ per cent). What Keynes meant by 'normal' unemployment was not made clear.

This order of magnitude, suggested by Keynes in 1930, was confirmed, rather remarkably, in a Memorandum written by Keynes in the Treasury in June 1942 about a draft Paper on 'National Income and Expenditure after the War'. In the course of the Memorandum Keynes wrote:

'Unemployment is due to –
  (a) the hard core of the virtually unemployable (100,000);
  (b) seasonal factors (200,000);
  (c) men moving between jobs (300,000);
  (d) misfits of trade or locality due to lack of mobility (200,000); and
  (e) a deficiency in the aggregate effective demand for labour.

Pre-war statistics are not a useful guide, because at all recent dates before the war (e) played a significant part, whereas the probable heavy demands for labour in excess of the supply indicated below suggest that the most convenient "standard" assumption for the post-war period is the virtual absence of this factor. An attempt which was made by an official committee in 1935 to estimate the probable minimum level of unemployment, excluding factor (e), arrived at a figure of 760,000 or 6 per cent. Subsequent experience suggests that this survey may have overestimated the number of the virtual unemployables, an actual count of insured persons who have been classified as unsuitable for ordinary industrial employment made on March 16th 1942 having brought out a figure below 25,000, compared with 150,000 *plus* 50,000 casuals' unemployment assumed by the Committee. In view of this a "standard" assumption of 800,000 men unemployed (or a somewhat larger aggregate of men and women together, 10 women reckoning as the equivalent of 7 men for the purpose of this calculation), which is about 5 per cent of the insured population, seems quite sufficient, made up as indicated above between brackets. It compares with about 120,000 equivalent men, or less than 1 per cent, unemployed at the present time, when factors (b) and (c) above are virtually inoperative. Experience after the last war shows that, apart from a brief transitional period in the spring of 1919, the above estimate would have been more than enough to cover the facts up to the end of 1920, although Professor Pigou reckons that the slump must be regarded as having commenced in the summer of 1920. This should, however, be regarded as a standard assumption rather than as a prophecy.'

The argument based on an over-estimation of the number of unemployables should have led to a figure less than, rather than greater than, 760,000. If 760,000 represented an unemployment percentage of 6, a percentage of 5 would mean a figure of 635,000. It seems to me that the figure of 800,000 must have been an error, and the correct figure was 600,000.[42]

Beveridge, in his 1944 *Full Employment in a Free Society*, pointed out that between the two wars unemployment had averaged 14 per cent. In the second war unemployment had been reduced to ½ per cent or less. For five months from June to October 1937, at the top of a cyclical fluctuation, the unemployment rate in London (one of the prosperous areas of Britain) was 6 per cent or a little less. 'By this calculation a figure of about 5 per cent is sometimes reached, as the minimum reserve of labour.' Beveridge, however, arrived at 3 per cent 'as a conservative, rather than an unduly hopeful, aim to set for the average unemployment rate of the future under conditions of full employment. In numbers it means about 550,000 persons.'[43]

In December 1944 Keynes wrote to Beveridge warmly congratulating him on his book. In a postscript he mentioned a point of criticism. 'No harm in aiming at 3 per cent unemployment, but I shall be surprised if we succeed.'

So in September 1930 Keynes regarded 6½ per cent unemployed, or 800,000, as 'normal', as opposed to 'abnormal'. In January 1937 he took the rather curious line, defended by his fear that the authorities might run out of ammunition for combating unemployment, that with unemployment at over 10 per cent – over 1 million – only regional measures for reducing it should be adopted. In June 1942 Keynes may have argued that 5 per cent – about 600,000 – was the probable minimum. By this Keynes did not mean that it would be unwise or dangerous to bring the figure down lower, but that this figure probably indicated the maximum success which could be expected from full employment policy. Hence his statement to Beveridge that there was no harm in aiming at an average of 3 per cent but it was an optimistic objective.

I have chosen these three occasions on which Keynes faced the question what, in some sense or other, constituted a quantitatively low level of unemployment – one in 1930, one in 1937 and one in 1942 – to illustrate my contention that the development of Keynes' thinking on the distinction between voluntary and involuntary unemployment, as published in the *General Theory* in 1936, is not matched by any parallel development of his method of arriving at full employment targets in terms of actual levels of unemployment.

POSTSCRIPT

In the course of the conference I became even more convinced that the distinction between voluntary and involuntary unemployment, while very important conceptually, had not proved important in relation to statistical measurement. Some of the time of the conference was devoted to the idea that, while some people did voluntarily give up their jobs, many of these before long became involuntarily unemployed.

NOTES

1 Dr Donald Moggridge (who, in October 1975, became Professor at the University of Toronto), the editor of the later volumes of Keynes' writings published by the Royal Economic Society, has been of great help to me in the preparation of this paper. Those of Keynes' writings to which I refer which have not yet been published will be published in due course in the Royal Economic Society edition.

For the extract near the end of my paper from a Memorandum written by Keynes in the Treasury, I thank the Controller of Her Majesty's Stationery Office (Public Records Office and Crown Copyright materials).

2 J. M. Keynes, *The General Theory of Employment, Interest and Money*, completed in December 1935 after five years' work (dating from the publication of *A Treatise on Money* in 1930) and published by Macmillan in 1936; republished in 1973 as Volume VII of the Royal Economic Society edition of Keynes' writings.

3 A. C. Pigou, *The Theory of Unemployment*, Macmillan, 1933. The manuscript had been read by Dennis Robertson, more pious in his attitude towards earlier economists than even Pigou, and Robertson had made very valuable suggestions for improvement. It is of interest that at the time when Dennis Robertson wrote his *A Study of Industrial Fluctuation*, published by P. S. King in 1915, his thinking was ahead of that of Keynes, who, criticising an early draft, seemed 'inclined to doubt a fall even in the monetary demand price for

consumable goods, and to refer the decline in the consumptive trades to a diversion of productive energy into constructional industry' (Robertson, ibid., p. 221n). Robertson commented on this view on p. xii of his new Introduction to the reprint of his book issued by the London School of Economics in 1948.

4   A. C. Pigou, *Unemployment*, Williams and Norgate, 1914, p. 14. (The italics are Pigou's.)

5   Ibid., p. 16.

6   Ibid., pp. 16, 17. Pigou referred in a footnote to the White Paper, Cd 5991, p. 3.

7   Dennis Robertson, op. cit., p. 210.

8   Pigou, *The Theory of Unemployment*, pp. 3, 4. (The italics are Pigou's.)

9   Ibid., pp. 252, 253.

10 Keynes, *General Theory*, p. 275.

11 Pigou, 'Mr J. M. Keynes' General Theory of Employment, Interest and Money', *Economica*, May 1936. In the course of this review Pigou reaffirmed his own attitude. He wrote (p. 131) that Keynes 'tacitly assumes that his full employment (above which no increase can be brought about by additions to effective money demand) is equivalent, allowance being made for frictions and so on, to maximum possible employment, i.e. to the situation at the peak of a boom. But this need not be so. Wage earners may exercise a continuous pressure directed to keep rates of real wages above what is compatible with maximum possible employment. So far as they do this, enhancements in money demand for labour will not be able to raise employment permanently to the boom level, because they will be offset by rising money wages.'

12 Keynes, *General Theory*, p. 7.

13 Ibid., p. 15. (The italics are Keynes'.)

14 The *General Theory* is based, on the whole, on the economics of the short period. It was assumed that short-period supply curves were rising curves. Work done by J. G. Dunlop and Lorie Tarshis threw doubt on this assumption. Keynes rightly attributed his error to me and pointed out that, if in fact the real wage remains constant when the demand for labour rises, 'it would be possible to simplify considerably the more complicated version of my fundamental explanation', particularly in Chapter 2, in which the concepts of 'voluntary' and 'involuntary' unemployment are explained. And 'my practical conclusions would have, in that case, *a fortiori* force' (*Economic Journal*, March 1939, reprinted in the Royal Economic Society edition of the *General Theory*, p. 401).

15 Keynes, *General Theory*, p. 16.

16 Ibid., p. 26.

17 Volume XIV of the Royal Economic Society edition, p. 56.

18 Keynes, *General Theory*, p. 6.

19 Ibid., p. 8.

20 Ibid., p. 277 (the italics are Keynes'). See also p. 13.

21 As a result of the adoption of a recommendation by an Inter-Departmental Working Party, whose *Report* (Cmnd 5157) was issued in November 1972, the number of those 'temporarily stopped' is now no longer included in the published figures for the total number and for the percentage of the unemployed, but is published separately. Nowadays it is usually a small percentage of the total, but in the early 1930s it was roughly one-quarter of the total.

22 Cmd 3331.

23 See Royal Economic Society edition, Volume XIII, pp. 528, 537 and 543.

24 Jacob Viner, 'Mr Keynes on the Causes of Unemployment', *Quarterly Journal*

of Economics, November 1936; reprinted in R. Lekachman (ed.), *Keynes' General Theory*, Macmillan, 1964.
25 Lekachman, op. cit., pp. 236–8. Incidentally Jacob Viner forestalled J. G. Dunlop and Lorie Tarshis in questioning Keynes' assumption that real wages and volume of output are inversely correlated (ibid., p. 237).
26 *Quarterly Journal of Economics*, February 1937; reprinted in Royal Economic Society edition, Volume XIV, p. 110.
27 It was circulated privately under the title 'Employment Theory and the Facts of Unemployment'. There is a copy among the Keynes papers.
28 For Keynes' comments in a letter to Beveridge, see Royal Economic Society edition, Volume XIV, pp. 56–9. For the 'mass of statistics' referred to in Beveridge's reply see *Economica*, November 1936 and February and May 1937.
29 W. H. Beveridge, *Full Employment in a Free Society*, George Allen and Unwin, 1944, pp. 93 and 97.
30 Reprinted in Joan Robinson, *Collected Economic Papers*, vol. 4, Basil Blackwell, 1973, pp. 176–98.
31 Ibid., p. 174.
32 Royal Economic Society edition, Volume XIV, p. 137.
33 Joan Robinson, *Collected Economic Papers*, Vol. 4, pp. 178, 182.
34 Ibid., p. 175.
35 Joan Robinson, *Essays in the Theory of Employment* (2nd ed.), Macmillan, 1947, p. 41.
36 Royal Economic Society edition, Volume XIV, p. 140. (The italics are Joan Robinson's.)
37 Joan Robinson, *Essays in the Theory of Employment* (2nd ed.), p. 42.
38 Royal Economic Society edition, Volume XIV, p. 142.
39 These three pamphlets are republished in *Essays in Persuasion*, Royal Economic Society edition, Volume IX.
40 When I prepared this paper, I was taken by surprise by these articles, which I had forgotten. Unfortunately I did not have time before delivering the paper to track down the following articles, etc. by Keynes: Chairman's annual address to the National Mutual Life Assurance Society, 24th February 1937; 'Borrowing for Defence', *The Times*, 11th March 1937; 'Borrowing by the State', *The Times*, 24th and 25th July 1939; 'Crisis Finance', *The Times*, 17th and 18th April 1939; 'Will Rearmament Cure Unemployment?', *The Listener*, 1st June 1939. These articles will be reprinted in due course in one of the volumes of the Royal Economic Society edition. This will also include relevant papers of the Economic Advisory Council, about which a book by Mrs Susan Howson and Professor Donald Winch will be published in 1976.
41 It thus becomes clear that one of the considerations in Keynes' mind in January 1937 was the importance of retaining a reserve army of unemployed to meet the requirements of a higher rate of rearmament, which Keynes thought it impolitic to advocate until the end of the following month, by which time the government had indicated a readiness somewhat to speed up rearmament.
42 These figures have been carefully checked against a xerox copy of the original stencilled version. The difficulty of reconciliation is enhanced if the 760,000 included women and the 800,000 was a 'male equivalent', indicating a considerably higher actual aggregate, ten women being reckoned equivalent to seven men.

43 This figure is based on a consistently higher post-war level for the insured population than existed in the 1930s. In his official Report, *Social Insurance and Allied Services*, Cmd 6404, 1942, Beveridge had assumed an average unemployment percentage of $8\frac{1}{2}$. This was partly due to caution. But in addition Beveridge had not yet appreciated the possibilities of a successful full employment policy.

Chapter 2

The New Micro-economics of Unemployment

MALCOLM R. FISHER

Keynes' massive analytical contributions of the thirties[1] seemed to deny traditional micro-economic studies of the firm and the household any meaningful functions in the explanation of the movement of the strategic factors in an economy, such as output and employment. At the hands of his most enthusiastic supporters resource allocation was accorded an insignificant role and the earlier emphasis accorded to relative prices as signals for expansion and contraction in largely decentralised decision-making economies was lessened, qualified or denied. Did Keynes provide adequate alternative sets of indicators to help frame individual firm and household decisions? Some would say that he did by his stress on income effects, which, in real terms, can be interpreted as quantity effects. Among these we may list changing levels of stocks of goods or of job openings in firms, and changing levels of stocks of goods or of reserve job potential in households.

Keynes' theory did, at least in part, clarify major sources of thrust, or the lack thereof, in an economy, but in conveying this important point tended to understress the need for the general acceptance of the 'product', which could not be taken for granted in a decentralised economy. In short, both macro-economic and micro-economic aspects have a part to play in the evolution of a decentralised economy. Keynes' contribution showed up the imbalance of thought in these matters, but the enthusiastic response for his correctives led to premature dismissal of the more traditional analysis. The new micro-economics of unemployment should be seen as an attempt to update micro-economics in the face of Keynes' strictures. It will be our claim

that concern for resource allocation is a *sine qua non* for successful
expansion of output and employment in a decentralised economy,
and that the signalling processes confronting firms and households
have important functions to perform. The nature of these signals is
imperfectly understood. Yet acceptable governmental policies cannot
result until the co-ordination mechanism is better appreciated.
Global policies for employment or inflation control may, without
adequate attention to micro-economic conditions, serve to intensify
the very strains they are designed to allay.

We shall begin then with a summary of the theory of the household
and of the firm, oriented in each case to the special problems arising
in employment markets. This means that the analysis is somewhat
one-sided, but we cannot hope to deal adequately with it all at one
time. What we must do is keep in purview the key interacting influences operating through product and other factor markets.

Right at the outset we must remind ourselves that a central feature
of our Society is investment, both in men and in goods, either or
both being undertaken by firms and by households. This means that
all participants in the economic process are involved in decision-
taking over time and in the processes of accumulation and decumula-
tion. Since these changes take place in a minimum of two already
distinguished classes of capital, human and non-human, there is an
important co-ordination problem to be resolved, one that occurs and
recurs as the range of products, factors and skills is broadened, and
the number of relevant time intervals is increased. For all practical
purposes a planning individual's lifetime is subdivided into many
points of review, so that the notion of consumption or depreciation,
and of investment or appreciation, is of relevance to each. We follow
convention in paying less attention to investment in numbers of men,
though we falter if we do not recognise that, at each moment of time,
Society comprises the activities of a mixture of generations, the composition of which is dependent upon the rate of population growth,
the character of migration and the mortality experience. We follow
the course of assuming that at any time the pattern of activity in an
economy is principally determined by those within the active
earnings span, though qualified by the actions of the remainder.
Since investment is important right across the community, both
short- and longer-run decisions matter. Dominance of the short run,
especially if pessimistic in tone as compared with earlier experience,

would serve to dry up investment. But all records show that the turnabout comes and investment resumes. We are concerned with the extent and speed of needed adjustments, rather than the extremes of the drying up of investment or of its unlimited pace.

Keynes' analysis sharply depicted problems of co-ordination between investment and savings markets, and between real and money markets, but, naturally for that time, he did not consider investment in human capital. Co-ordination problems across human–nonhuman investment categories, an important subset of the more general allocation set of products and factors, were not his concern. For some purposes this may not matter, but as a basis for more general policy prescriptions appropriate to all seasons it cannot be reliable. Since the economic conditions against which Keynesian corrective measures have been discussed have changed a great deal since the thirties, for which they were diagnosed, a good degree of caution is required.

THE HOUSEHOLD

The important issue here is how the individual detects patterns of likely developments in the economy, and of possible changes in the social environment, relevant to his own sphere of influence and livelihood. As a planning individual he is ascribed a set of goals, the relative evaluation of which he privately reaches, the whole being set out in the framework of a utility function. These include goods desired, services offered, assets sought, time allotted; all being combined within the preference set. This set, in a multi-period model, the only one relevant to investment decisions, contains within it intended capital totals at the termination of the planning horizon, while the formulation of the utility pattern itself is premised upon the past accumulated experience of goods, skills and assets, together with associated allotments of time. Bad investments, poor quality goods purchased, job dismissals, etc., all serve to qualify subsequent planning patterns. They enter the analysis through the 'givens' of the utility function in just the same way as entrepreneurial capacity enters the production function of the firm. But the latter is objective rather than subjective. The strict counterpart in a more general model of the firm would be the planning criteria or utility function too. On the other hand, the objective equivalent to the production function in household theory is the set of skill functions, which have only been recognised as relevant constraints on household behaviour in recent years. The characteristics here are also qualified by past experience. The multiple choice problems confronting an individual threaten to make any theory unwieldy if not tautologous. Yet this risk must be run unless we are to truncate the decision process in meaningless ways. This point has even more force when we face up to the problems posed by uncertain knowledge. The art – and it is an art – in theorising is to impose constraints in such a way as to retain the theory's essence without destroying, or excluding, relevant choice criteria. In this process the methods of pure science have merit, adding complication only when existing analysis is found wanting. In the present instance we have noted such a deficiency in relation to human capital acquisition. For this purpose we should recognise that there are several facets of immediate importance. These include investment in skill and accumulating work experience, and investment in information, for, even under assumptions of subjective certainty, training and experience can lift the quality of information upon which planning is premised. This is true *a fortiori* under uncertainty.

The main elements of such a theory have been set out by Becker[2] and Fisher,[3] both of whom impose a set of fairly strong restrictions on their models. With the latter as a base, we proceed to modify the analysis so as to bring out more clearly the role as signals assigned to price and quantity effects, and the motivations to job and occupation search, and to market withdrawal in particular.

If all individuals' decision-making under perfect certainty were consistent there would be no problem of search to consider. But such a circumstance if attained is not likely to be maintained for long, save in some type of Elysium where impediments of every kind, including access to knowledge, have been removed. Inconsistent plans tend to be sorted out through market changes, in which all potential participants may take part. Among the forms of participation may be the investment in trying to acquire better market knowledge.[4] Such investment requires both goods and time, each being affected by budget, time and skill constraints. This investment will only be undertaken if the prospect of utility gain exceeds expected costs. Further pursuit of search after some point will encounter rising costs, though there may be a range where added experience yields increasing returns. Were such increasing returns to persist without limit, all other activities would be forgone. This is not the case in practice and, even where time available seems the only effective constraint at any stage, search would be curtailed in any one direction because of the heterogeneity of search needs, not all of which benefit from complementarities, and because of the need for inputs to maintain productive search effort, many of which have to be financed through earnings from employment. This point is only made to answer those who point to the ever-increasing returns from search. There is here an essential parallel to the theory of the firm. Within any time interval, diminishing returns will set in for a firm, even though there are through time further gains to be made by investment in search. Search is really only an intermediate activity designed to improve access to other forms of activity. It is not often regarded as an end in itself. One is not really doing very much damage by omitting it from the utility function altogether. Yet we must admit that, over an interval, one may absolutely revel in search, or alternatively come to detest it. Where it matters is in the search (production) function, where the anticipated wage vintages for any input of skill are likely to be raised by search effort, current and anticipated. There comes a point in relation to the overall plan where further effort of this type yields diminishing returns as compared with other types of effort and eventually a balance is struck in relation to all activities that may be engaged in. Then there is no further pay-off, given the potential alternatives available, including those across anticipated price and wage vintages, from redirecting one's time, effort, goods and assets. Such an equilibrium may contain within itself an intention across time towards positive search for different wage vintages, because of anticipated deviations in skill opportunities, or because planned investment in skill, including that to offset depreciation, will require it. Not every participation in search is inconsistent with long-term planning under subjective certainty. The product of search can be a rapidly depreciating asset. Positive degrees of participation in search may be entirely consistent with equilibrium.

The interesting cases arise where this equilibrium pattern is disturbed. Disturbance takes the form of failure to attain in practice the characteristics of the plan. Let us concentrate upon disturbances that come through the labour market and produce diminished outlets for the skill offered. Initially these may show up as diminished work opportunities offered at existing rates of pay. For the individual this means that further search effort will be required to ensure the placing of any defined pattern of skill. Recontracting for an individual is no longer automatic and firms will be anxious to reappraise their labour force, in essence gaining more marginal value per unit of skill at the ruling wage rate. Maintenance of wage rates gives no prescriptive right to retention of labour services. Maintenance of labour services, as through tenure, gives no prescriptive right to the wage rate. This must follow, for the unit of engagement, the firm, has not got its own property rights guaranteed in real terms. This is as true of the State. Even where firms are forced to operate under a last in, first out arrangement by union pressure, rigidity thereby created only serves to increase costs of adaptation and extend the number of labour contracts severed. Whether a wage rate falls or not depends upon the way the occupational category as a whole is affected by the adjust-ment. If the effects are confined to a rearrangement of the relative profitability of firms, reshuffling in the labour market is likely to leave the wage rate patterns substantially intact, though, for some, active search is required to ensure reabsorption. When a downward move in profits occurs that affects one occupation or a range of occupations, the initial effects may be those of dismissal, layoff, or short-time, but the necessary reduction of costs by the firms serves to alter the relative plentitude of supplies of labour in such a way as to lower the relevant wage rates. This adjustment may take the form of the maintenance of money-wage rates but be associated with contracting of labour of higher relative efficiency, or the relative fall in wage rates in money with the maintenance of efficiency, or a mixture of the two. More people are inevitably going to pass through the unemployed pool and there will be greater participation in search than at equilibrium. Either way receipts of labour will diminish and, if they are a very important contributor to demands for products, the demand curve for labour will be pushed further to the left. Whether the adjustment process takes place predominantly through falls in wage rates, or through extended unemployment would seem in principle immaterial to this outcome. Rigidity of wage rates may serve to concentrate the unemployment upon particular categories of labour, which in welfare terms may be thought disadvantageous.

This adds another dimension to the controversy of the thirties over the relevance of wage cuts as corrective measures for unemployment in a closed economy – the relative stabilities of wage rates and unemployment during any adjustment process.[5] It would seem that the composition of the changing wage bill as between employment and wage rate changes may be less important than the variation in the total, depressing effects on the economy being fostered by a rapid fall in the aggregate wage bill through its further depressing influence on product revenues.

Where diminution in demand for labour falls with some severity on an occupational skill that is fairly clearly differentiated, it is only a matter of time before the wage rate gives. Something will depend upon the aggressiveness of any union organisation and its ability to order the supply of labour. In most cases its powers will be moderate and the general, more competitive, easing of wage rate pressures will apply. The important point to grasp is that a downswing in demand works through both employment and wage rates and, like an outgoing tide, takes longer to show its strength where the bottlenecks are greatest. But the tidal pressures eventually become dominating. Individuals' reactions will differ according to the degree of specialisation in their skills. Where these are readily transferable the effects will be less obvious in wage rate terms than where the persons are occupation-specific. Then wage rate cuts will be more readily accepted for, if improvement in trade is to be expected, investment costs are more likely to be recouped in this way unless unions can in some way ensure maintenance of employment by shifting the burdens of adjustment on to other workers.

But we move too fast. A fall in an industry's demand may not spread elsewhere. Labour of a range of skills is laid-off and we must distinguish the main alternative categories of reactions. These in turn will depend upon the anticipated length of the decline in trade. Where the effects are expected to be temporary, even though lengthy, labour without financial reserves, or which is unable to bolster income by other employment in the meantime, will search diligently for jobs outside the industry, in either the same occupation or a less desired one, paying a price through either a lower money-wage rate or utility forgone in the process. Labour that is not mobile will take cuts in pay either directly, to ensure recontracting as quickly as possible, or indirectly, where, through search, it endeavours to show that its quality, wage for wage, is better than that of alternative employees. Indirectly then the end result will be that the less efficient workers will be unemployed. Either flexible or inflexible wage rate systems will tend to concentrate unemployment on the least suitable employees. Put differently, in a declining market forces will operate so as to enable employers to detect more accurately patterns of heterogeneity in labour performance and then to select least-cost combinations of workers. The façade of homogeneity of work performance characteristic of more normal times cracks under strain. In this process both employers and workers will have played their part. The intensity of the search process is likely to undermine the coherence of any union organisation if the fall in the demand for the industrial product is considerable. But this argument assumes that the pressures for immediate recontracting for jobs are strong. Longer sighted employees who see a likely improvement in trading conditions may search for and detect vintages of firms who are likely to come out of the present situation with more robust profitability than others. After all some go bankrupt. This search takes time, but there may be rewards for waiting greater than making erroneous decisions for the longer term, if costs of subsequent switching are adjudged high. Hence in any group of workers there will be those who plan short and those who plan long, for assumed given background wealth conditions. Insofar as background conditions are more favourable the possibility of long-term planning, whether or not it is availed of, is greater.

What have we said then? Industry that is afflicted by slump may select employees from workers who differ in skills and in background conditions, whether of assets or of household reserves of labour, in potential for investment in search or in minimum time scales for adaptation. It is hard to draw general conclusions for such a complex pattern of workers. Slump hits markets first by short-time, layoff or dismissal and eventually by wage rate reductions. The lowest levels of skill, insofar as they are industry-specific, will suffer partly by decline in wage rates, but certainly by persistence of unemployment unless they can sufficiently reduce their acceptance wage. The more skilled workers will be prepared to take wage cuts if continuity of employment is vital to their skill status, otherwise they will divide according to length of planning horizon into those who must search and recontract speedily, though with some downgrading in skill, and those who can plan long, take note of the current industry experience and endeavour to gain a fresh contract in a firm that is likely to be more robust in future. Some in all skills will be tempted to quit the industry. Among these will be some who would do so anyway, but are induced by events merely to bring forward in time the date at which such transference is beneficial.

Where demand falls and unemployment becomes general, search will be the more pressing for the less well-endowed or the short-term planners. These must directly or indirectly suffer losses in net pay even if they regain employment. Those who have invested heavily in skill have much to lose and they will either react by taking pay cuts to maintain continuity in employment, or take time in searching for new jobs if the psychological and physical efficiency of their effort will not be impaired by unemployment. Persistent membership of the unemployed pool may go with the lower rungs of skill, where downgrading in job requirements does not keep step with the easing in wage rates, as well as with those who choose to use their time in unemployment to invest in search to improve their long-term position.

He would be a brave man who, in the event of falling demand, elected to forgo recontracting, period-by-period, to seek a better job, on the ground that complete specialisation on search is likely to be more productive. Such a behaviour pattern may be more common in times of fairly even trade or improving trade. If there is any gain from saying that one quit to get a better job rather than admitting one was laid-off, premature quitting may have some point. Where, as in the United States, distances may be large, it could be true that tapping a localised job market might require complete specialisation in search for a period. It is unlikely to be true in Britain save for very localised occupational activities. If the point of Alchian's argument[6] about the advantages of specialisation in search is that there is no need to distinguish between dismissal and voluntary recognition of unacceptable recontracting arrangements, we have no quarrel with him. What we do believe is that persistence in employment is desirable either for skill efficiency or for psychological reasons, and that the potential costs of discontinuity in employment through time must be weighed carefully before one elects to specialise in search.

In conditions of boom workers would presumably be willing to spend longer in search than they would in slump; psychological attitudes will be more favourable, budget constraints less severe, and longer-term planning more manageable for an enhanced number; voluntary unemployment should hence be more common. We presume, though we do not know, that the less skilled workers will be relatively more fussy about job selection in these circumstances than the more skilled. If so their resistance to premature acceptance of bargains is likely to push up the wage rate for a defined type of skill, or to lower the quality of skill acceptable to employers at a given wage rate, or a mixture of the two. Wage rate rises relative to price rises eventually put constraints upon further expansion in the economy.

This far we have assumed that the change in trading conditions was unanticipated. But it might have been foreseen, just as after two miners' strikes in three years firms and households can be expected in future to engage in contingency planning. If to a degree slump conditions are foreseen in intensity, though not necessarily in timing, a number of workers in the industry or industries will have taken precautionary steps already. We should not therefore be surprised if some, who have as it were paid the insurance premium, act less urgently to recontract. A general slump is a different matter. Even stockpiling of assets will not ensure liquidity of assets at an expected price. Here it is imperative that if any action is taken it should be taken by the State, for, as in the case of the public good, no-one has an interest in bearing the insurance cost unless the community as a whole participates.

This brings us up against the range of arguments normally discussed under uncertainty. Uncertainty relates to the nature of job openings, of product and asset market conditions, to the terms attaching to jobs and products on offer, and to the appropriate length of planning horizons. Investment in search, like investment in capital equipment or in skill, involves the weighing of an uncertain return against that available elsewhere both within and across categories. This may provide added motivation for diversification in allotment of time as between search and market activities at a moment of, or over, time. The regularity of return through time of the same unskilled persons to the unemployed pool may imply that the costs of search to lift themselves out of this situation, with its hazards of intermittent unemployment, are too high as compared with the lot they currently suffer. But this has got to be viewed against access to other, non-human, resources. To a degree these provide a means of reducing risk, by providing a degree of self-protection or insurance which enables employment transfers to be made that are not open to others. Yet the absence of non-human resources is not always an acceptable excuse. Some could reach this position if earlier they had forgone leisure or somewhat higher earnings in order to train or acquire experience. All choice involves risk of error, but many take decisions of this character even in adverse times. Nor is the willingness to take a long view inevitably confined to those with means. An important corollary for policy comes in here. Corrective measures for unemployment should not be framed in such a way as to discourage self-help through the provision of subsidies to those who could take these personal investment decisions.

Throughout this section we have omitted to mention the monetary subsidies available to the registered unemployed. In the short run these make unemployment more tolerable and extend the interval devoted to search. In the long run they may serve to raise the money-wage rates of employees, thus making the monetary differential between work and non-work greater than at the time of the introduction of benefits. Apart from this point, it is easier to handle the problem if we neglect such benefits and the effects of marginal tax adjustments.

EMPLOYER SEARCH

Employers have to match quality of product with price offered for all inputs they seek. We concentrate upon labour. Under competition the value of the marginal product of labour will be equal to the effective wage rate, differentials in quality being matched by differential wage rates, so that no cost reduction can be obtained by regrouping. But this assumes the absence of associated costs of hiring labour. Yet these may be important. Information on labour quality is not cost-free. Many firms may elect to maintain personnel departments, such are the relative cost-savings by a specialisation of this function within the firm. If information was cost-free there would be nothing to impede firms dismissing and hiring moment by moment, but even in the case where information costs tend towards zero, time of employers must be allotted to selection of inputs, and time is money. Even for stationary demand conditions this applies, for a worker's depreciation with age at some point exceeds any gains from experience. Hence grading and regrading is inevitable. Where product conditions are changing the argument is reinforced. As property rights of labour are vested in the worker, it is up to employers to adapt terms and conditions of employment to secure services at minimum cost for desired levels of output. As the choice of period over which their planning goals (presumably profit maximising) must be fulfilled is arbitrary, this criterion must be interpreted as relating to the associated period, and not to time periods selected in some unrelated context such as calendar months or years.

Firms then have an interest in limiting turnover, but to what degree? This is an extremely complex problem. As workers within an occupation class tend over a range to improve in performance through greater familiarity with the work, there are inducements to retain them until depreciation in effort tends to dominate. But firms are competing with other firms, often in different industries, for workers in particular occupational classes, and the cut-off point for recontracting as opposed to engaging fresh labour will depend upon the wage costs for the various categories. Further the workforce in a firm in any occupation will be a mixture of workers of different employment experience if the firm expects to remain in business for many periods. Added complexity arises when we note that workers have different take-off points for alternative opportunities, and we recognise that the problem of selection and grading of potential workers from outside the firm imposes costs of search, both in goods and in time. What we are saying is that time costs of screening a labour force sought by a firm can never be zero, more usually there are costs both in time and in goods. Yet minimising search costs for given product output is not an end in itself. As with labour–capital mixes it is the cost of the mixtures that must be compared, in this subsection concentrating for the present upon the balancing of marginal productive quality improvement against extra costs of search. Search costs are not a *deus ex machina* determining turnover. They serve to qualify the desired degree of turnover emanating from productivity considerations.

In the sphere of search there are also benefits to be gained from familiarity. The accumulating records of experience with previously contracted workers operates over a range to promote their re-engagement. The larger the firm and the more substitutable the occupational openings available the greater is the opportunity for a worker to secure regular re-engagement, period-by-period, with the firm. But for reasons indicated there comes a point where filling vacancies with fresh recruits from outside appears cheaper than re-engagement. The benefits from retention of those for whom the information costs are small are counteracted relative to cost by the anticipated extra productive contribution of new recruits, for whom the potential, but not yet the actual, quality can be assessed.

Search takes time, but production conditions are rarely so stringent that waiting costs become absolute in relation to labour inputs. Firms may elect not to re-engage, but await a favourable opportunity for hiring on the external market. The existence of positive vacancies at any time is not at odds with the theory of the competitive firm, even under subjective certainty. There would seem no reason to think otherwise for more monopolistic market situations either. Or again, sometimes a firm may retain for a period a worker whose services are less sought after, to keep production flowing until a suitable successor is found. This case is the counterpart for the firm to Professor Alchian's example of the worker who prefers to become unemployed to specialise in search.[7] Employers may leave vacancies in order to specialise in search, though, as with the earlier case, they can scarcely specialise completely without going bankrupt.

We have noted that internal labour markets may – over a range – enable costs of labour to be reduced. This will be more true the larger and more diversified the firm. On the other hand, the larger the firm the easier it is to amortise the costs of a personnel department, so that expertise in sifting new recruits works against this. There are always cost limits to the expansion of internal markets.

Our discussion has assumed that workers have exclusive property rights in the skills they possess. Hence the marginal productivity advantage of the worker must be assigned to him through the pay packet. It is a necessary reward to the worker to bring forth the degree of skill. But some skills provided by a worker can be exclusive to a firm, of no advantage in alternative opportunities for employment. For these the employer will be prepared to pay, expecting to amortise the cost through expected revenues from products. To secure these he must minimise the risk of transference of the labour offering the specific skill. A purely marginal extra wage may be paid to these people to inhibit turnover. In practice such cases are often dealt with by the offer of pensions, for which all benefits are deferred. The determination of the portion of a person's skill that is specific to a firm must be difficult to impute and one would expect to find a fairly competitive market in pensions, with graded deferment of benefits in operation.

Of more immediate concern is the action of a firm confronted with a fall in demand for its product. Will it try to reduce its labour force right across the board, or will it be selective in its retentions? The answer is implicit in the case discussed, but a few points deserve mention. If the firm expects to remain as a profit-making entity, it will be maintaining a certain establishment and still producing at least insofar as variable costs can be covered. We call non-labour inputs retained 'capital'. Certain types of labour are likely to be more complementary with capital than others over the output variation range involved. Dismissals or short-time will be concentrated elsewhere. It is impossible to say *a priori* whether these will be the more or less skilled. Insofar as some workers contribute specific services to the firm, they are likely to be retained also. Where discharge now is likely to result in deterioration of skills, and firms anticipate that the dismissals are likely to be common across the industry, they may consider that relatively greater ietention is desirable because search costs will be relatively larger for this category when trade recovers. This argument rests upon a degree of complementarity between overhead costs of a personnel department, and certain input categories in the search process. Such labour retentions under any head may involve fulltime or short-time (even zero-time) working. The last named has come to be known as labour hoarding.

When product demand falls in an industry which is occupation-specific, the reduction in new and recontracted demand for labour leads to unemployment and some possible reductions of minimum teims for re-engagement by workers themselves. We have argued that, where the loss of continuity in skill is deemed important to the worker, some sacrifice in pay may be made. These relaxations in terms of contract enable firms to adjust their patterns of demand for labour. Where no such shadings in terms occur, because of short-term rigidities imposed by unions, the rationing of jobs to labour that unemployment provides will enable a different pattern of selectivity to be pursued by firms. The pattern of relative wage rate adjustment merely qualifies the mix of labour openings offered, though it

may have some bearing on allocative efficiencies. These wage adjustments will be sensitive to the degree of occupation-specificity of
labour. Here we have concentrated on the totally specific case.

When demand declines become more general across industries at large, opportunities for alternative employment diminish
and downward revisions in labour demand in turn accentuate
product price falls. Unemployment becomes widespread, though its
pattern depends upon the differential movements in wage rates. The
important point to grasp is that large-scale unemployment is perfectly consistent with highly flexible prices and wages. Rigidity of
wages is in no sense fundamental to the argument. Naturally the
rigid and flexible price cases may well differ in the intensity and
length of the adjustment process.

The amelioration of the condition belongs to the discussion of the
lower turning point of the cycle upon which Keynes is very informative, though the Pigou effects have also some part to play.

The reverse case – that of expansion of demand – deserves brief
comment. Industry-specific expansion leads to greater demand for
labour, but, since selection takes time, vacancies will mount and
recontracting will become more common. Since industry-specific
workers see better prospects ahead, they may become more selective
as to job opportunities and in the interim they may prefer to remain
unemployed. Vacancies and unemployment can coexist. The selective
employment of workers will be important and is analysed elsewhere –
in brief it is largely the converse of the earlier case of industrial
contraction.[8]

Widespread industrial expansion means that search become harder,
costing more in time and in goods. Vacancies mount but workers,
faced with a wider range of good alternatives, may take longer in
choosing. It is here that Alchian's argument for the benefits of complete specialisation on search comes into its own, though the price of
discontinuities in work performance must be reckoned in. Bidding
for labour will drive up wage rates, and the more enterprising firms
may try and be ahead of their rivals in order to obtain the services of
the better qualified labour. We must note here the need to distinguish
between high and rising wage rates. A firm that offers higher wage
rates than its rivals will attract the higher quality labour, but it
cannot ensure that this will continue when other firms emulate it.
Property rights are vested in labour. Nevertheless, there may be

50   INVOLUNTARY UNEMPLOYMENT

segregation in equilibrium between high-paying and low-paying
firms, but the counterpart in quality will be the segregation into high
and low quality groupings; labour costs could be uniform per unit
of output across firms. In expanding demand, raising wage rates and
staying ahead may be a means of cost-saving for a firm through
reduced turnover, but as other firms fight back its competitive edge
can become blunted as the boom wanes. The use of a higher than
general market wage rate to lure workers and to reduce turnover only
makes sense in periods of expansion – it offers no advantage in
equilibrium, when it only raises labour costs of production differ-
entially unless matched by quality advantages.

MARKET INTERACTION

We have said enough to show that unemployment and vacancies may
be expected to coexist at any time, even under the most competitive
conditions and in equilibrium. Not all unemployment can be laid at
the door of disequilibrium forces. Nevertheless periods of diminishing product demand are likely to be periods of growing unemployment relative to vacancies, whilst periods of expanding demand are
likely to be periods of diminished unemployment relative to vacancies. The level of employment in an occupation and, a fortiori, an
economy does have an effect on search costs, at least in relation to
their distribution between employers and employees. At times of
substantial unemployment these costs are likely to fall especially
heavily on those seeking work. At times of labour scarcity the search
costs are likely to fall especially heavily on employers.

No theory of involuntary unemployment seems essential to explain
the emergence of unemployment, and even its persistence over
reasonable intervals of time, at quite high levels of intensity. The
problems of maintaining reasonable alignments between capital
stocks and flows, a central feature of trade cycle analysis, is enough
to account for the reinforcing effects of declines and expansions over
intervals of time. These are inevitable under conditions of changing
tastes and technology, quite apart from well-intentioned actions of
governments, working through monetary, fiscal or price instruments
internally, or exchange rates and tariff measures externally. Perhaps
the main new feature we have emphasised is that labour services
have an important capital aspect to them, as do inputs to facilitate

search. The capital stock adjustment problem is by no means limited to physical assets.

This leaves us with two aspects to consider. What role, if any, is left for a theory of involuntary unemployment? What policy measures should we favour to restrict the wide swings in economic activity that cause so much personal distress? These are large questions and our reactions must be brief, and somewhat provocative.

INVOLUNTARY UNEMPLOYMENT

Involuntary unemployment has been defined as a condition where a rise in product prices relative to wage rates would encourage employers to hire more labour and would induce more workers to offer their services. The theory implies that the economy has got locked into a situation where a movement in one direction would be beneficial to both workers and employers, to both consumers and producers; and yet the private interactions of participants cannot generate forces to push it in that direction. All actions become self-defeating. There seems little doubt that such a theory can be logically unassailable; what is at issue is its relevance. In my view Keynes' highly articulate theory is still in search of supporting empirical material. And this applies in two senses: first, there is no period when the 'fit' of this theory seems obviously better than that of others; secondly, there is no period when one could unequivocally say that the implied correctives for involuntary unemployment have worked. Obviously these two remarks are presented with too heavy a pen, but it does seem essential to downgrade the widely held view that involuntary unemployment is a basic tendency of our type of economy and that certain types of corrective are inevitably appropriate.

If we take the period between the wars in the United Kingdom, surely Lord Beveridge's description of the whole 20 years as being a period of 'chronic deficiency of demand' is succinct and acceptable. In discussing the period as a whole one cannot ignore history. The first world war had already heavily strained an economy, now past its zenith, both in manpower and through diversion of activities towards war production, and this enabled rapidly growing competitive economies such as the United States and Japan to make inroads into our competitive power. Apart from a short boom in the early twenties, Britain suffered from a painful and slow adjustment, which was not facilitated by repegging the pound to gold at a high rate. The United States boomed throughout the twenties, so it could hardly be maintained that investment opportunities on the world scene were becoming scarce. The excesses of the United States boom of the late twenties hit a Britain that was still in poor shape, but, by good fortune, inability to maintain the pound on gold gave her a sufficiently rapid benefit from depreciation to ride the first few years of the thirties more successfully than her more affluent competitors. These were the years of colossal unemployment, but the very worst of the levels were not maintained for long. But then came the long period of low activity and persisting unemployment, which, apart from the short boom of 1937, continued until the onset of the second world war, despite the rearmament programmes of 1938 and 1939.

The chief policy content of the *General Theory* was known at latest by 1934 – it was general knowledge even to members of the Australian Parliament about then – but the recuperative effects of fiscal spending did little to lift the level of economic activity before the second world war. If Keynes' message was so clear and convincing, one wonders why there was so much hesitancy. My point is that whether the theory was right or wrong there was little evidence, even after making all reasonable allowance for lags, of its success or even implementation before the second world war.

In the United States Roosevelt's accession to the presidency in 1932 brought a period of application of public works programmes, but we know from economic analysts of the time that there were increasing doubts as to the maintainable stimulus of fiscal correctives. After 1934 the United States entered a period of further malaise that continued till the second world war. In the United States we know there were other policy measures to which at least some blame can be attached for the patterns of the thirties: the banking collapse and the restrictive policies of the Federal Reserve Bank on money supply, National Recovery codes and other New Deal measures, which pushed up wages and prices despite mass unemployment, and federal legislation protecting the growth of trade unions. The international scene was one of disarray in consequence, and the mid-thirties was a time of beggar-my-neighbour policies through tariffs, bilateralism and other devices.

Since the second world war there have been consistently high

employment percentages by earlier standards. This war again de-
pleted the supply of skilled manhood in the earning span, but there
was much greater devastation of the industrial fabric of the competitive powers. Capital recovery was urgent. Moreover the number of
countries actively involved in the war was much greater – it was less
easy for some to improve their productive efficiencies whilst others
fought, though some suffered a minimum of direct bombing damage
to their industries. The nature of the armistice was one that shared
credit between opposing systems, so that the United States and the
Soviet Union were ready to bicker over the spoils of war, and to
spend a lot on defence provision and support of their erstwhile
allies in economic recovery in the process. It is hard to say how long
such a conjunction of events would maintain world activity at high
levels, but this must have continued into the sixties. Matthews has
argued that there has been a once-for-all non-Keynesian change to a
persistent scarcity of labour relative to capital in this country since
1945,[9] and he links this with the post-war rise in levels of demand
through continued habits of spending associated with war financing,
together with the high levels of investment induced by expanded
world trade and the restructuring of industries. The persisting
government surpluses do not suggest to him that Keynesian policies
can be credited with the post-war condition. Within the United States
fiscal policy has played a fairly small role as a policy corrective,
monetary policy taking the strain. H. G. Johnson has credited both
of them with some success,[10] presumably on Keynesian grounds,
though from the early 1960s the mounting expenditures for Vietnam
must have played a major part.

One must frankly admit that some of these forms of intervention
in the economy for what would seem extraneous reasons have to
some degree been consistent with Keynesian corrective measures. Yet
the whole period since 1918, in both the United Kingdom and the
United States, has been characterised by the upheavals and fears of
wars, the effects of which cut both ways – the absence of wars could
have led to easier adaptation and growth without accompanying high
unemployment. Further, many of the interventions of governments
undoubtedly made matters worse rather than better.

Hence, I would maintain that involuntary unemployment as a
phenomenon still lacks confirmation, and the success of implied
policy correctives is not clearly shown. To the extent that they do

seem to have been applied, and with some success, say in the early thirties, we note a petering out of effects, which may suggest a limit to their influence. To this we return.

The long-run footnote type argument of Keynes that investment opportunities were vanishing is belied by events.

From this scanty review we would make two points. Involuntary unemployment is a theory which as yet lacks adequate empirical support. At the least we should not be over optimistic as to its relevance. Yet we must admit that there is no rival theory that is intended to apply to the inter-war period, merely a series of special circumstances we have already enumerated. Secondly, in the period since the second world war, with its labour scarcity, we should expect to find different attitudes of mind from those applicable pre-war towards the process of search and tolerance of unemployment, and this demands some attention to the inter-dependence of unemployment and inflation. In recent years such discussion has taken place in the main against the framework of the Phillips curve, which Tobin has described as an empirical finding in search of a theory.[11]

UNEMPLOYMENT AND INFLATION

The controversy about the nature of unemployment continues at the present time against a backcloth of rising prices and wage rates as compared with fairly stationary indices pre-war. Monetary and fiscal corrective measures are now seen as contributing to both inflation and unemployment, so that, at least for an open economy, Society would seem to be confronted with some awkward choices. It has recently been affirmed, especially by Friedman[12] and Phelps,[13] that, within the full employment zone, rising aggregate monetary demand as a means for curing unemployment will produce a merely transitory effect; once people realise that widespread wage and price changes are occurring as a result of the added demand, they will correct their decision plans for initial monetary illusion and the previous unemployment patterns will reassert themselves. Unemployment cannot be corrected once the inflation consistent with demand expansion is correctly anticipated. Favourable effects on employment are transitory and not fundamental. Tobin has taken up cudgels on behalf of the Keynesian cause[14] by asserting that involuntary unemployment may as easily persist against a backcloth of rising prices and wage rates as against stable or falling movements characteristic of the time of publication of the *General Theory*. Attitudes to money illusion are not at the centre of the argument. I agree with him on this particular point. The key question is the relevance of involuntary unemployment as a theoretical specification related to the conditions of a market economy. If it is relevant, then some inflation must be forborne to bring about a reduction in unemployment; if it is not relevant, Friedman and Phelps are quite right to argue that the result may be that, or still more, inflation, with no reduction in unemployment. The central issue remains whether a capitalist economy has an inherent tendency from time to time to achieve some sort of stability with the maintenance of large pools of unemployed. The Keynesians have answered yes, the critics have pointed to a set of disparate events that fit with the rather tempestuous history since the first world war, or interventions of government that run contradictory to rules of sensible management of an economy for any school of thought.

Policy implications are heavily dependent on which of these views one holds. At times of relatively high employment, further reduction in unemployment inevitably involves tolerance of some inflation if the Keynesian view is accepted; on Friedman–Phelps criteria one will get inflation, but the reduction in unemployment will not prove lasting. In the latter account much store is placed upon the 'natural' level (percentage) of unemployment, presumably that which the basic forces of enterprise, accumulation and thrift characteristic of the economy will bring about over the longer term. This so-called 'natural' level of unemployment, named by analogy with Wicksell's natural rate of interest, may have some relevance to the depression zone also. Could it be that fiscal and monetary corrective measures will work within the range where unemployment is greater than the natural level of unemployment (related to the longer term), but not be very successful where activity proceeds at greater levels, save insofar as in this way the natural level is lowered? In the context of the thirties these measures would have served to lift current activity to a degree, but once spending plans lacked credibility in terms of normal patterns of economic growth they would prove abortive. It was widely held at the time that pyramid building and make-work schemes had only a limited corrective effect on unemployment, and that spending patterns that lifted enterprise, accumulation and thrift over time were the only effective policy measures. In a sense I am arguing that there may be output illusion effects to match money illusion effects. Certainly some of the evidence is not inconsistent with such a view. Another facet of this is where the State steps into the industrial sphere of activity, but in so doing only reduces the incentives of private producers. From this we conclude that output corrective measures will work so long as they are credible. This means they must operate quickly and with adequate intensity before normal levels of activity have declined to the point where there is a credibility gap – either because the schemes are merely demand and not supply creating, or because they are merely undertaken at the expense of private industry and hence do not reinforce economic recovery.

CONCLUSION

We have shown that a correctly stated theory of competitive activity would permit the coexistence of flexible prices, vacant job opportunities and unemployment even in stationary demand conditions. This points up the need for care in interpretation of unemployment statistics as a guide to policy formulation. Periods of falling demand are those when the unemployment pool is increasing relative to vacancies and the members of the pool are likely to spend longer in it. This will be particularly true of the lower grades of skill, who are likely to be outbid for jobs by displaced higher quality workers, even though wage rates for the lower skills are particularly flexible.

The theory of involuntary unemployment owes its strength to the need to explain the Great Depression. But, at least in terms of the implied policy correctives, there is some doubt as to the strength of fiscal and monetary policies. Alternative explanations of experience in the main capitalist countries after the first world war, related more closely to the historical events and forms of activity of governments, seem to offer as powerful interpretations as the theory of involuntary unemployment.

We would not deny that both fiscal and monetary measures may be used successfully over a range in reviving economic activity, but that range is limited. Those who are impressed by the explanatory power of the involuntary unemployment thesis will assign a larger range of opportunity to fiscal and monetary measures, both in slump and in boom with actual or incipient inflation.

Search unemployment theory serves to point out that there are more 'noise' effects in the separation of influences than had been thought. Nevertheless the central issue remains one of assessing the relevance, both as to analysis and for associated policy recommendations, of disequilibrium theories such as that of involuntary unemployment for the explanation of capitalist economies' periods of malaise, as opposed to explanations more reliant on equilibrating properties of the system disturbed by major events such as wars, and ill-chosen or wrongly applied corrective measures of governments.

Search theories of unemployment have much to offer in analytical improvement and as guides for econometric investigation before the formulation of policy measures. But they do not of themselves settle this fundamental policy dispute with which we have wrestled since the 1920s.

NOTES

1 J. M. Keynes, *The General Theory of Employment, Interest and Money*, Macmillan, 1936.
2 G. S. Becker, 'A Theory of the Allocation of Time', *Economic Journal*, September 1965.
3 M. R. Fisher, *The Economic Analysis of Labour*, Weidenfeld and Nicolson, 1971.
4 The rapidly expanding field of search literature is well illustrated in the recent publication E. S. Phelps (ed.), *Micro-economic Foundations of Employment and Inflation Theory*, Norton, 1970, especially the chapters by A. A. Alchian, E. S. Phelps, D. P. Gordon and A. Hynes, R. E. Lucas, Jr, and L. A. Rapping. See also G. J. Stigler, 'The Economics of Information', *Journal of Political Economy*, June 1961, and J. J. McCall, 'Economics of Information and Job Search', *Quarterly Journal of Economics*, February 1970.
5 J. Tobin, 'Money Wage Rates and Unemployment' in S. E. Harris (ed.), *The New Economics: Keynes' Influence on Theory and Public Policy*, Knopf, 1947.
6 A. A. Alchian, 'Information Costs, Pricing and Resource Unemployment, in Phelps (ed.), *Micro-economic Foundations of Employment and Inflation Theory*.
7 'Information, Costs, Pricing and Resource Unemployment'.
8 Fisher, *The Economic Analysis of Labour*, Chap. 3.
9 R. C. O. Matthews, 'Why has Britain had Full Employment since the War?', *Economic Journal*, September 1968.
10 H. G. Johnson, 'Major Issues in Monetary and Fiscal Policies', *Federal Reserve Bulletin*, November 1964. See also H. Stein, *The Fiscal Revolution in America*, University of Chicago Press, 1969.
11 J. Tobin, 'Inflation and Unemployment', *American Economic Review*, March 1972.
12 M. Friedman, 'The Role of Monetary Policy', *American Economic Review*, March 1968.
13 E. S. Phelps, 'Phillips Curves, Expectations of Inflation and Optimal Unemployment over Time', *Economica*, August 1967.
14 Tobin, 'Inflation and Unemployment'.

Chapter 3

The 'Micro-economic Foundations of Employment and Inflation Theory': Bad Old Wine in Elegant New Bottles[1]

A. G. HINES

Reading and reflecting upon the new 'micro-economic foundations of employment and inflation theory' as expounded in this book[2] is an intellectual experience which is simultaneously exciting and depressing. The essays contained therein constitute an excellent example of the analytic power, beauty and subtlety, but limited imaginative, conceptual and empirical domain, which is characteristic of so much of neo-classical economics. Although the authors cover a wide range of associated topics, this review will concern itself with the set of papers which deals with employment and wage dynamics. It turns out, however, that the essays which deal with other issues in price dynamics, such as optimal advertising, heterogeneous capital goods, output and price planning, etc., employ the same general principles which are used in the analysis of wage and employment dynamics.

Three related questions are dealt with in the analysis of wage inflation and employment:

(i) What is the rationale of the usual dynamic adjustment function which makes the rate of change of wages a function of the level of the excess demand for labour as measured by the level of unemployment?

(ii) Is the Phillips curve anything but a transitory phenomenon which is a result of expectational errors and their slow adjustment in time?

(iii) Given the answers which are offered in (i) and (ii), what is the appropriate interpretation of the aggregate level of unemployment which is observed in the real world?

THE BACKGROUND

The framework within which our discussion of these questions may be appropriately set is what has now come to be regarded as the neo-classical theory of the Phillips curve. I have set this out elsewhere,[3] but it is useful to repeat it here.

We have as equilibrium relationships:

$$N^d - N^s = f(\frac{W}{P}, Y) - g(\frac{W}{P}, Z) = 0 \qquad \text{(A)}$$

where $N^d \equiv E + V$, $N^s \equiv E + U \equiv L$,[4] Y and Z are vectors of exogenous variables, the elements of which are parameters of shift of the demand and supply functions, W/P is the real wage rate and E, V, U and L are the levels of employment, vacancies, unemployment and the labour force respectively.

The neo-classical dynamic adjustment hypothesis is

$$(\frac{\dot{W}}{P})/\frac{W}{P} = \lambda \, [(N^d - N^s) \, / \, N^s] = \lambda X \qquad \text{(B)}$$

where $X \equiv (V - U)/L$ is the level of excess demand and a dot over some variable, e.g. $(\frac{\dot{W}}{P})$ denotes the operator $\dfrac{d(W/P)}{dt}$.

Now $(\frac{\dot{W}}{P})/\frac{W}{P} = \dot{W}/W - \dot{P}/P$ \qquad (C)

Hence $\dot{W}/W = \lambda X + \beta \dot{P}/P$, where $\beta = 1$ \qquad (D)

If money-wages are absolutely rigid in a downward direction, a non-zero relationship between $\dot{W}/W$ and X, given $\dot{P}/P$, would only be defined for $X > 0$. Moreover, if equation (D) relates to an aggregate which consists of markets within each of which there is a downward rigidity in the money-wage rate, as Rees points out aggregate $\dot{W}/W$ would rise if in the ith market $X_i > 0$, even though in aggregate $X < 0$, because $U_j < V_j$ $(j = 1, 2, \ldots, n-1)$.[5] $\dot{W}/W$ could also be positive when there is some excess supply in each market because of competitive distortion in a situation in which the labour force is heterogenous in quality. However, even such minimal concessions to reality are absent from the literature which is under review.

If data on excess demand are not always available, it is assumed that there is a stable non-linear transformation between excess demand and the proportion of the labour force which is unemployed, $U' = U/L$, that is

$$X = \theta\,(U') \tag{E}$$

θ being such that when $X \to 0$, $U \to a$, $a > 0$ and when $X \to \infty$, $U \to 0$, then,

$$\dot{W}/W = \alpha U' + \beta(\dot{P}/P), \text{ where } \alpha = \lambda\theta, \text{ and } \beta = 1 \tag{F}$$

Before we begin our discussion of the three questions dealt with by the 'new' theory, a general observation may be useful.

The variables in the model that we have just outlined are economy-wide aggregates. However, the methodology of neo-classical economics enjoins us to derive our 'macro' equations from 'micro' theory. Specifically, we must have price theoretic explanations of functions such as equations (B) and (E), which are derivable from constrained optimising behaviour of the appropriate decision-making units (firms and households) in the labour market. According to this methodology, the correct next step is to obtain the macro relationships by consistent aggregation over the units. However, as is well known, the conditions for such consistent aggregation are in general so stringent as to make it almost impossible that they will be met in any aggregate data or relationships in the real world, or for that matter in any serious intellectual world. The alternative procedure, which is usually followed by neo-classical economists, including the theorists whose papers are under review, is to aggregate by analogy, that is to work out the theory for the micro unit and argue (or imply) by analogy that this holds for relationships which relate to economy-wide aggregates.

THE RATIONALE OF ADJUSTMENT

Now let us suppose that the model set out in equations (A) – (F) relates to a single labour market. We wish to focus attention on equation (E), as this is crucial to the derivation of a non-linear micro Phillips curve. How is this equation to be rationalised? Lipsey, who first attempted a rationalisation, argued as follows.[6] For various reasons – for example, it takes time for workers to move between jobs and a vacancy may exist in one place and the corresponding unemployed worker may be in another – zero excess demand is associated with positive unemployment and positive vacancies as illustrated by points a and b in Figure 3.1 (A). If this is the case, then we would expect that, over the cycle, V is positively related to X, U is negatively related to X, and V and U are inversely related provided that the quit rate does not exceed the hiring rate as excess demand rises. These relationships are given by the non-linear cuives in Figures 3.1 (A) and (B) for a given level of frictional and/or structural unemployment and vacancies at zero excess demand.

However, applying the neo-classical methodology, we can see that there is a flaw in Lipsey's argument. For, on reflection, it is apparent that it involves aggregation over at least two locationally distinct labour markets.

Indeed, from the standpoint of the pure theory of perfectly competitive markets, on which the conventional analysis of the Phillips curve rests, it is doubtful whether a non-linear Phillips curve derived from a non-linear mapping from X to U and which is defined for positive as well as negative levels of X (or a linear curve defined for positive values of X) can exist in 'true' micro markets. In a perfectly competitive model, firms which are identical, except for possible differences in entrepreneurial ability, employ homogeneous factors to produce homogeneous products. Given technology, the demand for factors depends upon their relative prices with a given market demand for output. Identical factor and product prices are parameters to each firm. If a 'true' market is defined with respect to a homogeneous commodity produced in a given location, it is difficult to see how vacancies and unemployment can exist simultaneously. In particular, V and U must both be zero in each firm when X is zero, and, if there is excess demand for (excess supply of) labour in one firm there must simultaneously be excess demand (excess supply) in

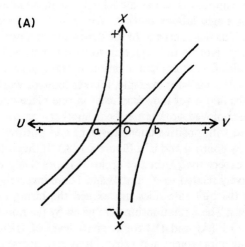

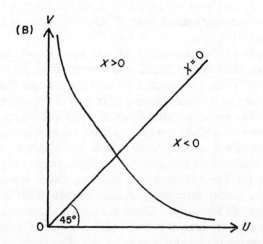

Figure 3.1. Relations between excess demand (X), unemployment (U) and vacancies (V)

all firms. In other words, in a true micro labour market equilibrium would be expected to occur at zero vacancies and zero unemployment. Unemployment (excess supply) would be zero when vacancies (excess demand) were positive and vacancies would be zero when unemployment was positive, that is $X = -U/L$ for $X < 0$ and $X = V/L$ for $X > 0$. The relationship between V, U and X would be given by the straight line in Figure 3.1 (A); that between V and U would coincide with the axes in the V, U plane in Figure 3.1 (B). Hence it would appear that a relationship between X and U/L and hence between $\dot{W}/W$ and U/L would only be defined in conditions of excess supply. If a 'true' labour market is defined over locational space as of a given homogeneous product, whether we can observe $V = U \neq 0$ when $X = 0$ depends on the level of aggregation, that is it depends on how wide is the locational space over which the 'true' market is defined.

To the extent that these arguments are correct, Phillips curves cannot exist in 'true' micro markets. For such curves to exist, there must be aggregation over at least two labour markets. The markets may either be defined over locational space as of a given homogeneous product, or over different commodities as of a given homogeneous supply of labour available in the same location. Positive vacancies and unemployment, and hence Phillips curves, can exist in the actual sectoral labour markets for which statistics are available. But such markets do not correspond to 'true' micro labour markets.

The authors of the 'new' micro-economics attempt to show how positive V and U, and hence a non-linear Phillips curve, may exist in a 'true' micro labour market. In their varied ways the authors provide us with a logically coherent theory. Stripped of all its mathematical complexity, calculus of variations and all, it is quite simple. It relies upon the explicit recognition of the absence of the Walrasian auctioneer and on the discretion over prices and/or quantities which transactors have and do exercise in disequilibrium situations. To be specific, if the rate of change of money-wage rates is to be positively related to the level of excess demand, and be negatively and non-linearly related to the level of unemployment in a micro labour market, we require that the vacancy rate should increase and that the unemployment rate should fall as the rate of change of money-wage rates increases. This is deemed to come about in the following fashion.

Consider a worker who is faced with the option of accepting a wage cut or accepting unemployment in his current occupation. His decision will be based on whether he regards the wage cut as localised or general. If he regards the change as general he will accept the wage cut, since he will not expect his real income to improve in an alternative occupation for which he will have to search, knowing full well that search is a costly activity. If, on the other hand, he thinks that the wage cut is localised – and this is assumed to be the more likely outcome – he will not accept the reduction in his real income which the wage cut entails. Consequently, he will quit and search for employment at the old wage rate, his reservation wage being a decreasing function of the length and cost of search. At each moment of time he must decide whether to accept the next best offer on the basis of the sample of offers on which he currently has information. We would therefore expect that, as unemployment persists, the acceptance wage and hence the actual wage will fall. In such a situation, what happens to the observed level of unemployment depends on the relative magnitudes of the numbers of newly quitting and laid-off workers, on the one hand, and the numbers of workers who are prepared to accept next best offers of employment at the lower wage rates which prevail on the other. It is assumed that the former exceeds the latter.

Similarly, consider the behaviour of the vacancy rate. As excess supply of output increases, employers increase the rate at which they lay-off workers for any reason whatsoever. Also, as employers plan to reduce their output, subject to stocks of hoarded labour they must reduce their rates of hiring. In the assumed dynamic monopsony situation, the hiring rate is reduced by lowering the wage offers made to marginal as well as to intra-marginal workers. The argument is symmetrical for positive and increasing excess demand.

The theory, therefore, rests upon the economics of imperfect information as developed by Stigler[7] and others, together with the implied theory of search behaviour, and upon a dynamic version of the theory of the monopolist or monopsonist. It appears to yield the conclusion that vacancies (positive excess demand in the conventional sense) and unemployment (excess supply) can exist simultaneously in the same micro labour market.

We observe in passing that, within this framework, the authors are able to provide a neo-classical rationalisation of the hypothesis that the rate of change of the price of any commodity is proportional to the excess demand for it.

However, it is doubtful whether the authors have succeeded in establishing that positive vacancies and unemployment can exist simultaneously in the same 'true' micro labour market.

The system which the authors construct is one of non-tâtonnement disequilibrium, in which every individual worker and employer is his own monopolist/monopsonist. Careful thinking suggests that in such a system there is no sectoral market corresponding to what is conventionally termed an industry. For, if we think through the logic of the 'new' micro-economics, in disequilibrium each such sector is segmented in such a way that the sectoral market reduces to the individual worker or employer. As Triffin pointed out in the static analogous context of monopolistic competition,[8] there appears to be no stopping place between the individual firm or worker and the whole economy.

One important implication of our comments is that it is not possible on any plausible set of assumptions to generate convex sectoral Phillips curves. In general, a convex *aggregate* Phillips curve can be derived by aggregation over n sectors if equation (B) is assumed to be piece-wise linear and $\bar{U} \neq U_i$ for $i = 1, 2 \ldots . n$. Such a model built on different foundations from those of the 'new' micro-economics of employment and inflation theory is developed by Hines and Muellbauer.[9]

THE PHILLIPS CURVE

The traditional neo-classical dynamic adjustment function which is given in equation (B) is concerned with the dynamic stability of markets rather than with the disequilibrium dynamics of ongoing processes. Alternatively, we could have postulated an adjustment function which is stated directly in terms of money-wages and which is concerned with how the participants in the wage bargain respond to a state of disequilibrium, irrespective of whether the responses are or are not equilibrating. Thus the adjustment function $\dot{W}/W = \lambda X$ simply states that when, for example, there is excess demand for labour, money-wages are bid up by buyers or advanced by sellers, the percentage rate of rise being proportional to the excess demand. On this view, the wage bargain in a non-tâtonnement situa-

tion is necessarily conducted in money terms whatever is the objective
of the participants. Money-wages are the only variable which the
workers can control or influence directly. This being the case, if the
wage bargain is a bargain for real wages, the expected rate of change
of prices enters the adjustment function. In place of equation (F),
we would then have

$$\frac{\dot{W}}{W} = \theta(U) + \kappa(\dot{P}/P)^*, \text{ where } 0 < \kappa \leqslant 1 \qquad (G)$$

Suppose that the adaptive expectations hypothesis is appropriate
to the formation of expectations about price changes. Then, using p
to denote the actual rate of change of prices $(\dot{P}/P)$ and p^* to denote
the expected rate of change of prices $(\dot{P}/P)^*$,

$$p_t^* = p_{t-1}^* + \psi(p_{t-1} - p_{t-1}^*) = \ldots \sum_{i=0}^{\infty} \psi(1 - \psi)^i p_{t-1-i} \qquad (H)$$

If, as is assumed in the real wage formulation in (B), the elasticity of
expectations is unity, $\psi = 1$ so that $\kappa = \beta = 1$, and if there is no
lag in the adjustment of $\dot{W}/W$ to excess demand so that $p_t = p_{t-1}$
for all t, the relationship between $\dot{W}/W$ and U would always be a
vertical line in the $\dot{W}/W$, U plane. However, empirical studies
usually yield historical Phillips curves with a non-vertical slope. This
suggests that there is some lag in the adjustment of money-wages to
the level of excess demand and/or that the elasticity of expectations
is not unity within the unit period. Hence, in the more usual case,
$0 < \psi < 1$ and p_t^* is some weighted function of all past values of p_t.

Now consider the behaviour of a system to which the adaptive
expectations hypothesis applies and in which $0 < \psi < 1$ so that

$$\frac{\dot{W}}{W} = \theta(U) + \kappa \sum_{i=0}^{\infty} \psi(1 - \psi)^i p_{t-1-i} \qquad (I)$$

In a situation in which $p_t^* \neq p_{t-1}$, the Phillips curve is downward
sloping. But, given sufficient time, such that the actual rate of inflation comes to be expected, $p_t^* = p_t$ for all t, and equation (I)
becomes

$$\frac{\dot{W}}{W} = \theta(U) + \kappa p \qquad (J)$$

$$\text{since } \sum_{i=0}^{\infty} \psi(1 - \psi)^i = 1.$$

In such a situation the real wage rate must be constant (or, with labour measured in 'efficiency' units, real wages must be growing at a rate which is determined by the rate of Harrod-neutral technical progress), that is $\dot{W}/W = p$, and

$$\frac{\dot{W}}{W} = \frac{1}{1-\kappa} \theta(U) \tag{K}$$

But, when expectations become fully adjusted so that the going rate of inflation comes to be expected, we also have $\kappa = 1$ and the Phillips curve becomes a vertical line in the $\dot{W}/W$, U plane. As Friedman put the matter,[10] the trade-off between $\dot{W}/W$ and U is temporary and is due to lags in the adjustment of expectations to the actual state of affairs. In the long run there can only be a trade-off between the level of unemployment and the rate of acceleration of inflation.[11] The economy can therefore be in equilibrium at *any* actual rate of inflation which is fully anticipated, such that $\dot{W}/W = \dot{P}/P$. The level of unemployment which is associated with such an equilibrium is called in this literature the 'natural' rate of unemployment.

This proposition, which is due to Friedman, is accepted by all the authors, even though some of them derive it in a mathematically elegant fashion and with many subtle embellishments.[12]

According to Friedman:

'The natural rate of unemployment . . . is the level that would be ground out by the Walrasian system of general equilibrium equations, provided there is embedded in them the actual structural characteristics of the labour and commodity markets, including market imperfections, stochastic variability in demands and supplies, the cost of gathering information about job vacancies and labour availabilities, the cost of mobility, and so on.'[13]

Here we can only repeat an observation which has been made by others. As yet, no-one has produced any such general equilibrium model with proofs of its existence, stability, etc. Moreover, there are some good grounds for wondering whether any such model can and will be constructed. Even if it was constructed, when and how would we be able to make estimates of *the actual magnitude* which corresponds to the 'natural' rate of unemployment? Given the policy conclusions which the 'new' theorists have already arrived at (and which we presently discuss), this is a question of some considerable importance.

THE LEVEL OF UNEMPLOYMENT

The question now arises as to the interpretation which is to be put upon the level of unemployment which is observed in the real world.

In the days before the 'new' theory, it was commonly believed that real world unemployment could be decomposed into frictional, seasonal, structural and demand-deficient components. There were problems with this classification. For example, is there more than a difference of degree between frictional unemployment and that structural unemployment which is due to changes in relative supplies and demands as of a given level of aggregate demand? Or, to put the point differently, is not structural unemployment simply frictional unemployment which for various reasons (such as inertia, expectational lags, immobility of factors according to their vintages, etc.) is drawn out in time? Again, the Keynesian notion of demand-deficient unemployment requires that we can define full employment. But to what level of actual unemployment does this correspond?[14] Moreover, is not the observed as distinct from equilibrium level of frictional–structural unemployment in part dependent upon the level of aggregate demand, as can be seen from the 'Beveridge curve' in Figure 3.1 (B)? Such problems remain within the old classificatory system. The new micro theory of employment and inflation simply by-passes them by the bold assertion that *all* unemployment is frictional. Moreover, it is voluntary.

We know that, in a static neo-classical model, utility maximising households determine the amount of leisure and goods which they will purchase as of a given number of available hours by equating their subjective rate of substitution between goods and leisure with the objective rate of transformation between them as measured by the real wage rate. In a disequilibrium situation, the theory of search unemployment implies that individuals *voluntarily* choose to work for an employer or to search for better options (which constitutes self-employment in the gathering of information about job opportunities and wages) in any given situation. This self-employment, so to speak, is not measured by the recorded employment figures, so that actual data overstate unemployment. Alternatively, if the individual is not actually observed to be engaged in search activity, it is to be presumed that he puts a higher valuation upon leisure than the real income which he could receive by accepting employment over the whole range of offers of real wage rates which he perceives.

Moreover, the unemployment which is associated with the long-run equilibrium of the system (the 'natural' rate) has no welfare costs. Such unemployment merely reflects the optimum 'off the job' search activity which optimising workers voluntarily undertake at full employment. Indeed if the monetary (and fiscal?) authorities pursue policies which result in generalised excess demand or excess supply (that is, they push the economy off the 45° line in Figure 3.1 (B)), so that actual unemployment is below or above the natural rate, they will impose a welfare cost on individuals in as much as they are induced to engage in less than or more than the optimal amount of search.

Lest the reader should think that I am putting up a straw man, I offer the following in evidence.

First there is the paper by Lucas and Rapping. They hold that at each moment of time the labour market is in equilibrium, in the sense that quantity demanded of labour equals quantity supplied *ex ante*. Measured unemployment is thus asserted to be not part of the short-run aggregate supply of labour. Such unemployment is to be viewed:

'not as an effective market supply, part of which cannot find employment, but rather as the supply of labour that *would be forthcoming* at perceived normal wages and prices. Measured unemployment (more exactly its non-frictional component) is then viewed as consisting of persons who regard the wage rate at which they could currently be employed as temporarily low, and who therefore choose to wait or search for improved conditions rather than to invest in moving or occupational change.'[15]

Moreover, on the basis of such a model, they proceed to fit an aggregate supply function for labour to United States data for the period 1930–65, which in its construction and rationale does not seriously face the question of deficient aggregate demand. The mean-

70 INVOLUNTARY UNEMPLOYMENT

ing of all this is clear. There was no involuntary unemployment in the United States economy in the Great Depression of the 1930s.

Secondly, nowhere in the volume is there a serious discussion of structural or demand-deficient unemployment. None of the authors make the usual assumption of the so-called neo-classical synthesis, namely that governments can (or do) always maintain full employment by the appropriate orchestration of monetary and fiscal instruments. In contrast, such an assumption is explicitly made by Reder,[16] a non-contributor to this volume. He makes it very clear that what he is providing is a theory of frictional unemployment at full employment. For these authors then, the economics of employment has come full circle; Keynesian demand-deficient unemployment is out. We are as it were in a time machine, back in the world of the economic theorists of the 1920s and 1930s. After all Hutt,[17] Hicks,[18] et al. all held the view that unemployment was voluntary.[19] What we therefore have in this book is old but bad wine, albeit in elegant new bottles.

CONCLUSIONS

What then are we to make of this new theory of unemployment?

Let us begin on the positive side. Neo-classical economists have always had difficulty making sense of Keynes' definition of involuntary unemployment. The definition is as follows:

'Men are involuntarily unemployed if, in the event of a small rise in the price of wage-goods relative to the money-wage, both the aggregate supply of labour willing to work for the current money-wage and the aggregate demand for it at that wage would be greater than the existing volume of employment.'[20]

How is such a phenomenon to be rationalised without invoking money illusion? There are two rationalisations, both set in the context of a non-tâtonnement disequilibrium process. In the first, in evaluating his human wealth the individual worker must have as reference points other individuals or groups of individuals in the economy. A reduction in the wage rate for the ith worker at a given price level of the appropriate basket of wage goods is perceived by him as a reduction in his relative real wage. He will therefore resist on his own or, more realistically, by organisation into a trade union. Thus he and his similarly placed associates will be forced into unemployment by his employer. The 'new' theory eschews this rationalisation from relativities. In the usual neo-classical paradigm, its prototype agent is an isolated and alienated individual who, independently of others, maximises his own utility. The 'new' theory therefore proceeds as follows.

If for example, the ith worker is faced with a wage cut in the firm in which he is employed, in a non-tâtonnement disequilibrium he must decide whether the cut is local and/or transient, or generalised and/or permanent. If he believes it is localised, it is assumed that he will quit and search for a better offer. If, on the other hand, the reduction in his real wages had been brought about by a rise in the aggregate price level, then this would be regarded as general (on the assumption that all workers consume roughly the same bundle of goods) and there would therefore be no incentive to quit and search.

Thus, in either of these two rationalisations Keynes' involuntary unemployment is not due to money illusion. It is due to the fact that, in a non-tâtonnement world which is in disequilibrium, the numerator and the denominator of the variable W_i/P (where W_i is the money-wage rate of the ith worker and P is an appropriately weighted index of the price of wage goods) do not transmit the same amount of information about real wages to the rational transactor. Specifically, P transmits more information than W_i. We therefore conclude, following Alchian,[21] that the new theory gives a possible price theoretic solution to Keynes' notion, which had previously appeared as a puzzle in the neo-classical paradigm.

However, as we have seen, and this is our first criticism of the new theory, it makes no reference to demand-deficient unemployment, even though, as I have argued elsewhere,[22] it could provide *one* choice theoretic underpinning of such a theory (should one be required). This is easily seen by exploring the implications for the necessarily inter-dependent structures of expenditures and income entailed by search on the part of agents with zero current income and zero or illiquid stocks of assets on which to draw in order to maintain current expenditure.[23]

The point can be restated in the language of the information framework. In the literature on the reappraisal of Keynesian economics it has been established that, in an integrated economy in which exchange, production, etc. are sequential activities occurring in *real* time, the appropriately weighted sum of information which individuals may acquire by quitting and searching will not in general be equal to the information that they fail to transmit to the system because of the reduction in their expenditures. Specifically, it has been shown that, in a situation of aggregate excess supply, actual expenditure rather than prices transmits the appropriate signals to economic agents. In such a situation, workers without assets who attempt to obtain information concerning an unknown vector of relative prices by quitting and searching may even succeed. However, if in so doing they are unable to transmit signals to producers via their expenditure, output contracts, with the familiar cumulative consequences. In that case, the information obtained on the supply side (with which the authors of the 'new' theory are exclusively concerned) will be less than that which is lost on the side of aggregate demand.

The second criticism relates to a crucial assumption of the 'new' theory. It is that, as a means of gathering information about job opportunities, off the job search is *invariably* more efficient than on the job search. This assumption is made by all the contributors but it is most explicitly formalised in the paper by Mortensen.[24] We must therefore examine the *a priori* and empirical justification of this assumption.

One could construct an *a priori* argument for it if the typical change of job were from one disjoint or non-competing group to another, for example, if dustmen were seeking to become barristers or vice versa. Unfortunately, not only is an insignificant proportion of job-changes of this kind, but it is also clear that this is not the typical case to which the authors wish the new theory to be applied.

As Tobin has observed, professors of economics in the United States seem to be quite capable of searching for better opportunities within their profession and achieving them on the job.[25] They do not quit to search. But this does not apply exclusively to the market for professional economists. To take another example, a worker, in say, the car industry is more likely to find out about job opportunities and wage prospects in another firm in the industry, or for that matter in firms in contiguous industries, by contacts with other workers at the place of work (for example, lorry drivers or messengers), in the canteen, in the pub, etc.

Even if one must be off the job to investigate a particular job prospect from among those which have been sampled on the job, one does not have to quit. The 'flu', 'the visit to the dentist', 'the unforeseen emergency cropping up in the home one morning' are all well-known facts of life.They facilitate or supplement on the job search. This is very important, especially since Gordon has found that in the United States unemployed workers spend no more than 2½ hours per week (of what may be called normal working hours in the case of the employed) in direct job search.[26] I would be prepared to hazard the guess that nearly all jobs offer sufficient flexibility for such supplementation. If they do not they should be made to do so, if one wishes to ensure that individuals are in jobs which, given their endowment of skills, maximise their lifetime income.

There is good reason for our contention that on the job search may in general be more efficient than off the job search. A profession or a trade is also a community of individuals or groups of individuals with well-defined networks of communication for the conduct of their affairs. These networks can be used by a member of the group to sample the job market without making the sacrifice of current income which off the job search entails. This proposition is derivable from more general considerations. It appears that their relevance to the question in hand has not been grasped by either the proponents or the opponents of the new theory.

In principle, we could imagine an economy in which the only contact between economic agents is through market or exchange relationships which rely exclusively upon vectors of relative prices. In principle also, we could contemplate an economy without markets, organised as a complete bureaucratic hierarchy of commands and the execution of orders. Each system would have its own distinct network of communications. Now, as Coase pointed out long ago, any actual market economy in which firms and similar bureaucratic organisations exist is an amalgam of the two systems.[27] We may add that the bureaucratic element and its modes of communication increase as the sizes of productive units and conglomerates increase, as they have in fact done under contemporary capitalism. In addition, there are of course other modes of communication associated with other aspects of social organisation, some of which are inseparable from activities in the sphere of production and exchange. It thus follows that to say, as we do, that, in general, on the job search is less costly and more efficient than off the job search, is to imply that these non-market networks of communication yield more, better and cheaper information to the individual and to the system than that which is obtained by using the pure market network, which involves the costs of quitting and searching.

It is not without interest that in their single minded pursuit of the 'endogenous' (identical with neo-classical for theorists in this genre) rationalisation of all economic phenomena, they ignore this alternative and more plausible scenario. Thus Phelps describes his agents as 'isolated and apprehensive' 'Pinteresque' men.[28] In the present context, that vision is only acceptable if one believes that the only relevant source of information available to economic agents is the vector of relative prices, and if one is prepared to ignore the many and varied sources of information and lines of communication which are necessarily associated with the process of production and exchange. It is hardly surprising that the new theorists take as the *institutional* setting for their parable a group of small, scattered and isolated islanders, with workers on the *j*th island having no information about wages or job opportunities on the *k*th. (Presumably the boatmen who ply from one island to another are for some unexplained reason forbidden to talk or carry news between the ports. Or perhaps no regular transport is available between the islands and each job-seeker sets out in his own canoe.)

We turn next to the empirical evidence, some direct and some indirect. It is worthy of note that the 'new' micro-economics does not present *any* evidence of either sort. We simply have the assertion by, for example, Mortensen, that 'the opportunity cost of time spent searching is higher for an employed worker than it is for an unemployed one'.[29]

According to the *Monthly Labor Review*, in the United States labour turnover as measured by gross accessions is at an average rate of 40 per cent per annum. The first question one needs to ask is what proportions of quits and new hires consist of people who move from one job to another without an interval of unemployment. Evidence cited in Tobin suggests that at least 25 per cent of workers who quit move directly into a job which they fixed up on their previous job.[30] Moreover, as Tobin also points out, if all accessions were new hires from the pool of unemployed persons, the mean duration of unemployment would have to be one-half of what it is actually observed to be. It is also well-established in the literature, at least since the paper by Eagly,[31] that the quit rate is *positively* related to the rate of change of money-wage rates and *negatively* related to the level of unemployment. This observation is in conflict with the new theory. Moreover, the literature on dual labour markets[32] suggests that most of the observed search by unemployed workers in the United States is concentrated in the so called 'secondary' labour markets, which are made up of blacks, women and similarly disadvantaged groups. Search by the unemployed in such markets is 'the unproductive consequences of dissatisfaction rather than a rational quest for self improvement'. Good jobs are very hard to come by in such segregated markets because of discrimination and similar social ills.

This is related to the data in Table 3.1, which shows unemployment by race, sex and age in the United States for the period 1964–72. Now suppose one did take the claim of the new micro-economics of inflation and unemployment seriously. How would it provide an explanation of the unemployment which is observed in these data?

We might be prepared to grant in part that a substantial proportion of unemployment among persons aged 16–19 is due to voluntary search activity. It may not be unreasonable to assume that a con-

Table 3.1   *Unemployment in the United States, 1964–72*

| | Percentages (annual average) | | | | | |
| | Whites | | | Negro and other | | |
	Male *20+*	*Female* *20+*	*Male & female* *16–19*	*Male* *20+*	*Female* *20+*	*Male & female* *16–19*
1964	3·4	4·6	13·2	7·7	9·0	27·2
1965	2·9	4·0	13·4	6·0	7·4	26·2
1966	2·2	3·3	11·2	4·9	6·6	25·4
1967	2·1	3·8	11·0	4·3	7·1	26·5
1968	2·0	3·4	11·0	3·9	6·3	24·9
1969	1·9	3·4	10·7	3·7	5·8	24·1
1970	3·2	4·4	13·5	5·9	5·3	29·1
1971	4·0	5·3	15·1	7·2	8·7	31·7
1972	3·6	4·9	14·2	6·8	9·0	32·8

Source: U.S. Department of Labor, *Monthly Labor Review.*

siderable number of young people enter the labour market as unemployed and search around for a job appropriate to their endowments, tastes and aspirations. But even here we have to ask, why are blacks in this age group better at this activity than whites? Or again, why should women, according to the interpretation which the theory would invite us to put upon the data, be more 'rational' than men, and black women more so than white women? Again, looking at the classification by race for all groups, why as compared to whites should blacks be better neo-classical optimisers, better informed, less subject to price or wage illusion, and hence making better use of the labour market by engaging in a more optimal level of search? It is blindingly obvious that the main explanations of the observed unemployment are fluctuations in the level of aggregate demand (demand-deficient unemployment) and that part of structural unemployment which is the result of the racist and sexist structure of the United States. There may be some elements of frictional unemployment in these data, but they surely are the minor part. In any event, no-one ever denied that there is such a thing as frictional unemployment.

It does not appear that the British data have been as carefully researched as those for the United States; neither are the data as adequate for investigating these matters. However, preliminary analysis of the available data which I have undertaken suggests that the duration of unemployment is positively related to the level of unemployment and negatively related to gross turnover holding the level of unemployment constant. These findings are also in conflict with the new theory. They are consistent with the hypothesis that the quit rate is negatively related to the level of unemployment. They are also consistent with the dual labour market hypothesis in the sense that, on average, some definable groups of workers stay longer in the pool of unemployment than do others. Moreover, their stay is positively related to the level of aggregate unemployment.

Let us finally observe that whether we regard unemployment as decomposing into demand-deficient, structural, seasonal and frictional components, the last being quantitatively the least important, or we regard all unemployment as voluntary and frictional, has serious implications for policy. The policy implications of the 'new' theory are quite clear. If unemployment is voluntary, no social disutility attaches to it. Such observed unemployment merely reflects the optimum off the job search which utility maximising workers voluntarily undertake in an economy which is implicitly assumed to be always at full employment. Phelps, in drawing out the policy implications of the Alchian contribution to the volume, writes as follows:

'It would be as senselessly puritanical to wipe out unemployment as it would be to raise taxes in a depression. Today's unemployment is an investment in a better allocation of any given quantity of employed persons tomorrow; its opportunity cost, like any other investment, is present consumption.'[33]

Aggregate demand management which interferes with this natural rate of unemployment results in non-optimality, in as much as it makes workers engage in more or less than the optimal amount of search. In any event, we have the assurance of the theorists that, given the self-righting equilibrating mechanisms of the economy, the government can only hold a level of unemployment below the natural rate in the long run by a monetary policy which results in an ever accelerating rate of inflation. If that is ruled out as being undesirable, the only beneficial policy open to the government consists in taking steps to improve the efficiency of the labour market by increasing the flow of information and perhaps reducing the costs of mobility and change. Interpreting this in the light of the work of Holt,[34] who is the author in the volume who appears most sensitive to the meaning and implications of unemployment, such a policy would, if successful, have the effect of shifting the Beveridge curve in Figure 3.1 (B) to the left, thereby reducing the amount of frictional unemployment which is associated with zero excess demand.

We have come full circle. The policy prescription is analogous to that of the 1920s in England: set up more and better labour exchanges. Can there be any more striking illustration of the intellectual and imaginative vacuity and irrelevance of this type of economics in the face of real and important social phenomena?

NOTES

1 I wish to thank my colleagues Richard Portes and John Weeks for helpful comments. I am, of course, responsible for all errors.

78 INVOLUNTARY UNEMPLOYMENT

2 E. S. Phelps (ed.), *Micro-economic Foundations of Employment and Inflation Theory*, Norton, 1970.

3 For example, A. G. Hines, 'The Phillips Curve and the Distribution of Unemployment', *American Economic Review*, March 1972, and 'The Determinants of the Rate of Change of Money Wage Rates and the Effectiveness of Incomes Policy' in H. G. Johnson and A. R. Nobay (eds), *The Current Inflation*, Macmillan, 1971.

4 It is assumed that L is measured in a manner which can accommodate changes in hours worked, changes in participation rates and changes in the working population. Moreover, questions such as the lag of desired employment behind actual employment are ignored.

5 A. Rees, 'The Phillips Curve as a Menu for Policy Choice', *Economica*, August 1970.

6 R. G. Lipsey, 'The Relation between Unemployment and the Rate of Change of Money Wage Rates in the United Kingdom, 1862–1957: A Further Analysis', *Economica*, February 1960.

7 G. J. Stigler, 'The Economics of Information', *Journal of Political Economy*, June 1961.

8 R. Triffin, *Monopolistic Competition and General Equilibrium Theory*, Harvard University Press, 1940.

9 A. G. Hines and J. Muellbauer, 'Wage Inflation and the Sectoral Distribution of Unemployment', Birkbeck Discussion Paper, 1974.

10 M. Friedman, 'The Role of Monetary Policy', *American Economic Review*, March 1968.

11 Theorists in the genre of which the present authors are the leaders are not disturbed by the failure of a host of investigators to find a vertical long-run Phillips curve. All the studies of the late 1960s, for both British and United States data, showed that there was in fact some sort of trade-off between unemployment and the rate of inflation, even though the trade-off was less favourable in the long run than in the short run. Apparently these theorists are also not disturbed by the fact that the experience of the 1970s in most countries is of simultaneously increasing rates of inflation and unemployment.

12 To take just one example, Phelps in *Micro-economic Foundations of Employment and Inflation Theory* shows that, given the extrapolative mechanism which is assumed to govern the formation of expectations, the speed of convergence towards the equilibrium rate of inflation is a function of the discrepancy between the actual and the desired rate of unemployment, which is held during the process of adjustment to the natural rate. Hence, given its preferences, Society can choose its path of adjustment from any actual non-equilibrium rate of unemployment to the natural rate, but this simultaneously involves a choice of the path of the (transitional) inflation rate.

13 Friedman, 'The Role of Monetary Policy', p. 8.

14 It should be noted that, before it was given its 'new' foundation, the Phillips curve could be used to provide one precise definition of full employment. Given some appropriate assumption about the growth of productivity, the slope of the curve can be interpreted as the technical rate of transformation of $\dot{P}/P$ into U. We can also postulate the existence of a well-behaved social ordering such that there are indifference curves which measure the subjective rate of substitution of $\dot{P}/P$ for U. Their mutual tangency gives the socially optimal level of unemployment and inflation. That level of unemployment corresponds to full employment.

15 Phelps (ed.), *Micro-economic Foundations of Employment and Inflation Theory*, p. 285.
16 M. W. Reder, 'The Theory of Frictional Unemployment', *Economica*, February 1969.
17 W. H. Hutt, *Theory of Idle Resources*, Jonathan Cape, 1939.
18 J. R. Hicks, *The Theory of Wages* (1st ed.), Macmillan, 1932.
19 An excellent discussion of the views of economists concerning the causes of and cures for unemployment in the 1920s is given in K. Hancock, 'Unemployment and Economists in the 1920s', *Economica*, November 1960.
20 J. M. Keynes, *The General Theory of Employment, Interest and Money*, Macmillan, 1936, p. 15.
21 A. A. Alchian, 'Information Costs, Pricing and Resource Unemployment' in Phelps (ed.), *Micro-economic Foundations of Employment and Inflation Theory*.
22 A. G. Hines, *The Reappraisal of Keynesian Economics*, Martin Robertson, 1971.
23 I would now argue that it is preferable to underpin the model with the relativities rationalisation of involuntary unemployment.
24 D. T. Mortensen, 'A Theory of Wage and Employment Dynamics' in Phelps (ed.) *Micro-economic Foundations of Employment and Inflation Theory*. An inspection of equations (78) and (90) in his paper shows that the magnitude as well as the sign of the 'optimal' level of unemployment depends critically on what is assumed about the relative efficiency of on the job and off the job search. (In his notation $U^* \gtrless 0$ according as $S_0 \gtrless S_1$).
   I am indebted to Mr T. Hazeldine of Warwick University for bringing this to my attention.
25 J. Tobin, 'Inflation and Unemployment', *American Economic Review*, March 1972.
26 R. J. Gordon, 'The Welfare Cost of Higher Unemployment', *Brookings Papers on Economic Activity*, no. 1, 1973.
27 R. H. Coase, 'The Nature of the Firm', *Economica*, November 1937.
28 *Micro-economic Foundations of Employment and Inflation Theory*.
29 Ibid., p. 174.
30 Tobin, 'Inflation and Unemployment'.
31 R. V. Eagly, 'Market Power as an Intervening Mechanism in Phillips Curve Analysis', *Economica*, February 1965.
32 For example, P. B. Doeringer and M. Piore, *Internal Labor Markets and Manpower Analysis*, D. C. Heath, 1971; R. E. Hall, 'Why is the Unemployment Rate so High at Full Employment?', *Brookings Papers on Economic Activity*, no. 3, 1970.
33 Phelps (ed.), *Micro-economic Foundations of Employment and Inflation Theory*, p. 17.
34 C. C. Holt, 'How Can the Phillips Curve be Moved to Reduce both Inflation and Unemployment?' in Phelps (ed.), *Micro-economic Foundations of Employment and Inflation Theory*.

Part II

WHAT IS IT THAT
WE DO MEASURE?

Chapter 4

Statistics of Unemployment in the United Kingdom

A. R. THATCHER

CONCEPTS OF UNEMPLOYMENT

The word 'unemployment' can be used in many different senses. It has been said that it can describe:

(a) a condition – being not at work;
(b) an activity – seeking work;
(c) an attitude – desiring a job under certain conditions;
(d) a need – that of needing a job.

Sometimes a distinction is made between 'voluntary' and 'involuntary' unemployment. In ordinary language the term 'voluntary unemployment' is generally applied to people who are thought to be capable of taking a job if they wish, but who prefer to remain unemployed. The term 'involuntary unemployment' is correspondingly applied to people who would like to have a job, but cannot manage to find one. But the term 'involuntary unemployment' is also used in a much more technical case, for example by Keynes.

Some people think of unemployment as a purely economic phenomenon and treat any numerical estimates of unemployment as an indicator of the pressure of demand for labour; whereas others think of unemployment as a measure of the number of people in need or distress, giving cause for social concern. These groups overlap but are not identical.

Anyone trying to compile regular statistics of 'unemployment' soon finds that he is forced to confine his activities to those types of unemployment which can be measured. The official statistics of unemployment in the United Kingdom, as in other countries, are based on the concept of 'seeking work'. Even within this definition, however, one obtains different results if one measures the number of people who tell an interviewer in a household survey that they are seeking work, or if one measures the number who seek work in a particular way, for example by registering as unemployed at an employment exchange. The numbers who register are easy to measure, regularly and quickly; they can be analysed in many interesting ways and they give information for local areas; for this reason they receive a great deal of attention. But they are not perfect indicators either of the demand for labour or of social distress. Of necessity the statistics are confined to the persons who register at the local offices and they have never been presented as anything more than this. Apart from the regular monthly statistics, there are also some limited data, described below, on the numbers who describe themselves as seeking work but who do not register.

PUBLISHED STATISTICS OF UNEMPLOYMENT

Every month the Department of Employment publishes a detailed count of the numbers registered as unemployed. The count includes all those who have reported to the employment exchange that they are seeking work, and who have been classified by the exchange (according to standard rules) as being 'capable of and available for work'. There is a continuous series on this definition since 1922, with only minor discontinuities. The rules are based on a type of 'case law' which has built up over the years. The series includes not only those who are entitled to unemployment or supplementary benefit, but also those who are not claiming benefit at all, provided that they come into the category of 'seeking work, and capable of and available for work'.

A distinction is drawn between those who have no employer at all (the 'wholly unemployed') and those who have an employer but who have been suspended on the understanding that they will shortly resume work (the 'temporarily stopped'). The latter are not now included in the official total of 'unemployed' but are given separately.

Statistics are compiled for each local office area, and they distinguish males, females and school-leavers. Detailed analyses are made monthly according to the industry in which the unemployed person last worked and (to a limited extent) according to the duration of his time on the register. Quarterly analyses are fuller in respect of duration of time on the register; they also classify by occupation in which employment is being sought and by whether or not unemployment and/or supplementary benefit is being received. Every six months the unemployed are analysed by age. Some specimen examples of these analyses are shown in Table 4.1, including a new occupational breakdown.

Table 4.1 *Specimen analyses of unemployment statistics*

	Numbers (thousands)	Rates[a] (percentages)
1 By industry (January 1974)[b]		
Agriculture, forestry and fishing	12·8	*3·0*
Mining and quarrying	17·9	*4·5*
Manufacturing	157·7	*2·0*
Construction	109·7	*8·0*
Gas, electricity and water	6·4	*1·8*
Transport and communication	37·6	*2·4*
Distributive trades	55·8	*2·1*
Financial, professional and miscellaneous services	100·5	*1·6*
Public administration and defence	32·2	*2·1*
Others not classified by industry	87·4	*..*
Total	618·0	*2·8*

		Percentages of totals
2 By occupation (December 1973)[c]		
Managerial and professional	31·3	*7·7*
Clerical, selling and security	60·4	*14·8*
Craft etc. in processing and production	40·9	*10·0*
Others in processing and production	30·3	*7·4*
Catering, cleaning, hairdressing and other personal services	10·4	*2·6*
Transport and materials, moving and storing	28·2	*6·9*
General labourers not classified elsewhere	197·8	*48·4*
Other occupations (including farming)	9·1	*2·2*
Total	408·4	*100·0*

	Numbers (thousands)	Rates[a] (percentages)
3 By age (July 1973)[d]		
Under 18	27·0	4·8
18–19	43·0	7·7
20–29	136·9	24·4
30–39	76·2	13·6
40–49	78·8	14·0
50–59	95·3	17·0
60 and over	104·1	18·5
Total	561·3	100·0
4 By duration of unemployment (October 1973)[e]		
Under 2 weeks	86·0	16·7
2–4 weeks	49·6	9·6
4–8 weeks	63·1	12·2
8–13 weeks	47·6	9·2
13–26 weeks	65·3	12·6
26–52 weeks	62·1	12·0
Over 52 weeks	142·6	27·6
Total	516·3	100·0
5 By entitlement to benefit (August 1973)[f]		
Receiving unemployment benefit only	163	28·6
Receiving unemployment and supplementary benefits	46	8·1
Receiving supplementary benefit only	219	38·3
Others registered for work	143	25·0
Total	571	100·0

[a] Unemployed persons last unemployed in an industry as a percentage of total employees in the industry (employed and unemployed).

[b] Condensed from analyses published monthly by minimum list headings of the Standard Industrial Classification.

[c] Males only; condensed from classification in *Department of Employment Gazette*, September 1972, pp. 799–803, as in *Department of Employment Gazette*, May 1974.

[d] From *Department of Employment Gazette*, August 1973, p. 778.

[e] From *Department of Employment Gazette*, November 1973, p. 1179.

[f] From *Department of Employment Gazette*, November 1973, p. 1148.

In 1971–2 the unemployment statistics were criticised, by some who said that the published statistics are too high because they include people who are not genuinely seeking work or who are 'unemployable', and by others who said that they are too low because they do not include people who seek work without registering as unemployed. A Working Party was set up to examine these arguments and its report was published in November 1972.[1] As regards criticisms about the genuineness or employability of those on the register, the main conclusions of the Working Party can be summarised briefly as follows:

(i) The 'temporarily stopped' are in a different category from the 'wholly unemployed' and should be shown separately; this is now being done.

(ii) It is not practicable to identify categories of those alleged to be 'not genuinely seeking work'. Between 1921 and 1930 it was a condition for the payment of unemployment benefit that claimants should be 'genuinely seeking work', but this criterion came to have emotional overtones, was extremely unpopular and was difficult to define and apply in practice. It was repealed in the Unemployment Act, 1930, which substituted the provision that a claimant should not refuse an offer of suitable employment without good cause.

(iii) There is no doubt that the register includes some people who might be described as 'unemployable', who are exceptionally difficult to place in work and who seldom hold down a job for more than a week or two. These tend to be found among the elderly, unskilled or socially disadvantaged, and people who find it difficult to adapt to the conditions of working life. However, although some individuals are clearly more employable than others, it is not possible to draw a clear line. It would be administratively impracticable to give an operational definition of 'unemployable' and, even if this were done, it would only identify the extreme cases.

(iv) Many of the unemployed are 'short-term unemployed' or 'just changing jobs', but one does not know in advance which of the people on the register are those who are going to get jobs quickly. It is, however, possible to identify those who have been on the register for only a short time – for example, in December 1973 some 23 per cent of those on the register had been unemployed for four weeks or less.

The Working Party made several recommendations for simplifying and improving the presentation of the statistics. It recommended that further studies should be made of the characteristics of the registered unemployed. It commented that the numbers on the register might be affected by administrative and legal changes, for example the introduction of redundancy payments in 1965 and of earnings-related benefits in 1966, the improvements in the employment service, and the forthcoming abolition of National Insurance cards and introduction of a new National Insurance scheme.

The Working Party brought together the available evidence on the 'unregistered unemployed' – those seeking work who are not registered – and stressed the importance of the United Kingdom participating in the E.E.C. Labour Force Survey, which was being planned at that time. It recommended that the possibility of instituting regular interview surveys to supplement the existing statistics should be considered further in the light of experience of the E.E.C. Survey and the General Household Survey.

UNREGISTERED UNEMPLOYED

At any one time there are always a considerable number of people who are looking for work but who are not registered as unemployed. This is not a new discovery. Figures were obtained in the Censuses of Population in 1966 and 1971. In between the censuses, estimates can be obtained from household surveys. Since the White Paper, some further qualitative information on the characteristics of the 'unregistered unemployed' has been obtained from the small-scale General Household Survey and more detailed estimates will soon become available from the E.E.C. Labour Force Survey which was held in 1973 and which covered a sample of over 80,000 households in Great Britain.

The censuses show the numbers who were economically active but who were 'out of employment' in that week. These include some who were sick, some who were seeking work and some who were waiting to take up a job which they had already obtained. The numbers from the 1966 Census can be seen in Table 4.2. In the Census of Population in April 1971 the questions on this topic were less detailed, yielding the information in Table 4.3. If we subtract from the 'out of work (other)' the known number who were registered as wholly unemployed and make various minor adjustments, it can be estimated that in April 1971 there were about 70,000 males and 230,000 females who described themselves as seeking work or waiting to take up a job, but who were not sick or registered as unemployed. These figures are broadly comparable to the 103,000 males and

133,000 females in this category in April 1966. Further information on the numbers of 'unregistered unemployed' will become available during 1976 from the E.E.C. Labour Force Survey.

Table 4.2 *'Out of employment' in 1966 Census of Population*

	Thousands Males	Females
Sick		
Registered as unemployed	20	8
Not registered	120	78
Seeking work		
Registered as unemployed	153	49
Not registered	60	66
Waiting to take up a job		
Registered as unemployed	47	18
Not registered	43	67
Total	444	287

Source: Department of Employment, *British Labour Statistics: Historical Abstract, 1886–1968*, H.M.S.O., 1971, Appendix A.

Table 4.3 *'Out of employment' in 1971 Census of Population*

	Thousands Males	Females
Out of work (sick)	192	104
Out of work (other)	667	344
Total	859	448

Source: *Department of Employment Gazette*, November 1973, p. 1084.

Qualitative information about the 'unregistered unemployed' has been found from the General Household Survey, which is a continuous interview survey covering about 15,000 households in the course of a year. Of those who described themselves to the interviewers as seeking work, about 7½ per cent of the men and 54 per cent of the women had not registered as unemployed. The proportion of non-registration among married women (two-thirds) was twice as high as the proportion for unmarried women (one-third). Out of the 103 persons in the sample who described themselves as looking for work but not registered, there were 23 who did nothing more than look at job vacancies in the newspapers or simply wait for something to turn up. The rest had taken active steps, such as registering with a private employment agency, advertising, or making a direct approach to a prospective employer, or they were waiting for the result of job applications.[2] The survey also showed the reasons why those who were unemployed had left their last job (see Table 4.4).

Table 4.4   *Reasons given by the unemployed for leaving their last job*

	Males	Percentages[a] Females	Total
Made redundant/sacked	55·8	21·4	43·1
Ill health	29·0	23·3	26·9
Dissatisfied with last job	11·0	20·4	14·4
Last job was temporary	3·7	7·3	5·0
Retired	1·7	0·5	1·2
Domestic reasons/pregnancy/other	4·8	33·0	15·2

Source: Office of Population Censuses and Surveys, *General Household Survey*.
[a]Columns do not sum to 100 because some people gave more than one reason for leaving.

REGISTERED UNEMPLOYED: TRENDS AND CHARACTERISTICS

Trends in the composition of the registered unemployed over the period 1954–72 were analysed in the *Department of Employment Gazette* for March 1973. A series of very informative charts brought out the following main points:

(i) The number of unemployed males has risen much faster than the number of unemployed females.

(ii) Around the trends, there have been marked variations, which have corresponded very clearly to the business cycle.

(iii) Among males, with a few exceptions, unemployment has moved more or less in parallel among the industries and regions. The main exceptions among regions were the Midlands regions, in which unemployment increased relative to the national average. Among industries, there was a tendency for unemployment to fluctuate with a wider amplitude in the production sector of the economy than elsewhere, and there were movements due to structural changes in shipbuilding and coalmining, and high rates in construction.

(iv) Most remarkably, unemployment among administrative, professional and technical workers rose even faster than unemployment among labourers. The increase in unemployment between 1954 and 1972 was not confined to unskilled workers but affected, almost equally, not only the labourers and administrative workers but also clerical workers, engineering and transport workers, and shop assistants; though among farm workers it rose less and among construction workers more.

(v) Analyses by age showed an above average increase for males in the younger age groups, particularly under 20, and a relative decline for males over 65, presumably as a result of earlier retirement.

The regular statistics show the numbers of people who have been on the register for various periods of time on the day of the count. These do not, however, tell us directly the time which individual people have spent on the register by the time they leave it, or the flows on and off the register. But they provide the raw material from which estimates can be made.

The flow of persons on and off the register is very large indeed. Some estimates obtained by actuarial methods were first published in 1968 in a paper by Fowler.[3] He estimated that when unemployment was at the average levels observed in the period 1961–5 the average flows on to the register were about 39,000 males and 16,000 females per week, with similar numbers flowing off, so that the average duration of a spell on the register was about 7·8 weeks for males and 6·2 weeks for females. More recent estimates obtained by similar methods suggested that in the period 1967–70 the flows for males were rather higher and the duration rather longer.[4] The same article showed the median and deciles of the duration of unemployment of those on the register in the period 1948–72, with some analyses by sex, age and region; it also gave further estimates of the 'survival curve' for unemployment, showing, for example, that out of cohorts of people joining the register in the average conditions of 1967–70 it could be expected that only about 50 per cent would remain on the register after 2 weeks, 25 per cent after 8 weeks and 3 per cent after 52 weeks.

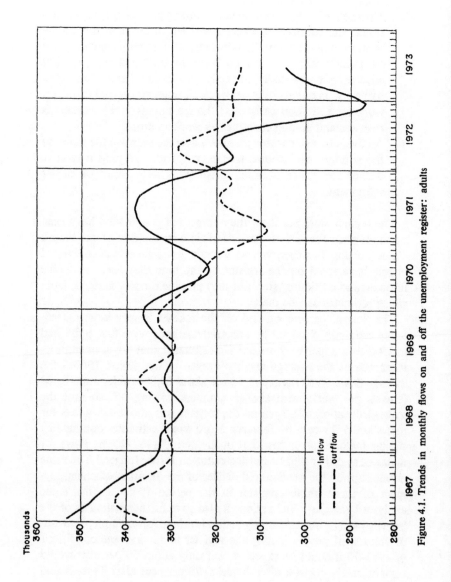

Figure 4.1. Trends in monthly flows on and off the unemployment register: adults

Meanwhile, approximate figures had been published of the actual flows on and off the register, based on management returns.[5] These proved to be even higher than the actuarial estimates, and the average duration slightly lower, probably because the flows include a high proportion of people who are on the register for only a very short time, many for only one or two days, and the characteristics of this group are not fully reflected in the assumptions used in the actuarial methods.

The further statistics of flows which have since been published[6] show in a very interesting way how the enormous movements in the level of unemployment in the period 1970-3 resulted from relatively small differences between the inflow and outflow to the register (see Figure 4.1). Each year there are some $3\frac{1}{2}$–4 million registrations of unemployed adults seeking work. In addition there are nearly $\frac{1}{2}$ million registrations of people who are seeking new jobs but who are not unemployed because they have existing jobs. The total number of occasions when people join a new employer in the course of a year is larger still; it varies with market conditions, but is probably of the order of 9 million a year. The proportion of people who register between leaving one job and starting another is higher for men than for women, and may also vary with time.

In 1961 and 1964 surveys were held in which the staff in Department of Employment local offices assessed the prospects and attitudes to work of those on the register. In 1964, for example, when unemployment was about 340,000, about 40 per cent of the men on the register were classified as 'should get work without difficulty' or 'will find difficulty in getting work because of lack of local opportunities'. The remaining 60 per cent were classified as 'will find difficulty in getting work on personal grounds', the majority because of age, or physical or mental condition. The assessments of the prospects were highly correlated with the age and duration of unemployment of the persons concerned.

Such assessments are subjective and the 1964 survey was later criticised by certain commentators. A similar survey was held in June 1973, but this time, in order to reduce the element of subjectivity to some extent, a follow-up survey was held in January 1974 to find out how many of those described as 'poor prospects' in June 1973 had since found employment.[7] The results are remarkably similar to those found in the 1964 survey: 40 per cent of those on the adult register in June 1973 were judged to have good or reasonable prospects of finding long-term work (though perhaps limited by local opportunities) and to be keen to find work; another 30 per cent were keen to find work but had poor prospects of finding it; and a final 30 per cent had poor prospects of finding work and were somewhat unenthusiastic in their attitude to work. About two-thirds of those men who were judged in June 1973 to have good prospects were successful in finding employment between June 1973 and January 1974, compared with only about one-third of those who were judged to have poor prospects.[8]

Unemployment has shown very large fluctuations in recent years. In early 1972 many commentators became extremely concerned about the level of unemployment and thought that it would never return to the levels of 1967–70. The characteristics of the unemployed were, however, not very different from before and the statistics did not show any obvious reason why unemployment should not fall considerably if the demand for labour revived. This was, in fact, what happened and by the autumn of 1973 the cry was that there were shortages of labour.

NOTES

1 Department of Employment, *Unemployment Statistics: Report of an Inter-Departmental Working Party*, Cmnd 5157, H.M.S.O., 1972.
2 Office of Population Censuses and Surveys, *General Household Survey: Introductory Report*, H.M.S.O., 1973, pp. 206–11. This report also gives analyses by socio-economic group.
3 Central Statistical Office, *Duration of Unemployment on the Register of Wholly Unemployed* by R. F. Fowler, H.M.S.O., 1968.
4 *Department of Employment Gazette*, February 1973.
5 Ibid., September 1972.
6 Ibid., September 1973.
7 See the *Department of Employment Gazette*, March 1974, for the main results.
8 Some further analyses by occupational group have been published in the *Department of Employment Gazette*, May 1974.

Chapter 5

Assessment of Unemployment in the E.E.C.

D. HARRIS

THE COMMISSION'S INTEREST IN STATISTICS OF UNEMPLOYMENT

The interests and activities of the Commission of the European Communities and of its Statistical Office, governed by the Treaties on which the Communities rest, are inevitably less wide-ranging than those of the administrations of member governments. (The information required by the Commission, however, may well be different or have a different dimension to that required by member governments.) It may therefore be best to indicate at the outset the policy and legal background to the Commission's interest and involvement in statistics of unemployment.

Article 46 of the Treaty establishing the European Coal and Steel Community requires the High Authority, in consultation with governments and the various parties concerned, to 'obtain the information it requires to assess the possibilities for improving working conditions and living standards for workers in the industries within its province, and the threats to those standards. . . . It may publish the studies and information mentioned above.' The Treaty establishing the European Economic Community does not expressly impose any such obligation. However a number of articles in the section of the Treaty dealing with social policy impose tasks which it would be impossible to carry out unless the necessary information were available.

Community endeavours in the field of social policy were given further impetus by the Paris summit meeting in October 1972, which asked the Commission to prepare and submit a programme for social action. This programme, approved by the Commission on the 24th October 1973 and submitted to the Council on the following day, includes full and better employment as one of the main objectives for concerted action in economic, financial, regional and social policies at both Community and national levels. Progress is also being made in the preparation of a Community regional policy to deal with sectoral or regional imbalances, a policy which was also given considerable impetus by the Paris summit conference, which regarded this objective as a top priority. The criteria proposed by the Commission to define the regions to benefit from regional fund aid include 'a persistently high rate of unemployment or a high rate of net outward migration'.

Finally, Article 213 of the E.E.C. Treaty states that the Commission may, within the limits and under the conditions laid down by the Council '. . . collect any information . . . required for the performance of the tasks entrusted to it'.

The Commission therefore has an interest in unemployment and is empowered, in consultation with governments and the social partners (representatives of both sides of industry), to compile any information necessary for its policy purposes. Indeed it may command resources for the task and its position in this regard – and because of the greater homogeneity of its member states – is somewhat different from say the United Nations or O.E.C.D. On the other hand, its requirements for information for policy purposes are different from those of member countries, and are certainly not the sum of all the information which member nations need for their own purposes. There is, for example, an important interest in securing broad comparability between data for individual States and this is an important part of the work of the Statistical Office in Luxemburg.

STATISTICAL SOURCES AND METHODS

Improvement in the comparability of data or – in the jargon of the trade – harmonisation, may be at various levels, depending on the possibilities in the series. The national series may be brought together as they stand, or edited as far as the data allow to render them more comparable. The next level of harmonisation occurs when consistent definitions and classifications are agreed beforehand by the countries and, at the level above this, uniform methods of collection and systems of processing are also agreed. Up to this point the ability of the Statistical Office to influence the outcome is much the same as that of the international organisations, and the national statisticians may quite honestly differ in their interpretation of the agreed methods and definitions. There is however a further level of harmonisation – the level of 'communitaire' statistics – that is, statistics derived from Community surveys, in which the timing and form of the survey and the involvement of the Office is laid down in a formal Regulation, agreed by the Council of Ministers, which may also provide for some payment being made by the Commission to the national Statistical Offices for work done. (Of course the Commission has to secure a broad measure of agreement among the government statisticians beforehand.) But the fact that the survey is in part, if not completely, being carried out for Community purposes and to an agreed timetable by agreed methods does considerably improve the prospects of securing statistics of a reasonable standard of comparability.

NATIONAL SOURCES

Effectively, the main statistical sources on unemployment used by the Commission are at each end of the spectrum described above. The national series of short-period statistics vary widely in definition and coverage, reflecting differences in unemployment insurance legislation, in the scope and definitions of registered unemployed, and in the very availability of employment exchanges at which to register. Some information on current schemes of unemployment insurance in the Nine is given in Table 5.1, but the coverage of the schemes change over time and there are discontinuities within series. Though the Commission has stated that it has no plans to harmonise national social security schemes, the publication of details in comparative tables tends, to the extent that best practice spreads, to bring about some convergence. Nevertheless, very substantial differences remain; the figures are not comparable between countries, and cannot be made comparable even in a very broad way without additional statistical information and investigation. The Commission therefore includes questions on unemployment in its 'communitaire' employment surveys, for which information is gathered from a sample of households.

Within countries, the figures coming from national censuses of population, national sample surveys and micro censuses, and the

Table 5.1 *Unemployment insurance in the E.E.C. countries*

	Belgium	Denmark	France	Ireland
EXISTING SCHEMES[a]	Insurance	Insurance (optional)	(a) Assistance (b) Supplementary insurance[b]	(a) Insurance (b) Assistance
LEGISLATION First law	1944	1907	(a) 1940 (b) 1958	1911
Basic instruments	Decree of 1963 (amended)	Law of 1970	(a) Law of 1940 and decree of 1951 (b) Agreement of 1958 and ordinances of 1959, 1967	Laws of 1952–74
FIELD OF APPLICATION	All employees covered by social security	Employed workers aged over 18 may be admitted to a fund	(a) All employees (b) All employees bound by contract to employers in the scheme[b]	All employees aged over 16 under a contract of service or articles of apprenticeship[a]
CONDITIONS FOR GRANT OF BENEFIT Main	Fit for work and registered for employment	Capable of work, available for work and signed on at employment office	Registered at employment exchange	(a) Capable of work, available for work and signed on at employment office (b) As (a), also seeking work, resident 6 months, inadequate resources and no right to insurance benefits
Qualifying period/ contributions	75 working days in last 10 months and 600 working days in last 36 months[d]	26 weeks' employment in last 3 years and 12 months' insurance with the fund	(a) Paid employment for 150 days in last year (b) 91 days' membership or 520 working hours in last year	(a) 26 contributions (maximum benefit paid only if 48 contributions in last year) (b) —

Italy	Luxemburg	Netherlands	United Kingdom	West Germany
a) Insurance b) Exceptional allowances	Assistance	(a) Interim allowance (b) Insurance (c) Assistance	Insurance	(a) Insurance (b) Assistance
1919	1921	(a) (b) 1949 (c) 1964	1911	1927
Decree – law of 1935 (amended)	Decrees of 1945, 1952	(a) (b) Law of 1949 (amended) (c) Law of 1964	Acts of 1965 (flat-rate benefits), of 1966 (earnings- related benefits) and of 1971 and 1973	Law of 1969
a) All employees b) Workers in certain categories and areas ineligible under (a)	Employed persons with some exclusions (e.g. agricultural workers)	(a) (b) All em- ployees (c) Employees not or no longer eligible under (a) and (b)	(a) Flat-rate benefits – all employees (b) Earnings- related benefits – all employees aged over 18, receiving (a) and earning at least £500 p.a.	(a) All employees including workers in vocational training (b) All employees in a state of need
Registered at employment exchange	Registered at employment exchange	Registered at employment exchange	Capable of work, available for work and signed on at employment office	Registered at employment exchange and having applied for benefit
a) 2 years' insurance and 52 weeks' contributions in last 2 years b) 5 weeks' contributions before 1949 or during last 2 years	200 days' employment in last year	(a) 130 days' paid employment in same occupational sector in last year (b) (c) 65 days paid employment in last year, or for last 36 days	26 contributions (maximum benefit paid only if 50 contributions in last year)	(a) 6 months' insured employment in last 3 years (b) 10 weeks' insured employment or having received unemployment allowance in last year

Table 5.1 – *continued*

	Belgium	Denmark	France	Ireland
CONDITIONS FOR GRANT OF BENEFIT–*cont.*				
Maximum age	65 for men 60 for women	65	65	68
WAITING PERIOD	None	None	(a) 3 days (b) None	3 days, and 12 days for pay-related benefits
DAYS FOR WHICH ALLOWANCE GRANTED	Working days and unpaid public holidays	6 days a week	Every day	6 days a week
DURATION OF PAYMENT	No limit*g*	Not more than $2\frac{1}{2}$ years, and 78 days in any year for pensioners or aged 67+	(a) No limit, but reduced by 10% after 1 year and 10% each further year[h] (b) 365 days, with extensions according to age	(a) Unlimited for aged 65–8 and 156 contributions paid; 156 days for under 18 and married women; 312 days in other cases. 147 days for pay-related benefits (b) Unlimited
AMOUNT				
Earnings taken as reference	Average gross earnings	Usually based on average earnings of last 5 weeks	(a) — (b) Earnings on which contributions paid in last 3 months	For pay-related benefits, gross taxable earnings in previous year
Ceilings	—	90% of average earnings	(b) F.F.9,280 per month	For pay-related benefits, £50 a week. Total benefits not to exceed weekly earnings
Rate	60% of earnings for a year, then 40% unless head of a household[k]	Maximum rates fixed annually by each fund[l]	(a) F.F.10.00 per day for 3 months, then F.F.9.10	(a) Married women £6.55 per week, others £7.75

Italy	Luxemburg	Netherlands	United Kingdom*f*	West Germany
—	65	65	(a) — (b) 65 for men 60 for women	65
(a) 7 days (b) 1 day	2 days if period of unemployment less than 1 week	None	(a) 3 days (b) 12 days	None
Every day	Every day	5 days a week	6 days a week	6 days a week

(a) 180 days a year
   (360 days in
   the building
   sector)
(b) 90 days with
   possible extension
	26 weeks in a year	(a) 40 days a year*i*
		(b) 130 days a year
		(c) 2 years
			(a) 312 days
			   (excluding
			   Sundays) for
			   for each
			   unemployed
			   period*j*
			(b) 156 days
			   (excluding
			   Sundays) for
			   each
			   unemployed
			   period
				(a) Proportionate
				   to employment
				   in last 3 years:
				   6 months – 78
				     days
				   9 months – 120
				     days
				   12 months – 156
				     days
				   18 months – 234
				     days
				   24 months – 312
				     days
				(b) Unlimited

—	Earnings on
	which sickness
	insurance
	contributions paid
		Daily earnings
		lost
			(a) —
			(b) Annual
			   earnings
			   divided by 50 to
			   give 'weekly'
			   rate
				Net earnings for
				last 20 days

—	L.frs 42,267 per month	(a) (b) Fl.155·70 per day*e* (c) —	85 % of weekly earnings in relevant year and 85 % of total flat- rate and earnings- related benefits plus family supplements	D.M.2,500 per month

L.800 per day	60 % of reference
	earnings
		(a) (b) 80 % of
		   reference
		   earnings
		(c) 75 % of
		   reference
		   earnings*m*
			(a) Married
			   women 18+
			   £6·05 per week,
			   all under 18
			   £4·75, others
			   £8·60
				(a) 62·5 % to 80 %
				   of net earnings
				   according to
				   family situation
				(b) 52·5 % to 80 %
				   of net earnings*n*

Table 5.1 – *continued*

	Belgium	Denmark	France	Ireland
AMOUNT–*cont.* Rate–*cont.*			(b) 50% of reference earnings for 3 months, then 35%⁰	(b) Urban areas £6.35 per week maximum, others £6.05
Family supplements	—	—	(a) F.F.4.00 per day for spouse and each dependant (b) —	(a) £5.05 per week for each dependent adult, £2.20 for each of first two children, £1.80 for each further child (b) £4.60 per week*f* for a dependent adult and £1.95 for a child

Source: Commission of the European Communities, 1974

a Family allowances (independent of unemployment benefit) are also payable in all nine countries.

b Originally based upon contracts, this scheme has in practice been extended to cover all employees with certain exceptions, e.g. in domestic service.

c There are a few exclusions from this scheme. Also additional pay-related benefits at 40% of gross taxable earnings are payable under the same conditions as sickness benefits.

d Varies with the age of the insured person.

e For a 5-day week.

f (a) and (b) in this column refer to flat-rate and earnings-related benefits respectively (see FIELD OF APPLICATION) rather than to EXISTING SCHEMES as for other countries.

g Except in certain cases where unemployment is protracted or recurs with unusual frequency, handicapped persons in a protected workshop or workers with reduced hours.

h Maximum reduction of 30% for workers over 55; no reduction when job lost over 55.

Luxemburg	Netherlands	United Kingdom	West Germany
		(b) 33 % of average weekly earnings £10–£30, plus 15 % of average weekly earnings £30–£42	
—	—	£5·30 per week for a dependent adult, £2·70 for a first child, £1·80 for a second child, £1·70 each for further children	D.M.12 per week for each dependant (can be combined with family allowances to maximum D.M.348 a week)

i Recipients of interim allowance still considered linked to occupation. Trade co-operation associations can extend the allowance beyond 40 days. When it ceases unemployment benefit may be paid for 78 days in the same year.

j A further 13 contributions in employment qualify claimant to another 312 days' benefit.

k Minimum B.frs 345 per day (household head), B.frs 276 per day (single person) for a 6-day week.

l Maximum D.Kr.132 a day.

m For household heads and single persons over 40, minimum 80% of Fl.72·38 under (a) and (b), 75% of Fl.76·15 under (c).

n Maximum for single persons, D.M.228·60 per week under (a), D.M.192 per week under (b).

o Minimum F.F.16 a day for 3 months, then F.F.13·92, reduced in the event of supplementary income to a total of F.F.1,200 a month.

p £4·50 only outside urban areas.

Community's Labour Force Survey always differ from the social security figures, and the direction of the bias varies from country to country and the size of the bias with time. The differences, of course, are well known and usually easy to understand against the legal and social background of the countries concerned, but there are difficulties even over fairly obvious explanations in such a politically sensitive area. In most countries the differences between series have been examined by one or more expert committees and there are numerous reports. The outcome generally has been to make some clear distinction in the terms used to describe the statistics from different sources, say to refer to 'unemployed' in data from censuses and other household surveys, but to refer simply to 'registered at employment exchanges' in the short-period administrative statistics. The Commission has adopted much the same solution, using the term 'registered unemployment' to describe the legal definition in the national short-period series and the word 'unemployment' to describe the economic definition used in the Labour Force Surveys which the Commission has carried out under formal Regulations.

The reasons for differences between the Labour Force Survey figures and those for registered unemployed vary widely from country to country, as do the methods of dealing with them. In some countries, national statistics for registered unemployed cover only those actually in receipt of benefits, and exclude both those too young to be entitled to benefits and those engaged on relief works (though where the missing figures are published separately, the Statistical Office includes them in Commission publications). In other countries, where the figures for registered unemployment are higher than the household survey figures, the reason may be that some who are not actively seeking work, and may indeed never work again, may need to maintain registration for pension reasons; or those registered may be seeking only specific employment, or employment in other countries, and, if not in receipt of benefits, may have accepted temporary work or family employment. In each case the numbers are large. In areas of very high unemployment, continued part-time studies may lead registered unemployed to return themselves as students in the household inquiries. In one instance, where the difference has been in the other direction, part of the explanation lies in a lack in some regions of employment exchanges at which to register.

So whatever is done, the national short-period statistics remain subject to a great deal of qualification in absolute terms and require some amount of expertise in use. But for some interpretative purposes it is the trend which is important and this is not likely to be affected to the same extent.

THE E.E.C. LABOUR FORCE SURVEY

The main purpose of the survey is to provide comparative figures on the structure of employment and to make good deficiencies in national sources. (In the early sixties, for example, only three of the Six produced regular statistics of the number of women in employment.) It is less satisfactory as a source of comparable statistics of unemployment, but is nevertheless a most important source and quite crucial to any comparison between national series.

By 1960, when the first Community Survey was held, the three large member countries already had national household surveys, on an annual basis in Germany and France, and quarterly in Italy. After the 1960 Survey, there was a gap until 1968 and then there were Community Surveys in 1969, 1970 and 1971; that for 1973 is now being processed. Luxemburg did not take part in the 1968 Survey and Holland did not take part in the Surveys for 1969 to 1971. Seven countries, the United Kingdom and the original Six, participated in 1973 and it is hoped that the Nine will all assist in 1975. Because their size of sample has to be proportionately so much larger if the same standard of reliability is to be achieved, the Surveys are always a problem for the smaller countries. The size of sample has been of the order of 100,000 for large countries, 50,000 for small.

The form of the Surveys is the subject of advice from a committee of statisticians from member countries, but neither the advisory committee nor the Statistical Office formulate the questions. This is because a straight translation of a standard questionnaire would not be universally understood, and because the national Offices prefer to work by modification of their existing and well-understood questionnaires and so to limit the extent to which interviewers have to be retrained. The method we employ is to let the national Statistical Offices know what is required in the form of answers codified for standardised processing and leave it to them to set the questions.

Coding instructions go out to member States in the form of a booklet in each language.

For the future: present intentions are to continue to take Labour Force Surveys at least biennially and to continue to use national material for short-period information. In the field of planning social action, however, and in the start of regional policy, the Commission is in an active phase, with projects and alternatives under discussion, many of which would require new and more detailed information about employment (for example, about migrant workers, school-leavers, the need for re-training and so on). So it is best to regard the present statistical programme as a minimum programme, which is unlikely to be reduced but which may well be augmented.

Part III

DOES WHAT WE MEASURE MATCH UP TO WHAT WE OUGHT TO MEASURE?

Chapter 6

Some Notes on Current Unemployment[1]

J. K. BOWERS

During the summer of 1973, before the oil crisis, there was an intensive discussion about whether the British economy was overheated. The actual unemployment rate was then only a little lower than the peak during the recession of 1962-3 and was actually higher than the peak in the recession of 1958. There were many who argued that the nature of unemployment had changed significantly, particularly since 1966, and that a rate which in earlier years would have been considered too high was now perhaps too low.

Much of the discussion of unemployment since 1966 has centred round the change in the relationship between unemployment and vacancies: the *UV* relationship. This paper adopts this approach and in particular considers the explanations of the shifts in this relationship over the period of the upswing since 1972.

THE DEBATE

The first detailed discussion of unemployment in the period since 1966 that I know of was by Cheshire, Webb and myself.[2] The task of hat paper was to explain the breakdown of the Phillips curve from 1966. It argued that the most appropriate measure of the level of excess demand for labour – the independent variable in the relationship – was the level of unfilled vacancies. Until 1966 unemployment, the variable normally used, had been a good proxy for vacancies, being related to it through a log–linear *UV* curve, but from the last quarter of 1966 the *UV* curve had begun to move outwards too. It was shown that, in the period up to the end of

1969, a relationship between the unfilled vacancy rate for men and the rate of change of average earnings of male manual workers remained stable.[3]

This argument led naturally to an attempt to explain the shift in the UV curve. The analysis was conducted entirely for adult males, for whom the UV curve from December 1958 to March 1970 was shown as Chart 4 in that article.[4] The approach adopted was to estimate UV curves for a set of industries and regions, and compare the pattern of shifts in these curves. Because UV curves are non-linear, the aggregate curve could shift as a result of redistribution of unemployment and vacancies between industries and regions, involving only movements along the disaggregated curves. More generally, the pattern of shifts in these micro-relationships might give some clues as to the sources of disturbance. Second, a relationship between change in unemployment and labour turnover was derived, and it was shown, mainly by means of a diagram but also with an equation relating turnover to vacancies,[5] that turnover was exceptionally high from the end of 1966 to the end of the period under consideration (1969). Finally, a list of possible causes – policy changes and other economic events – was drawn up. The plausibility of each as an explanation was then considered on the basis of its timing and compatibility with the observed pattern of shifts in the disaggregated UV curves, and with the behaviour of labour turnover.

For a number of reasons no clear-cut conclusion emerged from the exercise. First, the number of possible causes was large. Doubtless a considerable number of explanations might be suggested for the abnormal behaviour of any economic aggregate at any time, but the period of the 1964–70 Labour government saw the introduction of an exceptional number of new policies and policy measures. And, given that the probable time-lags between cause and effect were uncertain, it was difficult to rule out any explanation. Furthermore, a combination of causes was clearly possible and, since the UV curve continued, more or less, to shift outwards throughout the period and labour turnover remained high, perhaps necessary.

Secondly, the pattern of movement of industrial and regional UV curves was difficult to interpret. All of them followed the same general direction as the aggregate curve, but the extent of movement varied considerably. However, whether this differential pattern reflected the sectoral impact of the initiating cause of the shift, or was simply the result of differences in the recording of vacancies and the registration of the unemployed was not clear. The shift tended to be smallest in the high-unemployment regions, but the industrial shifts showed greater variation with no particular pattern. The diversity of shifts was less marked than the similarity; in no case did the *UV* curve move inwards and in only one (shipbuilding) was the outward shift from 1966 not significant.[6]

Two alternative explanations were suggested in the conclusion: 'a composite package . . . the main components of which are S.E.T., regional policy, some technologically or demand-induced shifts in certain industries . . . supplemented from the end of 1967 by the structural consequences of devaluation and perhaps also by the rundown of public investment programmes', and 'a "voluntary quits" hypothesis, where the main cause would seem to be incomes policy and perhaps a (related) change in workers' expectations about future employment prospects'.[7] The argument was that the imposition of a constraint on the rate of growth of wages led to an increase in labour turnover as workers sought to maintain their previous rate of growth of wages by finding higher paying jobs within their occupations in other firms and/or industries. This induced rise in voluntary quits would, particularly in a context of falling aggregate demand, cause unemployment to rise against vacancies. As an explanation of how incomes policy can shift a Phillips curve this still seems to me to be as theoretically coherent and as plausible as the analysis of Lipsey and Parkin.[8] Additionally, it explains the shift in the *UV* curve. It was not established, of course, that the rise in turnover was the result of increased voluntary quits.

In view of the subsequent debate it has to be mentioned that, as important parts of the explanation of events, a 'shake-out', the Redundancy Payments Act and the introduction of earnings-related benefits were rejected. It was felt that a 'shake-out' would explain the exceptional rise in unemployment in late 1966, but that it was difficult to reconcile with the evidence of high labour turnover in the succeeding three years, engagements as well as discharges as being high.[9] Redundancy payments, in view of the conditions of payment, were also thought unlikely to explain this phenomenon unless the Act induced employers to turnover labour rapidly to avoid liability, and here it was considered that the costs would exceed the possible benefits. Earnings-related benefits could explain high turnover were it not for the provision that a 'voluntary quitter' received no benefit at all for six weeks. With any positive rate of interest and with feasible expectations of higher wages from job-change, the benefit would be unlikely to induce voluntary quitting; at best it might soften attitudes towards redundancy.

In his paper published some 16 months later, Gujarati by-passed the discussion about the causes of the *UV* shift.[10] He simply asserted that the combination of the Redundancy Payments Act and the introduction of earnings-related benefit seemed to be responsible 'on grounds of logic and timing';[11] what the logic was he did not say. All the paper contains is a brief, loose, and in some respects inaccurate, summary of the provisions of the relevant Acts. The aim of the paper seems to have been to derive a 'simple correcting factor' which might be used 'to convert current unemployment rates to the old basis'.[12] This correcting factor he believed could be applied whatever the cause of the shift. If the aim had been simply to estimate what unemployment would have been at a given level of vacancies in the absence of the shift, then the adjustment would be unobjectionable although not very interesting. It could not be used to adjust unemployment for some level of effective demand or degree of capacity utilisation, however, unless the shift had not affected the relationship between vacancies and these variables, and no evidence was presented on this point. But Gujarati's aim was different: the social security legislation he says created an artificial increase in registered unemployment,[13] and the correction factor was to enable one to estimate the 'true' level of unemployment. If this is correct, it follows that the increased unemployment is voluntary, and it can be argued that the welfare implications of this 'new' unemployment are less severe than the old. But even then it does not follow that the full employment target level of unemployment needs revising upwards by the extent of the correction factor. The outward shift of the *UV* curve presumably implies a reduced allocative efficiency of the labour market, and there may be a welfare gain from running the economy at a higher level of excess demand for labour than was previously the case. But if Gujarati is wrong and the increased unemployment is not voluntary, stemming from changes in labour demand rather than supply, then no possible case can be made out for his 'correction'.

Taylor, in a comment on Gujarati, offered an alternative explanation.[14] He attributed the rise in unemployment over the period 1967–9 to a 'shake-out' of labour by employers at that time. As evidence he offered his estimates of labour hoarding for the economy and showed that hoarding, so defined, had fallen in these years in a number of index of production industries. Labour hoarding was measured by the ratio of actual labour productivity to its full capacity level, estimated as the trend through peaks. Taylor admitted that the evidence was equally compatible with a steep rise in the productivity trend, and this was the interpretation placed on events by the National Institute.[15] Either way it means that the rise in unemployment at that time was not matched by a fall in output. Taylor's technique amounted to a demonstration that the rise in productivity and in unemployment was not structural, that it was general across industries.[16] This is in accord with our findings in the 1970 article.[17]

While this alternative way of looking at the problem is useful, two comments are in order. First, the demonstration that there was a fall in labour hoarding does not establish that a 'shake-out' occurred; it is as compatible with a supply shift as a demand shift. Labour hoarding may have fallen (or labour productivity risen) because employers were unable to obtain the labour they desired as a result of increased voluntary quits. Provided that labour hoarding did exist – provided, that is, that the current employment levels were more than sufficient to meet current and immediate future output plans – increased turnover would not be matched by falling output.[18] Employers may have chosen to run down their labour stocks, or they may have had no choice.

If the dis-hoarding was involuntary, then one would not expect unfilled vacancies to have fallen in line with the rise in unemployment; indeed one might expect them to have risen. This is the second point: the 'shake-out' hypothesis has difficulty in accounting for the behaviour of vacancies.[19] Taylor suggests that vacancies remained high because employers became more selective in their employment policies, but admits that, while this will work for the period of dishoarding (1967–8), for later periods the argument is more difficult to sustain.[20] This also was a problem that we faced in our second article.[21]

In the light of the discussion in the *Economic Journal* and the difficulties of the previous attempt, our 1972 article abandoned the

attempt to identify specific events as causes of the behaviour of unemployment, and instead concentrated on deciding whether the
initiating force came from the side of labour supply or demand. This
is plainly the most important issue to be decided. As already noted
it affects attitudes towards unemployment and the benefits to the
community from a lower level of unemployment. Additionally, it
influences predictions about future levels of unemployment and
about the future behaviour of the UV curve.[22] If demand forces are
the cause, then the most important question is whether the rise in
productivity observed is permanent; perhaps labour hoarding was
the result of inefficiency coupled with ignorance, or perhaps it was
temporary. Most important of all, an answer to the question whether
demand or supply forces are paramount is required for judgements
about the levels of capacity utilisation in the economy, and hence
about the direction and extent of budgetary policy. In the last quarter
of 1972 this issue was plainly a real one.

The task as we saw it was as follows. First it had to be established
that indeed something had really happened to unemployment; that
it was not just something which had gone wrong with the recording
of unemployment or unfilled vacancies, or the result of a mis-
specification of the relationship between the two.[23] Then a theoretical
basis for the UV curve had to be developed and the results, with
such other evidence as was available, used to discriminate between
supply and demand forces as determinants of the higher unemployment.

It was also important to confirm the previous conclusion that
there had been no substantial structural shifts within the economy
that could account for events. To this end we estimated UV curves
for selected occupations. These were difficult to interpret and impossible to compare, since the unemployment and vacancies data
could not be put in the form of rates; but as far as they went they
tended to confirm previous conclusions. An alternative approach of
computing unemployment relatives by industry, occupation and
region also suggested that things looked much as they always had
done.[24] If there had been structural shifts in the economy, it seemed
that our techniques were too crude to detect them.

That unemployment was indeed at an abnormal level was established in the following manner. It was shown, following the work in
the 1970 article, that there was a stable relationship between the first

difference in registered unemployment and net labour turnover. Net labour turnover (discharges minus engagements) was then shown to be related to the first difference in industrial production (in fact a two-period distributed lag proved appropriate); substitution then gave a relationship between first differences in unemployment and in industrial production, and this relationship was shown to have shifted from the end of 1966, implying a positive time trend to unemployment from that date.[25] This relationship enabled an estimate of the extent to which unemployment was higher at recent dates than would have been expected from the output–unemployment relationship before 1966, and the estimates turned out to be almost identical to those derived from the *UV* curves. This established that indeed it was an exceptional level of unemployment that had to be explained. It also implied that the relationship between unfilled vacancies and output was stable over the period. The appropriate form of this latter relationship was again a first difference one, and this, on testing, was stable.[26]

Thus the problem was that of explaining why net labour turnover – in fact the (negative) change in employment – had risen against output and against vacancies. The previous article had suggested, in addition, that gross turnover had risen against these variables and this was confirmed. In other words, not only had discharges increased for given changes in output, engagements had increased also but not by so much. And, in this situation, vacancies had followed the movement in output and not the divergent movement in unemployment.

With regard to the *UV* curve it was reasoned that the relationship was indirect. Gross labour turnover was always very high compared with net movements in employment levels (or net turnover). This being so, any desired change in employment would have been quickly accomplished by minor adjustments in the flows were it not for the fact that gross turnover was itself a function of the level of aggregate demand for labour. An attempt at increasing employment levels by all firms would therefore be partially frustrated by increased voluntary turnover. Employment would rise and unemployment fall, not as a result of reduced rates of entry to and exit from the unemployment register, but because of a reduction in mean duration of unemployment amongst those on the register. But the increased rate of voluntary turnover would be reflected – given that workers did not move instantaneously to new jobs – by higher unfilled vacancies.

Any supply shift would appear as a rise in voluntary turnover, and hence vacancies, through an increased unwillingness to accept job offers, and perhaps a rise in unemployment levels (although most of the people involved would probably not pass through the unemployment register). The UV curve would thus move outwards, with higher V for any U or higher U for any V. Additionally, given the existence of some labour hoarding, vacancies could be expected to rise against output.

A reduction in labour hoarding (we called this a demand shift) would not, however, have opposite effects. This would entail a once-and-for-all reduction in employment. Once accomplished, however, the level of labour turnover would adjust to the level of unemployment; the result would amount to a move along the UV curve. This is not to say that the path of adjustment would be along the normal one of the UV curve. If the reduction of employment was dramatic and exceptional (as would seem to have been the case in 1966–7), then presumably more of the reduction would take the form of sackings and less of natural wastage. While the process was taking place therefore, discharges might be higher than normal. In its turn, this could be expected to induce more engagements and, perhaps for a time, some extra voluntary turnover, as some of the sacked men sampled the market and found jobs that suited them.[27] Additionally, it might take some while for the information about changed prospects in the market to permeate through to the relatively small section of the workforce that engages in voluntary quitting. Information flows in the labour market are very far from perfect.[28] Also, of course, part of the reduction in hoarding might be obtained by a tightening of recruitment policy – an increased reluctance to fill new and existing vacancies. For all these reasons one might expect that a shake-out would appear as an outward movement of the UV curve, and a rise in labour turnover – in fact a reduction in the allocative efficiency of the labour market – as a temporary phenomenon. Since, on the evidence of Taylor and the National Institute, the reduction in labour hoarding or the rise in labour productivity took place over a period of some two years, 1967 and 1968, one might expect the transitory movement to continue at least this long before settling down, with the UV curve returning to its previous position thereafter, although how long thereafter it is impossible to say.

Thus one cannot conclude anything about the causes of the higher unemployment directly from observation of the path of the *UV* curve or from the behaviour of labour turnover. The fact that vacancies did not rise against output, showing perhaps a once-and-for-all fall but no significant trend, argues for the 'demand shift' interpretation. But confirmation can only be obtained by looking at the causes of higher labour turnover; was there an increase in sackings over this period – or rather were sackings at an abnormally high level – or was it that voluntary quits were exceptionally high?

Unfortunately no direct evidence is available on these points; discharges are not classified by cause in United Kingdom data. Evidence must therefore be indirect, and three pieces were presented. First it was shown that, from 1968, the percentage of older workers on the unemployment register was greater than would have been predicted on past experience. A rise in voluntary turnover would have been expected to affect mainly younger workers; it is reasonably well-established that turnover declines with age. A shake-out, if taking place fairly quickly, would have been expected to embrace a cross-section of the labour force by age; the evidence being that in situations of redundancies 'last in, first out' principles do not normally apply. Given the lower probability of leaving the register of older workers, the change in the age composition of the register was what would have been expected from a shake-out and the reverse of the expectation for increased voluntary quits.

Secondly, because of the provisions of the National Insurance Acts, voluntary quitters have a lower incentive to register as unemployed than those who have been sacked. Examination of the relationship between rates of entry to the register and total discharges provides evidence for a higher proportion of labour turnover passing through the register in the period after 1966.

Finally, voluntary quitters, if they register, are less likely to receive benefits than sacked workers. Examination of the relation between recipients of benefit and the number of registered unemployed gave no evidence of a higher number of disqualified workers being on the register.

The article concluded therefore that the balance of probabilities was in favour of a shift in the demand for labour against output, and not a shift in labour supply, as being the explanation of the exceptional unemployment levels in the period since 1966.

THE UPSWING

The conclusion that factors on the side of labour demand rather than supply explained the rise of unemployment carried with it two implications. These, which held whatever one's beliefs about the nature and causes of the 'shake-out',[29] were that there was no need to revise the full employment target level of unemployment and that, with the fall in unemployment, the *UV* curve could be expected to return to something like its previous position. The second was, however, dependent on two assumptions: that the specification of the *UV* relationship was correct, and that there had not been and would not be any structural shifts within the economy. With these caveats, therefore, the behaviour of the *UV* curve in the upswing could be regarded as the acid test of the Taylor and Gujarati interpretations of events.

In the period of declining unemployment, there has been little sign of the *UV* curve returning to its previous position. Indeed if one fits a line to the observations from 1972 I to 1973 III,[30] its slope is considerably shallower than that of the line for the period up to 1966 II.[31] It would look therefore as though, with a constant regression, the relationship in the later period was still moving outwards. Such tests as could be carried out with so little data gave no evidence of a negative trend in the relationship.[32]

Should one therefore conclude that Gujarati was right and that the full employment target should be set at a markedly lower level of employment than was acceptable in the past – in fact at a level that was previously appropriate for a recession? Some commentators have drawn this conclusion. Certainly I do not. Rather, I wish to argue that the upswing of 1972–3 was marked by a substantial structural shift in the economy. This was tending to move the *UV* curve outwards and swamping any inward movement that might otherwise have resulted from a reversal of the shake-out. This view leads naturally to a reappraisal of my previous conclusion that structural change played a negligible role in the events of 1966–71. I think that structural factors were of more importance than I had previously allowed.

But before presenting the argument, a simpler explanation of events in 1972 and 1973 has to be considered. This is that the inward movement of the *UV* curve has been hidden by an increase in the efficiency of recording of vacancies – a consequence of administrative changes in the Department of Employment.

THE RECORDING OF VACANCIES

The question of the extent of spare capacity in the economy, and the related one of the full employment level of unemployment, were considered in detail by the National Institute in the *Review* for February and November 1973.[33] The latter repeats the arguments for an absence of structural change within the economy and attempts to provide additional evidence that the high level of unemployment is not voluntary.[34] Also a table is presented showing various indicators of spare capacity over the period 1964–73. The physical indicators suggest that, while spare capacity exists, it is at a level well below what would normally be expected in a slump, so that, while there is no reason to revise unemployment targets in the long term, a physical capacity constraint prevents that target being met in the immediate future, and a feasible short-term target of 300,000–400,000 registered unemployed is suggested.[35]

The other indicators of spare capacity are various parameters of the unemployment duration profile and derivatives from them,[36] and unfilled vacancies. Of these, only vacancies and one measure of the average duration of unemployment indicate a pressure of demand as great or greater than in the boom years 1964–6. 'So far as the vacancies series is concerned we are surprised at the continued faith placed in it by commentators . . . a significant part of the recent change is probably explained by increasing registration of vacancies as the government employment services are improved.'[37] The evidence given for this view is a publication by the Department of Employment, where it is stated that 'in one self-service experiment, vacancies notified by employers increased in the first year of operation by 30 per cent.'[38] This publication is a publicity and information pamphlet. Whether the experiments it mentions were controlled ones, and whether the increase in vacancies observed was standardised for variations in demand pressure and other factors is not clear. From the context it appears, however, that the emphasis in the experiments was more on increasing placings than on improving the recording of vacancies. The document is mainly about the future; it describes plans for the restructuring of the employment service. We learn that it is aimed to 'at least double' the number of vacancies notified in recent years;[39] that 'self-service will be provided in all new offices as a matter of course' and that it will be provided 'in any existing office where space can be made for it'.[40] Additionally, 'every local office will during 1972 install facilities for displaying the details of as many vacancies as possible.'

The effect of this on the recording of vacancies in 1972 is impossible to gauge. Certainly the trials at about 30 local offices, with five of them (in Cornwall) providing display for up to about 400 vacancies, which was the position in December 1971, must have had a negligible effect, and the Institute's assertion that these changes show that vacancies have 'been an *unreliable* indicator . . . over recent years'[41] is ludicrous. We have already quoted the Department's judgement at the Statistics Users' Conference in April 1973 that self-service exchanges had had little marked effect on vacancies so far.[42] Given the quality of evidence provided, I am, therefore, surprised that the Institute 'finds it surprising'.

These self-service experiments do sound a warning note that vacancies may become an unreliable indicator in future, but the same bell is rung with the unemployment series. The intention is to get more job-seekers to use the exchanges. Not all of these will be unemployed and unregistered, but some will be and, as the document makes clear, success in filling vacancies is dependent on success in registering job-seekers.

Having rejected this evidence, it is still worthwhile to test whether vacancies have shown an upward trend during the recent upswing. Our 1972 article produced evidence in the form of a first difference equation to show that vacancies were stable against output at least until 1971.[43] This evidence I suspect would not be acceptable to the authors of the *Review* article here considered, since they argue that, if demand factors explained the post-1966 rise in unemployment, then (given no structural shifts) vacancies should have fallen against output. Since they did not, then this was because they possessed an upward trend or at least were 'unreliable'. I have already suggested why this argument might not be correct.

Table 6.1 gives results for the period 1972 I–1973 III of applying

Table 6.1   *Actual and predicted changes in vacancy and unemployment rates: adult males, Great Britain*

| | | Percentages | | | | |
| | | Vacancies | | | Unemployment | |
	Actual	Predicted[a]	Residual	Actual	Predicted[b]	Residual
1972 I	+0·04	−0·02	+0·06	+0·35	+0·42	−0·07
II	+0·16	+0·15	+0·01	−0·82	−0·66	−0·16
III	+0·01	+0·02	−0·01	+0·21	−0·03	+0·24
IV	+0·14	−0·02	+0·16	−0·42	−0·02	−0·40
1973 I	+0·30	+0·17	+0·13	−0·34	−0·40	+0·06
II	+0·29	+0·15	+0·14	−0·81	−0·36	−0·45
III	+0·13	−0·06	+0·19	−0·10	−	−0·10

[a]Derived from the equation, estimated from data for the period 1958 IV–1971 IV,

$$\Delta V_t = -0·1559 + 0·0319\,Q_t{}^* - 0·0004\,Q_{t-1} - 0·0309\,Q_{t-2}^{\;*}$$
$$\quad\;\;(1·12)\qquad(2·62)\qquad\quad(0·02)\qquad\quad\;(2·56)$$
$$-0·0285\,D + \text{seasonals}\qquad\qquad(R^2 = 0·806,\text{D.W.} = 1·52)$$
$$(0·88)$$

where Q is a quarterly index of G.D.P., D is a shift dummy taking the value 1 from 1966 IV but omitted in the predictions given, t-ratios are shown in brackets and an asterisk indicates significance at the 1 per cent level.

[b]Derived from the equation

$$\Delta U_t = 0·5646 - 0·1648\,Q_t{}^* + 0·1134\,Q_{t-1}^{\;*} + 0·0492\,Q_{t-2}$$
$$\quad\;(1·63)\qquad(5·43)\qquad\quad(2·58)\qquad\quad(1·64)$$
$$+ 0·1670\,D^* + \text{seasonals}\qquad\qquad(R^2 = 0·906,\text{D.W.} = 1·37)$$
$$(2·86)$$

estimated from data for the same period and with the same conventions as for vacancies.

the equation relating first differences of vacancy rates to a distributed lag of the quarterly index of G.D.P.[44] estimated over the period 1958 IV–1971 IV. It is clear that from the last quarter of 1972 vacancies were rising much faster than this equation predicts.[45] Figure 6.1 shows this; there vacancy levels for the period 1972–3, calculated from the equation, are plotted against actual unemployment rates. The resulting curve has a much steeper slope than the observed one, and does not lie much above the actual *UV* path for the period 1969–71, when the *UV* curve was moving outwards. Thus, relative to previous experience, the trend in vacancy rates has been upwards during the recent upswing, this being discernible from the latter half of 1972.

The 1972 *Review* article also developed a relationship between out-

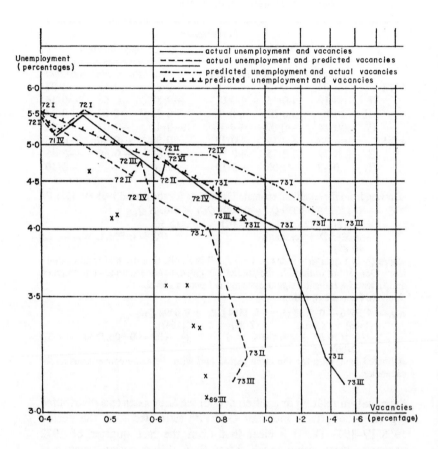

Figure 6.1. Actual and predicted unemployment and vacancy rates for adult
males: Great Britain
Source: *Department of Employment Gazette* (various issues).

put and the first differences of male unemployment rates. In this case there was a significant upward shift, described by a dummy variable, from 1966 IV; as well as rising against vacancies, unemployment rose against output. In Table 6.1 this relationship with the dummy omitted is used to predict the change in unemployment from 1972 I to 1973 III.[46] For most quarters (except 1972 III and 1973 I) the decline in unemployment is under-estimated; that is unemployment has declined compared with the relationship before 1966 IV. This is also shown in Figure 6.1, where unemployment rates calculated from the relationship (dummy omitted) are plotted against actual vacancy rates. This synthetic UV curve is shallower than the actual one. Figure 6.1 also plots predicted U against predicted V, calculated in the manner described above. This follows very closely the slope and positioning of the actual UV curve, but does not, of course, extend so far along the vacancy axis. Thus the outward trend in vacancies against G.D.P. has offset the inward trend in unemployment to give a UV curve which has not moved inwards. The contention of the National Institute that a trend in vacancies has masked the movement of the UV curve back towards its origin is in conformity with the evidence presented so far.

A STRUCTURAL SHIFT

But it is necessary to go a little deeper into the matter. The relationship between changes in output and in unemployment considered above is the result of two more basic relationships – between output and labour turnover, and between labour turnover and unemployment.

The output–turnover relationship itself has two aspects. Gross turnover – the level of discharges or engagements – is positively correlated with the cycle, being high when output is high relative to the trend, and low when it is low. Net turnover – engagements minus discharges – should be positively related to the change in output, because employment tends to rise with output and hence engagements exceed discharges. Implicit in this relationship between output and net turnover is, therefore, a trend in labour productivity. Any departure from this trend (or a change in trend) will cause the output–net turnover relationship to shift. A rise in the trend in productivity would seem to have been the proximate cause of the shift (change) in the unemployment–output relationship after 1966 III.

The relationship between net turnover and change in unemployment would, if all job-changers went through the unemployment register and all labour turnover was recorded, be an identity. Since the former condition does not hold and we have data only on manufacturing turnover, it takes on the nature of a behavioural equation. It can only shift, however, if the unemployment recording ratio changes, or the relationship between turnover in manufacturing and in other sectors of the economy alters. The 1972 article showed that this relationship was stable until 1971.[47]

Thus we would expect the fall in unemployment against output in the upswing to come from a rise in net turnover against output, as employers took back the labour that they had previously 'shaken out'. G.D.P. and manufacturing output were rising against trend from early 1972 to mid-1973. Gross labour turnover, as expected, rose also. The moving average of the discharge rate rose from 1·9 per cent in November 1971 to 2·7 per cent in November 1973 – the highest it had ever been – the engagement rate rose similarly over the same period from 1·6 per cent to 2·6 per cent. But throughout this period the discharge rate was greater than the engagement rate – net labour turnover was negative. Thus net turnover shifted sharply downwards against output – the reverse of the 'shake-in' expectation – implying a very sharp increase in the trend in labour productivity.[48] However, over this same period (1971 IV to 1973 III) the male unemployment rate fell sharply (from 5·1 per cent to 3·1 per cent) and male unemployment in manufacturing fell also (by 145,000). Thus the relationship between net labour turnover and the change in the total unemployment rate reversed itself: unemployment falling when net turnover (engagements minus discharges) was negative. Such a large and prolonged fall in unemployment cannot be attributed to changes in registration. It must be that over this period turnover (and hence unemployment) in manufacturing was moving in the opposite direction to turnover in the rest of the economy.

This conclusion is confirmed by Figure 6.2, where the quarterly first differences of the numbers of employees in employment in manufacturing and in the rest of the economy are plotted against time.[49] Manufacturing employment fell continuously from late 1969 until the end of the period. The rise in aggregate employment came

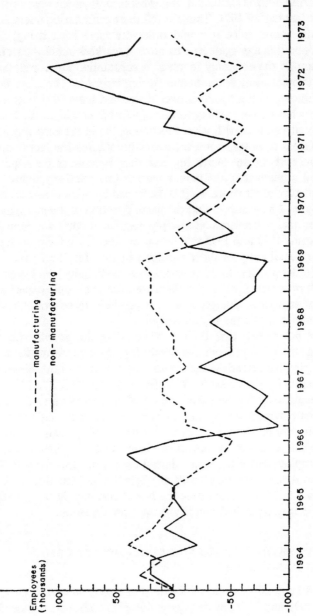

Figure 6.2. Quarterly changes in adult male employees in employment in manufacturing and non-manufacturing: Great Britain, 1963 IV – 1973 I

Source: *Department of Employment Gazette* (various issues).

entirely from outside manufacturing, where employment was growing from the last half of 1971. Thus the fall in manufacturing unemployment (and more, since it would otherwise have been rising) was brought about in aggregate by a transfer of workers out of the sector. Expansion of the economy involved a substantial 'structural shift' of employment away from manufacturing industry. The movement of manufacturing net turnover over the period from 1971 faithfully reflected what was happening to manufacturing employment. It was naturally at variance with what was happening in the economy as a whole. Gross turnover, however, correctly reflected the fact that, in aggregate, activity was increasing, and that, because of the required structural adjustments, the labour market was relatively tight.

This picture of structural shift is confirmed by other evidence. In a recent paper I have shown that the mean duration of unemployment for older males deteriorated sharply relative to that for younger males during 1971 and 1972.[50] This was not due to an increase in the relative rates of entry of older workers; in fact for these years the entry of older workers to the register was exceptionally low. Deteriorating job prospects for older workers are what one would expect in a period of structural change, since it is precisely these workers who are unable to make the adjustment.[51]

Figure 6.2 reveals that 1972–3, while being the period with the largest structural shift from manufacturing, is by no means the only one. Employment trends in the two sectors were in the same direction for substantial periods only in 1964, 1967 and from 1969 II to 1971 III. In aggregate, over the period of interest of the papers previously surveyed, male manufacturing employment was virtually static and the decline in employment took place entirely outside manufacturing. Structural adjustment was only possible in aggregate when manufacturing employment was rising – during early 1967 and from 1968 I to 1969 II – but the picture hardly suggests that no structural change took place in the economy over the late 1960s, merely that relative to 1972–3 it was gradual and in the opposite direction.

UNEMPLOYMENT AND VACANCIES IN AND OUT OF
MANUFACTURING

It should be possible to detect a period of strong structural change, such as 1972 and 1973, by disaggregation of the *UV* curve. Indeed if it is not, then the *UV* technique is of little use for analysis, because experience since 1966 has shown that it reveals little when similar movements are taking place in all sectors. In addition, it is worth examining the *UV* curves for manufacturing and for the rest of the economy for the period of slow structural change to see whether, and if so how, this is revealed.

A breakdown closely related to the one used here, in fact between manufacturing and services, was examined in the 1970 article,[52] and it was found that the outward shift, as measured by a dummy variable operating from 1966 IV, was of a roughly comparable order of magnitude in the two sectors. However, as a device for detecting structural change, this technique was misleading; the form of the movement in the two sectors was quite different. In manufacturing the period from 1966 IV to 1970 was marked by a large increase in vacancies but little increase in unemployment. With non-manufacturing the movement was the reverse – a large increase in unemployment and little change in vacancies. Then there was something like a 'normal' movement in both sectors until the end of 1971. The path of the upswing was shallower than in the period 1958–66 in both sectors, but steeper in manufacturing than outside it. This is shown by the equations in Table 6.2.

Between the first two periods in the table the change in constant between the two sectors is much the same, but in non-manufacturing

Table 6.2 *Equations for* UV *curves in manufacturing and non-manufacturing: adult males, Great Britain*

	Manufacturing				Non-manufacturing			
	a	*b*	R²	D.W.	*a*	*b*	R²	D.W.
63 III–1966 II	6·649 (0·143)	−0·608 (·0037)	0·964	1·78	8·485 (0·385)	−0·728 (0·091)	0·867	1·77
69 III–1971 IV	7·462 (0·153)	−0·646 (0·041)	0·968	1·06	9·290 (0·604)	−0·852 (0·156)	0·789	1·31
72 I–1973 IV	7·065 (0·129)	−0·482 (0·034)	0·972	1·85	7·798 (0·265)	−0·396 (0·062)	0·870	1·59

Notes: (i) The equations are of the form $\log U_t = a + b \log V_t$.
(ii) Standard errors are shown in brackets.
(iii) All coefficients are significant at the 1 per cent level on a t-test and all equations are significant at the 1 per cent level on an F-test.

the slope of the line becomes relatively steeper,[53] implying a larger change in unemployment for a given change in vacancies.[54] Between the second and third periods both curves become shallower and the constants decrease. The constant decreases by much more in non-manufacturing and the slope is reduced by more. Thus, relative to manufacturing, the *UV* curve in non-manufacturing became steeper between the first two periods and swivelled back the other way between the two second periods. The structural shifts between the sectors appeared as movements in the slopes and positions of the curves rather than as divergent movements along stable curves. This is perhaps not surprising. Structural shifts requiring abnormal movements in both sectors are marked by a decline in the efficiency of both markets. And there is really no reason to expect that the movements should take any particular form; only perhaps that, unless it is accompanied by a very sharp decline in aggregate employment in both sectors, it should be outwards.

CONCLUSIONS

Thus, properly interpreted, and with the benefit of hindsight and other sources of evidence, the *UV* analysis does reveal that structural change has taken place in the labour market in Great Britain. The detection of this is, however, not as simple as might previously have been thought. Nor is it obvious that structural factors have been more significant in keeping the *UV* curve from moving inwards in the recent upswing than they were in moving it outwards during the previous long downswing; the evidence from data on labour turnover suggests that this is probably so. It may be, of course, that the appropriate division is not between manufacturing and the rest of the economy; this breakdown was suggested simply by the turnover statistics. But the question of the appropriate form of disaggregation is an insoluble one with *UV* analysis; it can only be decided by external evidence on likely causes of events. Concluding comments would seem to be called for on two issues: the explanation of events in the British labour market since 1966 and the utility of *UV* analysis in providing such an explanation.

The latter is easily dealt with. The *UV* relationship reveals nothing that is not revealed better by some or all of the other variables I have used here and elsewhere. In my view it is a derived relationship, dependent on the more fundamental flow variables I have considered; as such it can be discarded. It may give an indication that something is going on in the labour market; to find out what, one must lay it aside. Its sources of instability are manifold. Like the Phillips curve, to which its affinity is more than cultural, it is surprising not that it has broken down, but that it ever held up. To the explanation of events this paper contributes little. Structural shifts are not acts of God and raise as many questions as they answer. The recent shake-out in manufacturing cannot be explained in the same terms as the previous one; it is not a response to prospects of a depression. It may in some way be a consequence of a previous prolonged depression. Statements about employers' expectations do not help much either. As well as two rises in the trend in labour productivity in manufacturing, we have had a rise in the productivity trend outside (this can in fact be shown to have taken place in services) and recently a fall in productivity trend there also.[55] The trends in services I believe can be explained by a combination of S.E.T. and the pattern of substitution of women for men in industry, but I intend to develop this argument in another paper.[56] Another UV shift is clearly that between women and men. The female UV curve, apart from a brief pause in early 1972, appears to have moved inwards throughout the 1960s and early 1970s. On the explanation of trends in manufacturing productivity I have nothing to offer except for a feeling that, in this respect, the current unemployment is inextricably bound up with the current inflation.

NOTES

1 I am grateful to Mr A. S. Fowkes and Mr D. Harkess of the School of Economic Studies, University of Leeds for invaluable assistance in the preparation of this paper. The blame for what is written, however, rests entirely on me.
2 J. K. Bowers, P. C. Cheshire and A. E. Webb, 'The Change in the Relationship between Unemployment and Earnings Increases: A Review of Some Possible Explanations', *National Institute Economic Review*, No. 54, November 1970.
3 It broke down, along with almost every other wage-inflation equation, with the wage explosion after that date. But it could be argued that the nature of the inflationary process underwent a change at that time: the normal situation of the late 1950s and 1960s, of change in average earnings leading change in basic wage rates, reversed itself.
4 *National Institute Economic Review*, No. 54, November 1970, p. 52.

5 This was obviously unsatisfactory both econometrically and conceptually, but the point was demonstrated in a more satisfactory manner in a later paper (see note 21).

6 In that case the equation was highly auto-correlated.

7 Bowers, Cheshire and Webb, 'The Change in the Relationship between Unemployment and Earnings Increases', p. 60.

8 R. G. Lipsey and J. M. Parkin, 'Incomes Policy: A Re-Appraisal', *Economica*, May 1970.

9 We subsequently revised this view (see below).

10 D. Gujarati, 'The Behaviour of Unemployment and Unfilled Vacancies: Great Britain, 1958–1971', *Economic Journal*, March 1972.

11 Ibid., p. 202n.

12 Ibid., p. 198.

13 Ibid., p. 198.

14 J. Taylor, 'The Behaviour of Unemployment and Unfilled Vacancies: Great Britain, 1958–71. An Alternative View', *Economic Journal*, December 1972.

15 See the discussion in the *National Institute Economic Review*, No. 63, February 1973, pp. 29–31.

16 In fact across index of production industries. Reddaway's work on S.E.T. suggests that it also took place in service industries (see W. B. Reddaway, *Effects of the Selective Employment Tax. Final Report*, Cambridge University Press, 1973, pp. 55–6).

17 Bowers, Cheshire and Webb, 'The Change in the Relationship between the Unemployment and Earnings Increases'.

18 This, of course, is one reason why labour hoarding is not necessarily a sign of inefficiency or of non-cost-minimisation by employers.

19 And, as already noted, the rise in labour turnover where this involves rising engagements as well as discharges.

20 Gujarati in his reply to Taylor rejects the arguments and concludes that he finds his original explanation more convincing. He still offers no evidence in favour of it.

21 J. K. Bowers, P. C. Cheshire, A. E. Webb and R. Weeden, 'Some Aspects of Unemployment and the Labour Market, 1966–71', *National Institute Economic Review*, No. 62, November 1972.

22 This is obviously of secondary importance.

23 While several commentators discovered at this time that the unemployment figures were not all that they seemed and, indeed, that unemployment itself was a slippery concept (see especially J. B. Wood, *How much Unemployment?*, Institute of Economic Affairs, 1972), the only suggestion that the nature of the data had actually changed was in N. Bosanquet and G. Standing, 'Government and Unemployment 1966–1970: A Study of Policy and Evidence', *British Journal of Industrial Relations*, July 1972. However several people were suggesting that the vacancy statistics had ceased to be reliable (see the comment by the Department of Employment in National Economic Development Office, *Labour Statistics: Report of a Conference held under the General Auspices of the Standing Committee of Statistics Users*, 1973, p. 7 and the discussion on pp. 119–20).

24 These are reported in the *National Institute Economic Review*, no. 59, February 1972, pp. 18–21. Further relatives for unemployment and vacancies are reported in the *Review* for November 1973.

25 This, in fact, is a sort of inversion of normal output–employment relationships, but the employment–unemployment relationship is implicit in it.
26 The shift was if anything downwards though it was not significant. There was a large negative residual in 1966 III-IV, implying that a relationship between levels of vacancies and output (industrial production) had a negative constant shift (vacancies falling against output). This, however, was not significant in the levels equation, which, because the appropriate specification was in first differences, was highly auto-correlated. Thus vacancies probably showed a once-and-for-all negative shift against output, but no trend. Unemployment, on the other hand, showed positive trend against output.
27 On this, see D. I. MacKay and G. L. Reid, 'Redundancy, Unemployment and Manpower Policy', *Economic Journal*, December 1972, where the distinction is drawn between 'snatchers', who take the first job available to them and use this as a base for finding a better job, and 'stickers', who wait on the register until they find a job that suits their requirements.
28 If information lags are normal, then delayed response of quitting to demand could be a normal cyclical phenomenon. This would account for observed 'loops' in the *UV* curve.
29 There are broadly two schools of thought, the second with two variants. The first holds that labour hoarding is rational cost-minimising behaviour in a world characterised by uncertainty and indivisibilities. Dis-hoarding is thus the result of a change in the relative costs and benefits of holding stocks of labour because of changed expectations of future demand, or changed costs of holding labour (taxes, wage–price movements), or changes in the appropriate discount rate. The second regards hoarding as an indication that firms are not cost-minimisers. One variant then holds that this is because of ignorance and that once firms have seen that they are inefficient they will not return to their old ways (this could be called the Wilson thesis). The other, derived from managerial and behavioural theories of the firm, sees non-cost-minimising as rational, either yielding utility to the management, or being a division of monopoly profit with the labour force, or being necessary for the reconciliation of conflict between decision-makers. On only the Wilson thesis would the dis-hoarding be permanent.
30 This was the last observation available when the exercise was performed.
31 The equations relating log U_t to log V_t are, for 1972 I–1973 III:

$$\log U_t = 1 \cdot 5012^* - 0 \cdot 4629 \log V_t^* \qquad (R^2 = 0 \cdot 956, \text{D.W.} = 2 \cdot 25)$$
$$\quad (28 \cdot 9) \qquad (10 \cdot 5)$$

and, for 1963 III – 1966 II:

$$\log U_t = 0 \cdot 3639^* - 0 \cdot 6431 \log V_t^* \qquad (R^2 = 0 \cdot 833, \text{D.W.} = 2 \cdot 10)$$
$$\quad (16 \cdot 5) \qquad (8 \cdot 67)$$

with t-ratios in brackets and an asterisk indicating significance at the 1 per cent level.
32 Mainly these consisted in sequentially omitting the last observation, fitting lines to the rest and testing whether the omitted observations could come from a population exhibiting the observed relationship. Collinearity precluded the simpler procedure of including a trend in the equation.
33 *National Institute Economic Review*, No. 63, February 1973, pp. 25–33 and No. 66, November 1973, pp. 24–33.
34 These arguments are difficult to follow. Thus the one based on Table 15 (p. 27), purporting to show that earnings-related benefit is not a cause of

increased stay on the unemployment register, seems to rest on a misunderstanding about the rules for payment. It is payable for a maximum period of 26 weeks.

35 This was of course written before the three-day week was introduced. The probability of reaching the suggested short-term target was, of course, then reduced (perhaps eliminated), but the target itself was not affected.

36 These do not seem to me to be indicators of spare capacity in any meaningful sense, but a critique of them would be the subject of another paper.

37 *National Institute Economic Review*, No. 66, pp. 25–6.

38 Department of Employment, *People and Jobs: A Modern Employment Service*, H.M.S.O., 1971, p. 14. In another case the increase in vacancies was described as 'substantial'. The self-service system 'has so far been tried out at about 30 offices and, without exception, the results have been encouraging'.

39 Ibid., p. 7.

40 Ibid., p. 15.

41 *National Institute Economic Review*, No. 63, February 1973, p. 16.

42 National Economic Development Office, *Labour Statistics*.

43 Bowers, Cheshire, Webb and Weeden, 'Some Aspects of Unemployment and the Labour Market, 1966–71'.

44 In 'Some Aspects of Unemployment' the index of industrial production was the independent variable; this gave similar results.

45 The equation contains a non-significant shift dummy operating from 1966 IV which is omitted in making the predictions. This was done to maintain comparability with the unemployment equation also shown. Very similar results are obtained using equations for the periods 1958 IV–1966 II, before the shift, and for 1966 IV–1971 IV.

46 The omission of the dummy in effect assumes that, after moving upwards against output over the period 1966 IV–1971 IV, unemployment stabilised and the relationship between first differences of unemployment and change in G.D.P. returned to that existing before 1966 IV. Use of the relationship for the period 1958 IV–1966 III gives results very similar to those reported in Table 6.1.

47 Bowers, Cheshire, Webb and Weeden, 'Some Aspects of Unemployment'.

48 The growth of output per man–year during 1972 and 1973 was described in the *National Institute Economic Review* for November 1973 as 'very disappointing . . . in the light of the gradual acceleration of productivity growth that we and other commentators had thought we had detected over the last ten or fifteen years'. At that time the estimate was $3\frac{1}{4}$ per cent per annum. In fact productivity was rising very rapidly in manufacturing (same *Review*) at an annual rate of $5\frac{3}{4}$ per cent and the labour turnover statistics were reflecting this.

49 Manufacturing employment is a quarterly series, seasonally adjusted, derived from the monthly 'L' return series. This is subtracted from the seasonally adjusted historical series for total employees in employment to give the non-manufacturing series. The 1972 and 1973 figures are the employment census figures scaled to make them comparable with the earlier card-count data. The scaling factors are derived from the dates when the two series overlapped. While the methodology is open to criticism, it is hoped that the pattern of employment movements, if not the magnitude, is faithfully recorded.

50 J. K. Bowers and D. Harkess 'Duration of Unemployment by Age', University of Leeds Discussion Paper, 1974. A trend against older males is discernible throughout the 1960s. There was a large additional deterioration in 1971 and 1972.

51 Even if they are both able and willing, employers are unwilling to accept them. The conventional explanations for this are well known.

52 Bowers, Cheshire and Webb, 'The Change in the Relationship between Unemployment and Earnings Increases'.

53 Few of these differences are significant on conventional tests. With so few observations this is scarcely surprising. The comments should be treated as descriptions of tendencies. More data could of course be obtained by taking monthly observations.

54 These comparisons can be made because, although the data are absolutes not rates, the equations are logarithmic.

55 On the former see Treasury, *Effects of the Selective Employment Tax: First Report on the Distributive Trades* by W. B. Reddaway, H.M.S.O., 1970; Reddaway, *Effects of the Selective Employment Tax. Final Report* and the subsequent dispute in the *National Institute Economic Review*. On the latter see the *National Institute Economic Review* for November 1973 (p. 24): 'in the last three years, productivity has risen by only $\frac{1}{2}\%$ per annum in those industries (mainly services) outside the index of production. Indeed in 1972 and early 1973 it appears to have fallen.'

56 The conference version of this paper contained some thoughts (and graphs) on this issue. It was excessively terse and evoked bewilderment rather than opposition. I have decided to leave this out of the published version. In so doing the paper, I hope, comes closer to the issues considered by the conference.

Chapter 7

UV Analysis

A. J. BROWN

The object of this paper is to present briefly the salient points of an approach to the study of the labour market through the published statistics of unemployment and vacancies. Although a number of other writers have adopted this approach – some independently at about the same time, some subsequently – the lines of thought summarised here are essentially those developed from 1967 onwards by a group who were then working on regional economics at the National Institute of Economic and Social Research.[1]

The original concern of our group in experimenting with this approach was to provide a measure of the differences in degree of imperfection between the labour markets of the United Kingdom regions; we wanted to be able to say something about the extent to which the regions' different rates of unemployment could be attributed to differences in labour-market imperfection, as opposed to differences in level of effective demand. How consideration of the relation between the unemployment rate (U) and the unfilled vacancy rate (V) might be expected to help us in this is perhaps best seen by paraphrasing and slightly expanding the exposition that appears (in a rather different context) in Webb's paper.

If we had a homogeneous labour supply with perfect information and mobility, so that no worker remained unemployed so long as there was a vacancy and no vacancy unfilled so long as there was an unemployed worker, and if we could measure demand for labour (D) in the straightforward sense of the number of workers employers want on their pay-rolls, then the numbers of vacancies (V) and of unemployed (U) respectively would be related to demand in the ways shown in Figure 7.1. (We assume for the time being that these numbers are recorded in full.) The vacancy line would coincide with the horizon-

tal axis up to the point where the available labour force (which we are
taking as being unambiguously fixed) was fully employed and would
then rise at an angle of 45°. The unemployment line would descend
at an angle of 45° to reach the full employment point on the horizontal axis, and then continue horizontally along that axis. Since we
cannot in practice measure *D* in any direct way, the best we can do
with data on vacancies and unemployment is to plot them one
against the other, either as absolute numbers or as rates. In the pure
case of a perfect labour market just described, this yields a line
coinciding with the two (*U* and *V*) axes, with a right-angled kink at
the origin.

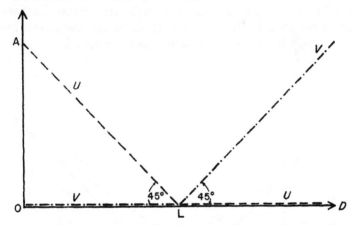

Figure 7.1. Relations between demand for labour (*D*), unemployment (*U*) and
        vacancies (*V*) with a homogeneous labour supply and perfect
        information

What will now be the effect of introducing market imperfections?
As *D* rises from a very low level, it may be at first that all posts are
filled almost as soon as created or vacated, because the choice of
candidates is so wide, and thus that, though the number of engagements (including replacements) may be high, the average duration of
a vacancy is so short that the stock of vacancies is negligible. But,
as *D* moves up further towards the total size of the available labour
force, the first acceptable candidate for a post just created or vacated
becomes less likely to be waiting on the employer's doorstep; he is
more likely to have to be sought further afield. He is also more likely

to be someone already in employment, who creates one vacancy by filling another. At some point demand, for first one kind of candidate, then for progressively more, exceeds the total supply in the market, so that the net addition to vacancies per hundred extra employees demanded rises. When total labour demand is equal to total supply, however, this figure will still be well below a hundred, because, it being the nature of the case that demand and supply are qualitatively (and perhaps geographically) mismatched, excess demand in some trades or districts will be equalled by excess supply in others. It is only at some high level of excess aggregate demand for labour that excess supply will vanish in the last submarket, and further additions to demand will create equal additions to unfilled vacancies. The V curve therefore, in practice, rises from the horizontal axis a long way short of the point L where demand equals supply, and merges into the 45° line, LB, a long way beyond it, as in Figure 7.2.

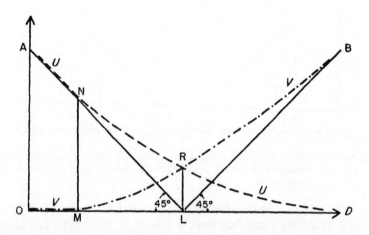

Figure 7.2. Relations between demand for labour (D), unemployment (U) and vacancies (V) with an imperfect labour market

A parallel argument applies to unemployment, which, because of market imperfections, starts to diverge upwards from the 45° line, AL, a long way before demand reaches L, and merges into the D axis a long way to the right of that point. It is unnecessary, however, to trace the arguments about V and U independently, because, on

our definitions and assumptions, unemployment is identically equal
to excess aggregate supply of labour *plus* vacancies; put otherwise,
unemployment *minus* excess supply of labour (or *plus* excess demand)
must equal vacancies. This means that the *U* curve can be deduced
from the *V* curve, or vice versa. In Figure 7.2, moreover, the *U* curve
rises above AL at the same level of demand at which *V* ceases to be
zero, crosses the *V* curve where $D = OL$ (that is where there is no
aggregate excess supply or demand), and sinks to zero at the same
value of *D* for which *V* merges with LB. The assumption of a fixed
labour force, all of whom are either employed or unemployed,
with complete recording of both unemployment and unfilled
vacancies, also implies that the slopes of the *U* and *V* curves,
both taken as positive, must sum to unity at all levels of demand
for labour.

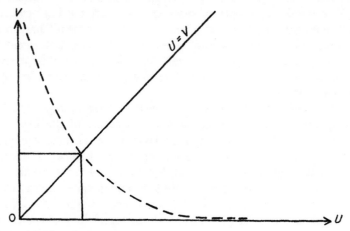

Figure 7.3. The *UV* curve

What this implies for the *UV* curve – the curve of *V* plotted against
U – is that it is convex to its origin, and also, in a broad sense, further
from it the more imperfect the market is (Figure 7.3). This, however,
is an imprecise statement. If, of the curves for, say, two different
regions, one lies wholly outside the other, there cannot be much
doubt about which market is the more imperfect, provided that we
are still dealing with complete recordings of *U* and *V*. But if the curves
cross, questions arise about the proper method of measuring distance

from the origin, and the difficulties are greatly increased if we do not know how complete are the recordings of U or V or both.

Let us, however, postpone the problem of incomplete recording. What is the best way of measuring, or comparing, degrees of labour-market imperfection, assuming that our data on unemployment and vacancies are complete? The most obvious answer is that they should be measured by the rates of unemployment and of vacancies (U and V) at which the two are equal. This, on our assumptions, is the point of zero labour demand deficiency (or excess) in aggregate, at which the fact that anyone is unemployed can be ascribed to his not yet having found some vacancy suitable for him which does in fact exist (frictional unemployment), or being in the wrong place to accept a known and otherwise suitable vacancy (locational unemployment – a subdivision, perhaps, of frictional), or having the wrong skills (structural unemployment) or personal characteristics (personal deficiency unemployment) for acceptability in any existing vacancy, even though the total number of vacancies matches the total number of unemployed. In other words, the existence of the unemployment is ascribable wholly to what are usually regarded as market imperfections, not to the sheer numerical supply of labour exceeding the numerical demand.

This value of 'non-demand deficiency' or 'market imperfection' unemployment, if it is to be used as a measure of the inherent imperfection of labour markets, must be measured at some standard level of demand, since in any given market the number of unemployed that would be assessed as attributable to any of the varieties of market imperfection mentioned in the last paragraph is clearly a function of the pressure of demand. Cheshire's paper points this out. If, for instance, one divided both demand and supply into a number of internally homogeneous 'trades', ignoring for the moment the qualitative differences between people within a trade and the existence of some people who are doubtfully suitable for any employment at all, then frictional (including locational) unemployment may be defined as the sum for all trades of the overlap between the number of vacancies and the number of unemployed – that is the sum for all trades of the number unemployed in the trade or the number of vacancies, whichever is fewer. Structural unemployment, similarly, consists of those for whom there is no vacancy in their own trade, but for whom there would be a place elsewhere if they could change their

trade – that is whichever is the smaller of (a) the sum across all trades
of the excess of vacancies over unemployment, where there is such
an excess, or (b) the sum across all trades of the excess of unemployment over vacancies where this excess exists. At very low levels of
demand there will be no vacancies anywhere, so that neither of these
kinds of unemployment can exist; all unemployment will appear to be
ascribable to demand deficiency, the excess of aggregate supply over
aggregate demand. At higher levels, some vacancies will appear in
spite of the existence of unemployed in the same trade. Higher still,
vacancies in some trades will exceed unemployment in them, while
in others the opposite is true, so that structural unemployment exists.
When total demand and total supply are equal, there will be no
aggregate demand deficiency unemployment; all the unemployment
in existence will be attributable to market imperfections. As demand
increases further, both structural and frictional employment will
decrease; the former will vanish altogether when no trade shows a
deficiency of labour demand, the latter at some still higher (perhaps
indefinitely high) level of aggregate demand at which unemployment
vanishes. The point at which vacancies and unemployment are equal
in aggregate may, therefore, be expected to be that corresponding to
a *maximum* level of unemployment (and of vacancies) attributable to
market imperfections. In terms of Figure 7.2, market imperfection
unemployment at any level of demand is represented by the vertical
height of the *U* curve above the 45° line AL, or, to the right of L,
above the horizontal axis. Alternatively, it may be thought of as the
height of the *U* or the *V* curve, whichever is lower, above the horizontal axis. It is plain that it reaches a maximum RL when demand is at L.

The point is made in Cheshire's paper that a set of definitions that
makes the maximum level of market imperfection unemployment
occur only at the level of aggregate demand at which it equals
aggregate supply of labour (the level which might for some purposes
be thought of as in some sense the 'full employment' level of demand)
may seem anomalous. If demand is lower than this, so that some
demand deficiency unemployment exists, it may seem more sensible
to ascribe to that demand deficiency, not an amount equal to the
whole excess of supply over demand, but simply that amount of
unemployment that is in excess of the *maximum* market imperfection
level RL (Figure 7.2). This could be defended on the ground that,
whereas at a level of demand represented by M, for instance, the

whole of unemployment can in one sense be attributed to demand
deficiency, if demand were increased so as to eliminate that deficiency,
a level of market imperfection unemployment represented by RL
would be found to exist. How one deals with this essentially
semantic problem, however, is not material to the main point I am
trying to make: namely, that the level of unemployment existing
when 'true' unemployment and vacancies are equal is uniquely
qualified to serve as a measure of the imperfection of a labour
market.

The real problem of applying this proposition in practice arises
from three sources: the imperfection and possible variability in the
recording of both vacancies and unemployment, the fact that some
labour markets provide no evidence relating to a time when U and V
were equal, and the variability of the true UV relation over time.
Imperfection in statistics of registered unemployment as measures of
true involuntary worklessness is a well-known difficulty about which
much will no doubt be heard at the conference, and I shall not pursue
it here, except to recall that the National Institute study noted the
problem. In the 1966 Census, the number of people describing themselves as economically active, but who were neither in work nor
registered as unemployed at the time, was considerably greater than
the number so registered. We noted that, among men, the unregistered percentage was correlated across regions with the registered,
but with a much smaller interregional variation. Among women, the
unregistered were four times as numerous as the registered, and there
was no correlation between the two across regions. Cheshire regarded
this as a reason for confining his analysis of registered unemployment
mainly to men. It is plain that, even with men, there is scope for the
number of registered unemployed as a percentage of the true number
of involuntarily unemployed (however that might be defined or
ascertained) to vary a good deal over time.

Vacancy statistics have been suspected of this kind of variation. It
is known that the proportion of engagements that take place through
employment exchanges is quite low. Cheshire recalls, however, that
Dow and Dicks-Mireaux concluded,[2] on the basis of relative ampli-
tudes of fluctuation of V and U, and of variations in V, when com-
pulsory use of employment exchanges was first removed, then re-
imposed, then removed again in the 1950s, that the proportion of the
stock of total vacancies represented by the number registered was at

that time close to unity – the vacancies that remained in being for longer periods were likely to be registered, while those never registered were mostly of short duration. Considering that, as we have just noted, registered unemployment provides a considerable under-estimate of involuntary worklessness, there does not seem to be any clear presumption that registered vacancies understate the 'true' figures of vacant posts to a greater extent.

The fact remains, however, that the 'recording ratios' for both U and V are uncertain and are less than unity, and that they may vary over time or between regions sufficiently to distort comparisons of market imperfection that we want to make. This is a ground for caution in making such comparisons, but it does not seem to me to invalidate them, any more than similar possibilities of error invalidate many other economic comparisons that we find useful as contributions to a composite picture of reality.

The fact that in some labour markets in some periods U and V are persistently very far from equal is clearly an obstacle to estimating at what level they would achieve equality. In some cases, where the statistical relation between the two over time is close, one may boldly extrapolate it, but, where it is not very close and the necessary extrapolation is a long one, this is clearly hazardous. Cheshire, whose object is to compare the degrees of imperfection of regional labour markets, tries not only those values of U at which it is equal to V, but those at which it equals $2V$ and $3V$. This is a method of ranking regional markets for degree of imperfection, or of checking the consistency of their ranking, on the assumption that their UV curves lie roughly parallel to each other. It is also useful for seeing whether his conclusions would be vitally affected if vacancies were understated by the registration statistics, in comparison with unemployment, by such ratios as $\frac{1}{2}$ or $\frac{1}{3}$. If this is not the case, however – if the degrees of understatement are not widely different – then, one should no doubt insist on the unique virtue of the point where $U = V$ as an indicator of market imperfection. If the UV curves of two regions cross, it is their values when $U = V$, not the values of U at which, beyond the crossing-place, it equals, say, $2V$, that in principle give a correct indication of the relative *maximum* amounts of market imperfection unemployment that would be encountered in the two regions in the course of raising labour demand in them from low to high levels.

The third source of difficulty mentioned above is that, quite apart from possible changes in the recording ratios, the relation between the 'true' values of U and V may vary over time, so that one has to hunt for other variables responsible for the variation if a UV relation appropriate to a stated condition of the labour market is to be discovered, and the corresponding point where $U = V$ ascertained. Cheshire tried, with mixed success, on the strength of very short time-series, to explain apparent shifts of the curve by inserting measures of rate of change of industrial structure and dummy variables for acts of policy, such as the introduction of redundancy payments and earnings-related benefits.

To enter into this subject further would take me, without adequate equipment, into areas which will doubtless be very fully discussed in the light of more recent work. The only point I wish to add is as follows. It is well known that, since 1966, the UV curve for the British economy as a whole seems to have moved far outwards from its origin, and there has been much discussion of whether this represents a true increase in market imperfection, and if so why, and whether the change is likely to be permanent. Some years ago, I pointed out how much lower the unemployment rate had been in the first post-war decade than Beveridge, Saunders, and others who had tried to assess the minimum level of frictional, seasonal and other kinds of non-demand deficiency unemployment had thought it could possibly be, and that the Dow–Dicks-Mireaux estimate of the average level of excess demand seemed inadequate to explain the difference.[3] My suggestion was that, once some critical degree of labour shortage seems to have established itself on a quasi-permanent basis, employers change their habits and become hoarders of labour. I believe that there is evidence that, by various stages in the years since 1966, this hoarding habit has broken down in the famous 'shake-out' of labour,[4] and that employers now behave much more as the writers of the pre-war and war period, basing their thoughts on experience of a demand deficiency, seem to have anticipated.

Now a reduction in the demand for labour normally increases unemployment and diminishes unfilled vacancies, but the 'shake-out' presumably represents something additional to, or different from, a mere reduction in the demand for man–hours of active work; it consists in a reduction of internally held labour reserves. Pushing one's reserves out into the labour market will, of course, make it easier for oneself and other employers to get extra labour when needed, and this in itself will tend to reduce the duration and thus the stock of vacancies. But if everyone has got rid of reserves that could be drawn upon to meet contingencies, then everyone will have to meet those contingencies by going to the labour market more often – there will be many more vacancies. It may also be that, in a period when labour is not regarded as chronically scarce, employers exercise greater discrimination in making engagements, thereby going some way towards offsetting the effect on the average length of a vacancy of a more plentiful supply. In short, a move to hold labour reserves externally to firms instead of internally may increase both unemployment and vacancies at the same time. It is a question for discussion and investigation whether this, quite apart from any increased willingness of labour to remain unemployed (because of redundancy payments and earnings-related benefits), any increase in the mismatch between skills and requirements, and any change in the recording ratio for vacancies, may not provide a large part of the explanation of the otherwise puzzling behaviour of the *UV* curve in the last seven years.

APPENDIX: LABOUR HOARDING AND THE *UV* CURVE

In this paper, I have suggested that the tendency of employers to 'shake-out' their labour, so that their reserves have come to be, in effect, held more outside the firm and less inside it than in the mid-1960s, may be responsible for at least a substantial part of the outward movement of the *UV* curve since that date. The following simple model may help to substantiate this suggestion.

Consider an economy in which the working population, N, and the employment desired by employers, N_r, are constant – that is to say a static economy, since this argument is limited in the first instance to a comparative static form. If, then, the number of vacancies is V and the number of unemployed is U, we have:

$$U = N - N_r + V \qquad \text{(A)}$$

Now consider, across the whole field of employment, the number of vacancies arising per year. Expressed as a proportion of the number in employment, $N_r - V$, this can be represented as the sum of total retirements or deaths in service, w, total voluntary quits, q, and total redundancies, r. The total stock of vacancies, V, at any time, will be the product of these vacancies arising per year and the average duration of a vacancy, t_v, so that:

$$V = (w + q + r)(N_r - V)t_v$$

or

$$V = \frac{(w + q + r)N_r t_v}{1 + (w + q + r)t_v} \qquad (B)$$

From this and (A) above

$$U = N - N_r + \frac{(w + q + r)N_r t_v}{1 + (w + q + r)t_v} \qquad (C)$$

Now suppose that our comparisons are always made at the value of N_r where $U = V$, i.e., from (A), where $N - N_r = 0$. Then both U and V have the value given in (B).

The next question is what can be said about the average duration of vacancies, t_v. It seems likely that, *ceteris paribus*, the time taken to fill a vacancy will vary directly with the number of existing vacancies and inversely with the number of unemployed. It does not seem too implausible, therefore, to suggest that it is a function of V/U, and will accordingly always have the same value (which we can call $\bar{t}_v$) when $V = U$. Another probability is that the number of voluntary quits, q, will vary, at least in part, with the state of the labour market. But again, it is not implausible to suggest that it (or the variable part of it) varies as a function of V/U, so that it also can be taken as having a standard value when $V = U$.

If all this is so, what will happen if employers modify their labour requirements so as to tune them more sensitively to short-term variations (which can be taken as random) in their strictly technical needs for employees with particular qualifications – that is, reduce the extent to which they keep on people who are not fully occupied because they think they will want them when the market picks up again, or people who have less than ideal qualifications because 'they'll do' or in the hope that their performance will improve?

The effect of such a modification will be to raise r. (It will also, *ceteris paribus*, raise U, but that need not concern us, because we are supposing that the system is brought back to the point where $U = V$ again before we examine it – we are working at the level of effective demand at which $U = V$.) The partial derivative of V with respect to r is $N_r \bar{t_v}/[1 + (w + q + r) \bar{t_v}]^2$, which is necessarily positive, so that less labour hoarding and more redundancies per year are bound to increase the value of V (and of U) at the point where $U = V$. Exactly the same is true, of course, of an exogenous increase in the rate of voluntary quits, or in the death or retirement rates.

NOTES

1 The chief publications bearing on this for which members of the group were responsible are Paul Cheshire's 'Regional Unemployment Differences in Great Britain', in N.I.E.S.R. *Regional Papers II*, Edward Webb's paper 'Unemployment, Vacancies and the Rate of Change of Earnings: A Regional Analysis', in N.I.E.S.R. *Regional Papers III*, and two articles in the *National Institute Economic Review*: (No. 54, November 1970), 'The Change in the Relationship between Unemployment and Earnings Increases: A Review of some Possible Explanations' by Bowers, Cheshire, and Webb, and (No. 62, November 1972) 'Some Aspects of Unemployment and the Labour Market, 1966–71' by Bowers, Cheshire, Webb and Weeden. In addition, I referred to this approach in the National Institute study of regional matters, *The Framework of Regional Economics in the United Kingdom*, Cambridge University Press, 1972, pp. 221–6.
2 J. C. R. Dow and L. A. Dicks-Mireaux, 'The Excess Demand for Labour: A Study of Conditions in Great Britain, 1946–56', *Oxford Economic Papers*, February 1958.
3 A. J. Brown, 'Inflation and the British Economy', *Economic Journal*, September 1958.
4 For a development of this evidence see the Appendix to this paper.

Chapter 8

The Unemployment Gap in Britain's Production Sector, 1953-73[1]

JIM TAYLOR

Registered unemployment used to be regarded as an accurate indicator of 'involuntary' unemployment in Britain. Consequently, the rate of registered unemployment was extensively used by policy-makers and economists as a measure of the excess supply of labour. Recent research has indicated, however, that the registered unemployment rate has become an increasingly unreliable and misleading measure of the pressure of demand in the labour market. It is the purpose of this paper to investigate why this has happened.

Previous work has indicated that a possibly useful approach to understanding movements in registered unemployment is to divide it into two component parts: a deficient-demand component and a residual.[2] The residual is attributed to frictions in the labour market, which give rise to short-run search unemployment and long-run structural unemployment. For convenience of exposition, the residual is henceforth referred to simply as frictional unemployment. Voluntary unemployment other than the 'voluntary' short-run search activity of workers is assumed to be negligible and is therefore ignored. An attempt is made in this paper to construct a method of dividing registered unemployment into a deficient-demand component and a frictional component. The approach suggested here, however, is different from the previous work on this problem, which is based on the '*UV* method'.[3] The aim of the exercise is to answer questions such as:

(i) Was the upward trend in registered unemployment during the period 1953–73 due to an increasing deficiency in the aggregate demand for labour, or was it due to an increase in frictional unemployment?

(ii) Why was the registered unemployment rate over twice as high during the period 1967–73 as during the period 1953–66?

The paper is in four sections. In view of the vital importance of the concept of full employment to the measurement of involuntary unemployment, we begin by discussing the view of full employment taken in this paper. The second section analyses the structure of the excess supply of labour, which is henceforth referred to as the 'unemployment gap'. The analysis of the unemployment gap and its individual parts will be seen to be a crucial step in the method developed to divide registered unemployment into a deficient-demand component and a frictional component. This is followed by an explanation of how each component of the unemployment gap can be estimated in practice. The final section analyses the position with regard to the excess supply of labour in the British production sector over the period 1953–73 with a view to answering the questions posed above.

THE CAPACITY VIEW OF FULL EMPLOYMENT

The concept of full employment used in this paper is based on the capacity view,[4] which asserts that a situation of full employment will have been reached only if a further increase in aggregate demand would not result in an increase in employment. This assertion can alternatively be expressed in terms of unemployment: a situation of full employment will have been reached only if a further increase in aggregate demand would not result in a decrease in unemployment. If the situation is such that an increase in aggregate demand would cause unemployment to fall, there is a demand deficiency, hence the label 'deficient-demand unemployment' for any unemployment that would be eliminated as a consequence of an expansion in aggregate demand.

The capacity concept of full employment can also be explained in terms of lost output.[5] If an increase in aggregate demand results in an increase in output, the short-run ceiling on output has not been reached. The difference between the output ceiling and actual output is the output gap, which is the output equivalent of deficient-demand unemployment. An assumption of the capacity concept of full employment is that the short-run ceiling on output could be sustained provided aggregate demand was maintained at a sufficiently high level. The sustainability of output at its capacity level refers here to the technical production possibilities of the economy and, of course, to the willingness of workers to provide labour services. Whether or not a capacity level of output or employment can be sustained in practice (and we know it cannot because it conflicts with other policy goals) is irrelevant to the capacity view.

The primary concern of the capacity view of full employment is with deficient-demand unemployment. The capacity view fully recognises, however, that the attainment of full employment does not mean that unemployment will fall to zero. Due to labour-market frictions, such as a skill mismatching or a geographical mismatching in the demand for and supply of labour, unemployment and job vacancies will coexist in a fully employed economy. This frictional unemployment will be affected by:

(a) structural changes in the economy (which will affect the degree of mismatching in the demand for and supply of labour);
(b) changes in the search behaviour of workers.

It will be useful to examine briefly the factors determining job-search activity in order to construct hypotheses about the likely behaviour of the frictional component of unemployment.[6] It must be pointed out, however, that little is yet known about the search activity of workers.[7]

Let us first examine the meaning of 'search activity'. A person who is offered a job is faced with the decision of accepting the offer and in so doing terminating his search activity; or, alternatively, he can reject the offer and continue his search for a job. At the point in time when he makes this decision, he will (in theory) compare the expected benefits with the expected costs arising from further search activity. If he judges the present value of the benefits to outweigh the present value of the costs, he will continue to search for a job. By waiting longer he expects to receive a better job offer than the one he has just received – better in terms of remuneration, job satisfaction and working conditions. On the cost side of the equation, a longer period of search will result in a loss of earnings, plus other costs incurred in the search process, such as the effort expended in looking for a suitable job.

This description of search activity implies that job-seekers will accept jobs more readily whenever the estimated costs of searching rise relative to the estimated benefits. One possibility is that workers will be more ready to quit their jobs and search for another job when job openings are relatively plentiful.[8] Those already unemployed will also be more willing to extend the duration of their search activity at times when the job market is in their favour. To use Reder's terminology, workers may become more 'fussy' about their choice of a job when jobs are in plentiful supply.[9] Search activity can therefore be expected to vary directly with short-run movements in the excess demand for labour. In addition to these short-run changes in job prospects, there may be factors affecting the 'fussiness' of workers over the longer run. As wealth increases with economic growth, for example, those searching for work may be prepared to wait longer to find a suitable job. Government measures designed to raise the absolute standard of living of the unemployed will also tend to increase the duration of job search. Finally, there are forces working in the opposite direction. Any reduction in labour-market frictions, through schemes to improve the matching in the demand for and supply of labour, will reduce the search duration of the unemployed.

The main purpose of this section was to explain the capacity view of full employment. Specifically, we have defined unemployment as consisting of two components: a deficient-demand component and a frictional component (defined to include unemployment that is commonly referred to as 'structural'). One of the aims of the following analysis of unemployment is to construct a method that will provide time-series estimates of the two components of unemployment. Our next task, however, is to investigate the structure of the unemployment gap, which we earlier explained to be the unemployment resulting from a deficiency in aggregate demand. This analysis of the structure of the unemployment gap will be seen to be an essential step in the estimation of frictional unemployment.

AN ANALYSIS OF THE UNEMPLOYMENT GAP

The unemployment gap is defined in this paper strictly in terms of the capacity view of unemployment. If an increase in aggregate demand results in an increase in the amount of labour services used up in production, there exists deficient-demand unemployment. When additional aggregate demand does not cause an increase in the amount of labour used up in production, the unemployment gap is equal to zero. As already pointed out above, full employment is therefore defined analogously to capacity output,[10] which is the output that would be achieved in the short run if the economy were to be run at very high levels of demand relative to productive potential (for example, as at business cycle peaks when the man–hour input reaches a relative peak).

Since the meaning and derivation of the unemployment gap has been investigated in detail elsewhere,[11] it will only be necessary to summarise the concept briefly in this paper. Nonetheless, it will be useful to show how the unemployment gap and its component parts can be generated from a simple model of employer–worker behaviour in the face of a reduction in product demand (and thus output). The following assumptions form the basis of the model:

(i) The firm is a price-setter and output is exogenously determined.
(ii) The firm is a short-run cost-minimiser subject to certain constraints (to be explained below).
(iii) We are in the short run, with all factor inputs fixed other than the labour input, which is defined in terms of man–hours.
(iv) Workers and hours worked per worker are substitutable in the short run (as depicted by the isoquants in Figure 8.1).
(v) The wage bill (W) is defined as follows:
$$W = n(t_n w_n + t_o w_o) + nf$$
where n = number of workers employed, t_n = normal time hours worked per worker, t_o = overtime hours worked per worker, w_n = wage rate for normal time working, w_o = wage rate for overtime working and f = fixed costs per worker employed.

Expressing the number of workers (n) in terms of hours worked per worker, we obtain $n = W/(t_n w_n + t_o w_o + f)$, which is depicted by the kinked isocost curves in Figure 8.1.[12]

Let us now suppose that the employer aims to produce an output of x_o, which is depicted as an isoquant in Figure 8.1. The optimum combination of workers (n) and hours worked per worker (t) will

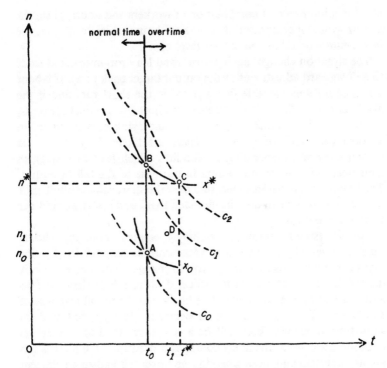

Figure 8.1. The choice between workers and hours with adjustments to changes in output

Note: n = no. of workers employed; t = average hours worked per worker; x = isoquant; c = isocost.

be at $A(n_o t_o)$, given the isoquants and isocosts as depicted, and assuming that there are for the time being no constraints preventing the employer from achieving this optimum combination of n and t. We should note that no overtime is being worked at this particular combination of n and t. The situation changes, however, when demand suddenly increases, with the result that the firm is now faced with a new and higher output target of x^*. To minimise labour costs, the firm will aim to purchase the combination of n and t given by point B. But, if we assume that there is a limit in the short run to the number of workers available to the firm (for example, an upper limit of n^* in the production period), then the firm will have to move to combination $C(n^* t^*)$ if the output x^* is to be produced. Combination

C is the minimum cost combination of workers and hours, given the labour availability constraint. Overtime hours equal to $t^* - t_o$ are now being worked at the output level of x^*.

The situation changes again when a sudden drop in demand leads to a downward adjustment of the output target back to x_o. If labour was a completely variable factor input in the short run, and if the firm's aim was simply to minimise its short-run production costs, the firm would produce output x_o by employing n_o workers at an average workweek of t_o hours. There are likely, however, to be several constraints operating on the firm which lead to a sluggish adjustment of workers and hours in response to the fall in output. The firm may find, for instance, that over the short run the number of workers employed can only be cut back to n_1, and hours worked per worker cut back to t_1.

But why should employers willingly employ more man–hours than they actually require to produce current output? Briefly, the input of labour tends to be insensitive to changes in output, especially during the initial phases of a cyclical downturn.[13] If demand falls and output has to be curtailed, it is likely that the initial response of employers will be a reduction in overtime working, followed by short-time working. There will be a reluctance to dismiss workers until forecasts about the likely course and duration of the recession are more certain and, even when the employer has gathered sufficient information to revise his production plans (downwards in this case), there may still be sound reasons for a slow and prolonged reaction of employment levels to changes in output. These include legal and/or institutional constraints resulting from contractual agreements between employers and workers about the dismissal of workers and the length of the workweek, technical constraints resulting from indivisibilities in the production process, economic constraints resulting from the transaction costs of hiring and firing workers and the retraining costs resulting from hiring new workers when output recovers.

If it is accepted that employers will tend to purchase more labour than is actually needed (to produce current output) during recessions, such as the man–hour input of $n_1 t_1$ at output x_o in Figure 8.1, we can now complete our discussion of the unemployment gap. But first we require an assumption about the workweek desired by workers. We shall assume that workers desire to work t^* hours per week.[14]

In other words, workers are assumed to prefer overtime to working a normal workweek, which is in fact a standard result in labour supply theory, provided premium rates are paid for overtime.[15] This is a useful assumption, since it makes it possible to express unemployment in terms of man–hours rather than in terms of the number of workers, and by so doing to add to our understanding of the structure of the unemployment gap. Returning to Figure 8.1, the following components of unemployment can be derived:

$$n^*t^* - n_o t_o = \text{the total unemployment gap}$$
$$n^*t^* - n_1 t^* = \text{unemployed man–hours}$$
$$n_1 t^* - n_o t_o = \text{under-employed man–hours.}$$

These two components of the unemployment gap, namely *un*-employed man–hours and *under*-employed man–hours, can each be subdivided into two further components. Let us take the unemployed man–hours component first. Not all those who become unemployed are registered as such, with the result that the official statistics of the wholly unemployed are an incomplete statement of this first component of the unemployment gap. It appears that many secondary workers (mainly married women) do not register their unemployment in recessions, with the result that there exists *hidden* unemployment. The second component of the unemployment gap, namely under-employed man–hours, can be divided into *paid-for* and *unpaid-for* varieties of hoarding:

$$n_1 t^* - n_o t_o = (n_1 t_1 - n_o t_o) \qquad + (n_1 t^* - n_1 t_1)$$

or total hoarding = paid-for hoarding + unpaid-for hoarding.

The unpaid-for component arises because workers are working a shorter workweek than they desire. It is therefore the consequence of short-time working. The paid-for component of hoarding is self-explanatory: it is the man–hours purchased by the employer but not used.

THE MEASUREMENT OF THE UNEMPLOYMENT GAP

As with our treatment of the concept of the unemployment gap, the following discussion of the measurement of this gap will be kept brief. More detail of the construction of these methods of measurement, and their related conceptual and practical problems, can be found in Taylor.[16]

The unemployment gap (U) was defined above as the sum of unemployment and under-employment (see Figure 8.1), that is

$$U = (n^*t^* - n_1 t^*) + (n_1 t^* - n_o t_o)$$
$$= n^*t^* - n_o t_o.$$

Expressing this as a percentage of the full employment supply of labour (n^*t^*), the unemployment gap becomes:

$$u = \left(1 - \frac{n_o t_o}{n^*t^*}\right) \times 100. \tag{A}$$

On the assumption of constant short-run returns to labour,

$$\frac{x_o}{n_o t_o} = \frac{x^*}{n^*t^*} \tag{B}$$

or

$$\frac{x_o}{x^*} = \frac{n_o t_o}{n^*t^*}. \tag{C}$$

Substituting (C) into (A), we obtain $u = [1 - (x_o/x^*)] \times 100$, or, more generally, $u_t = [1 - (x_t/x_t^*)] \times 100$, where x is actual output, x^* is the full employment level of output and t is time. In this paper, the full employment output level has been calculated by using the Wharton method.[17] Linear segments are fitted across peak output levels in a time-series of the output index. Full employment output levels can then be interpolated from the linear segments for the time period between full employment peaks in the output series. This procedure was applied to each of the index of industrial production industries for the period 1952–73 (using quarterly data, seasonally adjusted). The variable u was then estimated for each industry, and an aggregate index was constructed by summing the estimates across industries, using employment levels for weighting the industry estimates, that is, $u = \Sigma[u_i(n_i/\Sigma n_i)]$, where u = aggregate estimate of the unemployment gap, u_i = estimated unemployment gap in industry i and n_i = employees in employment in industry i.

It should be noted that the procedure used here for estimating the unemployment gap is subject to a number of drawbacks. First, no evidence has been offered in support of the assumption that the short-run returns to labour are constant in each of the index of production industries. Secondly, the trend-through-peaks procedure relies heavily on the selection of peak output levels. The estimates of full employment levels of output will suffer to the extent that the selected peak output levels are not of 'equal strength'. Thirdly, the absence of a full employment output peak at the beginning or at the end of the time period necessitates extrapolation of the appropriate linear segments. Fourthly, the fitting of linear segments between the peaks in output is itself open to question, since this implies that productive capacity moves along a linear time path between the peaks.

We are now ready to begin the job of dissecting the unemployment gap (U) into its three component parts:

$$U \equiv R + H + D$$

where R = deficient-demand component of registered unemployment; H = hidden unemployment (arising from a demand deficiency) and D = labour hoarding (arising from a demand deficiency). Since the hoarding component of the unemployment gap is obtained in a similar way to the unemployment gap as a whole, it will be convenient to begin by explaining how this component is estimated. Using Figure 8.1, we earlier defined labour hoarding (D) as follows:

$$D = n_1 t^* - n_o t_o. \tag{D}$$

From equation (B), we have $n_o t_o = (x_o/x^*) \, n^* t^*$. Substituting this equation into (D), we obtain

$$D = \left(1 - \frac{x_o/n_1}{x^*/n^*} \right) n_1 t^*.$$

Expressing D in terms of the full employment supply of labour $(n^* t^*)$, we obtain the rate of labour hoarding (u_d):

$$u_d = \left(1 - \frac{x_o/n_1}{x^*/n^*} \right) \frac{n_1}{n^*} \times 100$$

or, more generally,

$$u_{d_t} = \left(1 - \frac{x_t/n_t}{(x/n)_t^*} \right) \frac{n_t}{n_t^*} \times 100 \tag{E}$$

where $(x/n)^*$ is the ratio of full employment output to employees, and n^* is the level of employment assuming that the economy is at a position of full employment. As in the calculation of x^* (the full employment level of output), the Wharton trend-through-peaks procedure was again used to estimate a time-series for both $(x/n)^*$ and n^* for the period 1952–73, using quarterly, seasonally adjusted data. The aggregate estimate of u_d was then constructed by:

(a) estimating labour hoarding in each industry, expressed in terms of the number of employees;
(b) aggregating across industries; and
(c) expressing the result as a percentage of the full employment supply of employees (n^*).[18]

A restriction had to be added to the method used to calculate labour hoarding. In some industries, the underlying growth in labour productivity was found to be exponential, which means that the fitting of linear segments to the peaks in the x/n time-series leads to an over-estimation of the full employment estimates of x/n. This in turn leads to an over-estimation of labour hoarding, and in some industries labour hoarding was estimated to be greater than the unemployment gap as a whole (during recessionary periods). Since this is impossible by definition, the estimate of labour hoarding was constrained so that it could not exceed the unemployment gap (that is, $u_d \leqslant u$).

The final task in the process of dividing the unemployment gap into three components is to estimate the hidden unemployment component (u_h). First, a full employment level of the workforce was calculated by fitting linear segments between peaks in the time-series of the registered workforce. In view of the fact that hidden unemployment is likely to be quite small for males, linear segments were fitted to the peaks in the annual time-series of the registered female workforce for Great Britain over the period 1951–73 (Figure 8.2). Hidden unemployment is then estimated as:

$$H = F^* - F$$

where $F =$ registered female workforce and $F^* =$ estimated full employment level of F. Expressing hidden unemployment as a percentage of the full employment supply of employees (n^*), we obtain

$$u_h = \left(\frac{F^* - F}{n^*}\right) \times 100 \qquad\qquad (F)$$

By deliberately ignoring hidden male unemployment, hidden unemployment is being under-estimated. But this under-estimation is likely to be quite small,[19] since nearly all males are permanently attached to the workforce throughout their working lives. By comparison, a large proportion of married female workers are not permanently attached to the workforce and unemployed females are

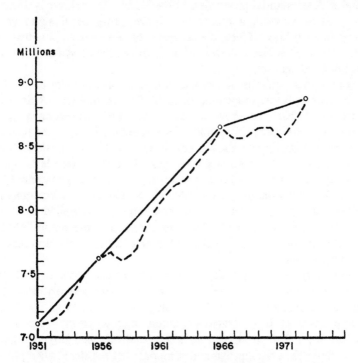

Figure 8.2. Estimation of hidden unemployment: Great Britain, 1951–73

Sources: Department of Employment, *British Labour Statistics: Historical Abstract*, 1886–1968, H.M.S.O., 1971, table 115; *Department of Employment Gazette*, April 1974, tables 101 and 106.

Notes: (i) The dotted curve shows the registered female workforce (employees in employment plus wholly unemployed).
(ii) The straight lines join the points on that curve in 1951, 1956, 1966 and 1973.

158   INVOLUNTARY UNEMPLOYMENT

consequently more likely to be discouraged from registering as
unemployed during recessionary periods than are unemployed males.
On the other hand, the method of applying the trend-through-peaks
procedure to the registered female workforce in order to calculate
hidden unemployment will tend to over-estimate the amount of
hidden unemployment. This over-estimation of hidden unemployment arises because we have ignored the fact that the desired workweek for many of those in the hidden unemployment category will
be considerably lower than the workweek desired by, say, prime-aged
males. A substantial proportion of the hidden unemployed will want
only part-time work, and only a small proportion are likely to want
overtime working. Hence, the estimates of hidden unemployment in
this paper are subject to errors of over-estimation as well as to errors
of under-estimation.

Since this paper is concerned only with unemployment in the
production sector, the estimates of hidden unemployment derived
in the way described above had to be corrected. Hidden unemployment will vary between sectors of the economy because the female
intensity of employment varies considerably between industries. The
1961 Census of Population showed that the ratio of female to male
employment in the production sector was then 32/100 compared to
48/100 in the economy as a whole. The estimates of hidden unemployment for Great Britain were consequently multiplied by two-
thirds (using the ratio of 32/48) to correct for the possibility of
proportionately less hidden unemployment in the production sector
of the economy.

Our only remaining task in this section of the paper is to show
how registered unemployment can be split into deficient-demand
unemployment and frictional unemployment. Since two of the three
components of total deficient-demand unemployment have been
estimated, and since we have an estimate of the unemployment gap
as a whole, the deficient-demand component of registered unemployment (u_r) is determined as a residual. Since $u = u_r + u_h + u_d$,

$$u_r = u - u_h - u_d. \tag{G}$$

The frictional component, z, of registered unemployment, w, is
determined analogously. Since $w \equiv u_r + z$, $z = w - u_r$, where u_r is
calculated from equation (G) and w is obtained from official sources.
A note of caution, however, must be added: z is simply a residual;

it is not estimated directly. This means that it will contain any error arising from the method of estimating the deficient-demand component of registered unemployment, u_r. If the cyclical fluctuations in u_r have been over-estimated, for example, this will generate contra-cyclical fluctuations in z; and conversely if the cyclical fluctuations in u_r have been under-estimated. Short-run movements in z must therefore be regarded with suspicion, at least until we know more about the accuracy of the other estimated variables.

UNEMPLOYMENT IN BRITAIN, 1953–73

The estimates of the individual components of the unemployment gap constructed in this paper indicate that it is misleading to use any one component as a proxy for the gap as a whole. The ratio of registered unemployment to the unemployment gap as a whole, for example, remained fairly stable from 1953 to 1963 (Figure 8.3). But since 1963 this ratio has been subject to sudden and considerable shifts. In addition, the registered unemployment rate indicates that there was a rising trend in the excess supply of labour during the period 1953–73. Yet according to our estimates of the unemployment gap as a whole (as shown in Figure 8.4), the excess supply of labour was definitely not subject to an upward trend. This result means one of two things: either that unemployed man–hours were shifting from one component of the unemployment gap to another, or that the trend increase in the rate of registered unemployment was due to a trend increase in frictional unemployment. From an examination of the two components of the rate of registered unemployment in Figure 8.5, we can see that the upward trend in the rate of registered unemployment is explained entirely by the upward trend in the frictional component. There is no discernible long-run trend in the deficient-demand component of the rate of registered unemployment, which means that an explanation of the upward trend in registered unemployment as a whole requires an explanation of the upward trend in the frictional component. We shall return to this question later.

The years 1968–9 provide us with perhaps the most vivid example of the inadequacy of the rate of registered unemployment as an index of excess supply in the labour market. According to the estimate of the unemployment gap as a whole, 1968 and 1969 were years of

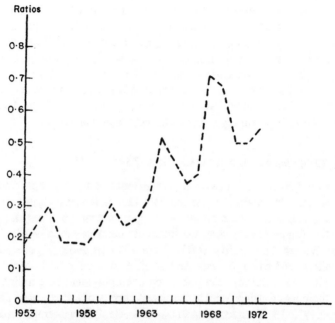

Figure 8.3. The ratio of registered unemployment (*w*) to deficient-demand unemployment (*u*) in the production sector: Great Britain, 1953–72

Note: Rates for *w* and *u* calculated as explained in the text.

labour scarcity (see Figure 8.4). Yet the average rate of registered unemployment was at its highest post-war level up to that time. Apparently the expansion of 1967–8 was not reflected at all in the rate of registered unemployment. Previous experience would have suggested that the 1967–8 expansion should have been followed (with a lag of about six months) by a fall in registered unemployment. Another example of the inadequacy of the registered unemployment rate is that the 1971 recession gave rise to a rate of registered unemployment that was twice as high as it was in the recessions of 1958 and 1962. Yet the estimates of the unemployment gap suggest that the 1971 recession was, if anything, less severe than the 1958 recession, and of similar strength to the 1962 recession (Figure 8.4).

A feature of the rate of registered unemployment in Britain that has attracted attention in recent years is the prolonged upward movement that occurred in this variable, from 1·1 per cent in the

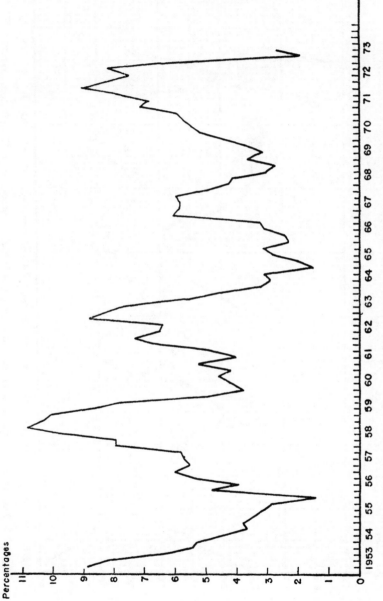

Figure 8.4. Estimated deficient-demand unemployment in the production sector (u): Great Britain, 1953–73

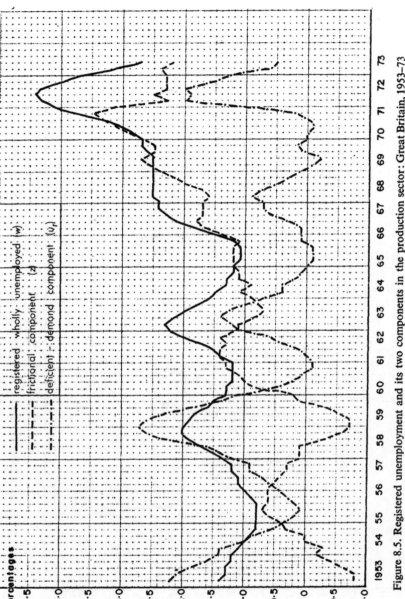

Figure 8.5. Registered unemployment and its two components in the production sector: Great Britain, 1953–73

first quarter of 1966 to 4·4 per cent in the first quarter of 1972.[20] At no time during this six-year period did the registered unemployment rate actually fall, apart from seasonal fluctuations. The question arises: how much of this persistent increase in the registered unemployment rate was the result of a demand deficiency and was thus removable by raising aggregate demand? The answer appears to be that about one-half of the high rate of registered unemployment in the first quarter of 1972 can be attributed to a demand deficiency. The rapid fall in the unemployment rate in response to an expansionary fiscal and monetary policy during 1972–3 provides additional support for the theory that a large part of the high rate of registered unemployment in the 1971–2 recession was the result of a demand deficiency. Yet the fact that the unemployment gap reached the very low level of 1·9 per cent in the first quarter of 1973 indicates that unemployment was approaching its short-run minimum level during 1973 (falling towards the 2 per cent mark, but not quite reaching it in spite of a strong expansionary policy).

Let us now take a look at the frictional component of registered unemployment. A feature of this variable that stands out above all others is the marked long-run upward trend that was present during the 1960s. This trend appears to have been levelling-off during the period 1969–73. The implication of this upward trend in frictional unemployment is that the minimum level to which the registered unemployment rate will fall, under conditions of full employment, is currently in the vicinity of 2 per cent. This minimum level was apparently 'jacked up' during the 1960s.

We ought now to ask why there has been an upward trend in frictional unemployment, since this may provide us with a guide as to its likely future course. One possible explanation can be found in Reder's work.[21] If workers in their search for a job become more 'fussy' in accepting job offers, the duration of their search activity will lengthen and frictional unemployment will consequently increase. Under what circumstances, though, will workers become more 'fussy' in accepting a job offer? One possible explanation is that the economic hardship of being unemployed has been reduced over time as the real value of unemployment and supplementary benefits available to unemployed workers has increased. Perhaps a more plausible explanation is to be found in Hill's work.[22] An increase in unemployment and supplementary benefits will have the effect of raising the reservation wage of workers. For many low-paid (usually unskilled) workers, this could mean that the income incentive for seeking a job actually disappears. Firm conclusions are not yet forthcoming on this question and more detailed survey work is clearly needed.

The second dominating feature of the frictional component of registered unemployment is that it fluctuates contra-cyclically. This result supports the view that search activity will tend to increase when the job market is favourable (to workers) and decrease when it is not. A situation of labour scarcity raises the probability that a worker will receive an acceptable job offer, and so workers will tend to become more 'fussy' as the job market moves in their favour. The contra-cyclical fluctuations in the frictional component of registered unemployment suggest that workers do in fact increase their search activity during booms and reduce it during recessions. But this contra-cyclical behaviour of frictional unemployment must be treated cautiously. As explained earlier, it may simply reflect the fact that the cyclical fluctuations in the deficient-demand variety of registered unemployment have been over-estimated.

CONCLUSION

The aim of this paper was to analyse unemployment in Britain during the period 1953–73. Earlier work on unemployment has indicated that a greater understanding of the behaviour of *registered* unemployment can be obtained by examining the whole of the unemployment gap, which is defined as the total unemployed man–hours resulting from a demand deficiency. Another strand of research has suggested that the division of registered unemployment into a deficient-demand component and a frictional component provides valuable insight into the behaviour of registered unemployment. This paper has attempted to fuse these two approaches together. Knowledge of the unemployment gap and its structure has been used to construct a method of dividing registered unemployment into a deficient-demand and a frictional component. This method was then applied to the British production sector to obtain quarterly estimates of the two components for the period 1953–73.

The main findings of the analysis of unemployment in the British production sector were as follows:

(i) The rate of registered unemployment is a completely unsatis-factory indicator of the excess supply of labour.

(ii) The upward trend in the rate of registered unemployment during the period 1953–73 was due entirely to the upward trend in frictional unemployment.

(iii) Frictional unemployment rose from around zero in the period 1953–9 to around 2·3 per cent in 1973. This implies that it will not be possible, in the short run at least, to achieve the low rates of registered unemployment that prevailed in the production sector during the mid-1950s (0·8 per cent), or during the mid-1960s (1·1 per cent).

(iv) Frictional unemployment fluctuated contra-cyclically over the period 1953–73, indicating that the search activity of workers tends to increase when market conditions are favourable to workers.[23]

(v) The upward shift in registered unemployment that occurred in the second half of the 1960s can be partly explained by the absence of a 'shake-in' during the short period of expansion in 1967–8.

(vi) About one-half of the high level of registered unemployment reached in the first quarter of 1972 (that is, one-half of 4·4 per cent) can be accounted for by a deficiency of aggregate demand.

The main policy implications of these findings are, first, that the policymakers cannot rely on the registered unemployment rate as an indicator of the pressure of demand in the labour market. If aggregate demand is to be efficiently regulated, then alternative indicators (such as the 'unemployment gap') will have to be used. Secondly, if frictional unemployment is now at a permanently higher level, then it follows that the policymakers will have to accept a higher average rate of registered unemployment than was experienced during the 1950s and early 1960s, unless, of course, the efficiency of the labour market can be improved through, for example, regional policy measures and re-training programmes.

Finally, it is necessary to end on a note of caution. The methods developed in this paper for the purpose of (a) measuring deficient-demand unemployment more accurately, and (b) segregating deficient-demand unemployment and frictional unemployment, are still in their infancy. It would be wrong to leave the impression that the empirical estimates presented here were anything other than a 'first try'. Much more work will have to be done before firm policy implications can be drawn from this type of analysis.

NOTES

1 The author is grateful to the Nuffield Foundation for providing the funds to support the research reported in this paper, which is part of a larger project investigating the behaviour of unemployment in Britain. Thanks are also due to my colleagues at Lancaster, to participants in the Royal Economic Society conference at Durham (March 1974), and to John Corina, John Flemming and Stuart McKendrick. The errors are my own.
2 R. G. Lipsey, 'Structural and Deficient-Demand Unemployment Reconsidered' in A. M. Ross (ed.), *Employment Policy in the Labor Market*, University of California Press, 1965.
3 See R. Perlman, *Labor Theory*, Wiley, 1969, for a useful description of the '*UV* method', and A. P. Thirlwall, 'Types of Unemployment, with Special Reference to "Non-Demand-Deficient" Unemployment in the UK', *Scottish Journal of Political Economy*, February 1969, provides an example of its use.
4 See J. Tobin, 'Inflation and Unemployment', *American Economic Review*, March 1972, for a discussion of the different views of the concept of full employment.
5 Following L. R. Klein, 'Some Theoretical Issues in the Measurement of Capacity', *Econometrica*, April 1960, and A. M. Okun, 'Potential GNP: Its Measurement and Significance', *Proceedings of the American Statistical Association (Business and Economic Statistics Section)*, 1962.
6 The 'natural' rate of unemployment is not considered here. See M. Friedman, 'The Role of Monetary Policy', *American Economic Review*, March 1968, and E. S. Phelps, 'Money Wage Dynamics and Labor Market Equilibrium' in Phelps (ed.), *Micro-economic Foundations of Employment and Inflation Theory*, Norton, 1970, for discussions of the 'natural' rate, and see Tobin, 'Inflation and Unemployment' for a critique.
7 See D. I. MacKay and G. L. Reid, 'Redundancy, Unemployment and Manpower Policy', *Economic Journal*, December 1972, and M. H. Fisher, 'The New Micro-economics of Unemployment', Chapter 2 above.
8 See B. A. Corry and D. E. W. Laidler, 'The Phillips Relation: A Theoretical Explanation', *Economica*, May 1967.
9 M. W. Reder, 'The Theory of Frictional Unemployment', *Economica*, February 1969.
10 See Klein, 'Some Theoretical Issues in the Measurement of Capacity', and Okun, 'Potential GNP'.
11 See J. Taylor, *Unemployment and Wage Inflation, with Special Reference to Britain and the USA*, Longman, 1974.
12 See F. P. R. Brechling, 'The Relationship between Output and Employment in British Manufacturing Industries', *Review of Economic Studies*, July 1965.
13 For a more detailed discussion, see Taylor, *Unemployment and Wage Inflation*; for an inter-industry analysis see A. S. McKendrick, 'An Inter-industry Analysis of Labour Hoarding in Britain, 1953–72,' *Applied Economics*, June 1975.

14 Although the desired workweek is a constant in the static analysis presented here, the workweek desired by workers appears to have been subject to a long-run downward trend. This point is not important in the present discussion, and it becomes important only if the labour hoarding component of the unemployment gap is to be split into a paid-for component and an unpaid-for component.

15 See Perlman, *Labor Theory*.

16 *Unemployment and Wage Inflation*.

17 See L. R. Klein and R. Summers, *The Wharton Index of Capacity Utilization*, University of Pennsylvania, 1966, and J. Taylor, D. Winter and D. Pearce, 'A

19 Industry Quarterly Series of Capacity Utilisation in the United Kingdom, 1948–1968', *Bulletin of the Oxford University Institute of Economics and Statistics*, May 1970, for an explanation of the method and a discussion of its major drawbacks.

18 The rate of labour hoarding for the production sector as a whole was calculated as:

$$u_d = \frac{D}{N} \left(\frac{N^*}{N} \right) \times 100$$

where D = total hoarding in the production sector, expressed in terms of employees and calculated as explained above; N = total employees in employment in the production sector; N/N^* = ratio of total employees in employment to full employment level of employment for the economy as a whole. So that all the components of unemployment are expressed as a proportion of the same base, the same procedure was applied to the rate of registered unemployment, that is:

$$w = \frac{W}{N} \left(\frac{N}{N^*} \right) \times 100$$

where W = wholly unemployed in the production sector.

19 See 'Regional Activity Rates as a Measure of Potential Labour Reserves'. *Department of Employment Gazette*, January 1971, pp. 67–71.

20 See, for example, the discussion of the upward shift in the rate of registered unemployment in J. K. Bowers, P. C. Cheshire and A. E. Webb, 'The Change in the Relationship between Unemployment and Earnings Increases: A Review of Some Possible Explanations', and J. K. Bowers, P. C. Cheshire, A. E. Webb and R. Weeden, 'Some Aspects of Unemployment and the Labour Market, 1966–71', *National Institute Economic Review*, No. 54, November 1970 and No. 62, November 1972.

21 'The Theory of Frictional Unemployment.'

22 M. J. Hill, 'Can we Distinguish Voluntary from Involuntary Unemployment?', Chapter 9 below.

23 More recent research by the author suggests that the contra-cyclical fluctuations in frictional unemployment were induced by an under-estimation of hidden unemployment, which resulted from the exclusion of males from those estimates (see p. 157). Until further research is undertaken it would be prudent to treat frictional unemployment simply as a trend variable. The short-run behaviour of this variable should be ignored.

Chapter 9

Can we Distinguish Voluntary from Involuntary Unemployment?

MICHAEL J. HILL

INTRODUCTION

This paper is based upon some research on the characteristics and attitudes of unemployed men which was sponsored by the Department of Health and Social Security and the Department of Employment. It was designed to throw light upon long-term and frequent unemployment by examining the factors that were correlated with these phenomena. It took the form of a study of 1,018 men who were registered as unemployed in Newcastle-upon-Tyne, Coventry and the London borough of Hammersmith in October 1971. These men were a random sample of those unemployed in these areas at that time, close to the peak of the 1971–2 recession. They were all interviewed (the 1,018 being about 75 per cent of the initial sample) and their employment, sickness and (where applicable) criminal records were examined. The main findings of this study were reported in *Men Out of Work* published in the summer of 1973.[1]

This research project, which arose out of Miss Olive Stevenson's spell as Social Work Adviser to the Supplementary Benefits Commission,[2] was expected to throw some light upon the efforts made by civil servants in the Department of Employment and the Supplementary Benefits Commission to distinguish between those amongst the chronically unemployed who can be said to be making little effort to find themselves work and those who are unable to obtain work. There are a number of sanctions which officials can use against the voluntarily unemployed, their problem is to distinguish the individuals for whom such treatment is appropriate, or justifiable. In *Men Out of Work* it was argued that there is no satisfactory way of drawing a distinction between the voluntarily and the involuntarily unemployed, and that the attempt to do so within the current social security policies has the unfortunate effect of maximising the impact of the sanctions upon those who are in the weakest positions in the labour market. For this reason it is a little disturbing that economists should want to make use of the voluntary–involuntary distinction. While it is recognised that these are used as technical terms, it does seem to be the case that (a) the popular and the technical usages of these concepts are often confused, and (b) that this confusion often rests upon an underlying desire to use differential motivation to work as an explanatory variable with reference to key contemporary labour-market problems. In this paper, therefore, two things will be attempted. First, an examination of ways in which data from the survey of unemployed men may be related to some popular hypotheses about voluntary unemployment, and second, an explanation of how some of the difficulties in disentangling voluntary from involuntary unemployment led us to take up the position described above.

HIGH SOCIAL SECURITY BENEFITS

Quite the most widespread popular theory about voluntary unemployment is that social security benefit levels close to potential earnings levels deter individuals from seeking work. The regulations concerning both earnings-related supplements to unemployment benefit and (until 1975) supplementary benefits contained wage-stop clauses to prevent benefits exceeding potential earnings, but clearly these did not prevent many situations arising in which the actual increases in income individuals gained from going to work were very slight. There is no absence of anecdotal evidence to support this disincentive hypothesis. Some of those in a sub-sample of men who were given second intensive interviews were themselves quite ready to ascribe their employment problems to low earnings relative to their benefits. For example one young man said:

'When you go down to the dole they've either got a job for you that is behind the standard of pay, and therefore I find myself getting more dole money than I get wages, or their standard of skill required is above my grade anyway.'

Another man who had recently gone back to work explained he was contemplating throwing up that job once he had moved out of his in-laws' home into a house, where social security help with his rent would raise his out-of-work income:

'Well that [supplementary benefit] on top of me dole, it'll work out about five bob less than me wages, so it's a waste of time me working for that, because I'm rushed off me feet all day and I'm really aching and tired when I come home and I'm filthy.'

In *Men Out of Work* some evidence for this hypothesis was considered, leading to some very tentative and guarded conclusions, in which it was suggested that, since the men with high benefit incomes relative to past wages had been low wage earners, probably characteristics such as advanced age, low skill and poor health were 'likely to have been the main determinants of both low pay in the past and their long unemployment in the present'.[3]

For this paper more detailed attention has been given to the impact upon unemployment duration of high benefits relative to past earnings. Table 9.1 sets out the number of men in each area, in each of three unemployment duration groups, with benefit incomes higher than £1 below their last weekly earnings. The figures in italics represent these numbers as percentages of all the men in each area in each unemployment duration group. In all three areas the relationship

Table 9.1   *Unemployment duration of those with benefit incomes higher than £1 below their last weekly earnings*

Unemployment duration	Coventry Nos	%a	Hammersmith Nos	%a	Newcastle Nos	%a
Under 6 months	9	*8·3*	14	*15·6*	10	*12·7*
6 months to 1 year	27	*16·3*	24	*25·8*	50	*32·3*
Over 1 year	19	*21·3*	18	*43·9*	33	*28·2*

aPercentages of all men in each area in the unemployment duration group.

apparent from the table between high out-of-work income relative to earnings and unemployment duration is statistically significant at the

5 per cent level, and in Hammersmith it is so also at the 1 per cent level.

Bearing in mind the qualification made in *Men Out of Work* that the linking factors here are likely to be factors known to be associated with prolonged unemployment, like advanced age and low skill, some calculations were done with these factors taken into account. In Coventry and Hammersmith the breakdown of the sample into two age groups, under and over 50, eliminated the statistically significant association in all cases. In Newcastle, however, the association was statistically significant at the 1 per cent level for the under 50s.

Similar calculations were done with the samples divided into two skill groups (as defined by their last jobs), one of these contained the non-manual and skilled workers, while the other contained semi- and unskilled manual workers. In two of the groups thus produced statistically significant associations appeared, amongst the low skilled in Hammersmith and amongst the more skilled in Newcastle. These are interesting associations because both these groups were comparatively advantaged in the labour market; the low skilled in Hammersmith were shown in *Men Out of Work* to be but little disadvantaged by comparison with the more skilled in that area, while in Newcastle skilled and non-manual workers were shown to have much better job prospects than low skilled workers. However, before jumping to any conclusions about motivation, it must still be remembered that dividing a skill group by past income level may still be a process of distinguishing the better from the worse favoured within that group.

Another factor to be taken into account in relation to this hypothesis is marital status, since the single very rarely have benefit incomes close to their potential earnings levels. Calculations were done dividing the currently married (including those in common law relationships) from the rest. When this was done the associations between the variables continued to appear in all cases, but were only statistically significant at the 5 per cent level amongst both groups in Hammersmith and the married in Newcastle.

Finally, an attempt was made to control for age, marital status and skill, by looking at the two skill groups within the married under 50s. Unfortunately in Coventry and Hammersmith this tended to reduce the numbers to too low a level, but in Newcastle the results for both groups showed clear associations, the one for the non-manual and skilled being statistically significant at the 5 per cent level.

These calculations indicate a much stronger association between high benefit income relative to last pay and prolonged unemployment than was suggested in *Men Out of Work*. Furthermore they do, to some extent, suggest that this association is, at least partly, independent of those strong correlates of prolonged unemployment, advanced age and low skill. However one other reservation expressed in *Men Out of Work* is still applicable, this is 'that with inflation any pay rate from a year or more ago will tend to seem rather low, and that therefore the longer men were out of work the more likely that their past earnings would be below their current income levels.'[4] Finally it must be emphasised that the proportions of the unemployed in a 'low incentive' situation are relatively low, being about 15 per cent of the Coventry sample and around 22–24 per cent of the Hammersmith and Newcastle groups.

EARNINGS-RELATED SUPPLEMENT

Earnings-related supplement to unemployment benefit, introduced in 1966, has been seen by some as playing a part in reducing incentives to go to work. This benefit only lasts for the first six months of unemployment; it can only be argued, therefore, that it may influence the behaviour of the relatively newly unemployed.

In an attempt to test the hypothesis that earnings-related supplement deters men from returning to work quickly, the lengths of unemployment after 1st October 1971 (the date for which income information was collected for the sample) were compared for those who were and those who were not getting earnings-related supplement. This produced no evidence in support of the hypothesis, and in fact, in one area, Newcastle, there was a statistically significant tendency ($p = <0.01$) for those without earnings-related supplement to remain unemployed the longest. This is not surprising, since those without the supplement were a mixture of men with no entitlement, on account of either very low earnings or very irregular employment before the onset of the spell of unemployment they were in, together with men who had exhausted their six months' entitlement. In other words, men without earnings-related supplement tended to be the men who were least likely to be attractive to employers.

The difficulty with any hypothesis about the impact of earnings-related supplement is, therefore, the absence of a comparable group getting nothing who can be compared with those receiving the supplement. The supposition must be that, at most, the impact of earnings-related supplement will amount to no more than an increase in the selectiveness of men who are in any case able to get more work fairly easily. It will be seen that similar considerations apply to those who obtained redundancy pay.

REDUNDANCY PAY

To be entitled to a redundancy payment of any size an unemployed man will have to have lost, in circumstances that reflect no discredit on him as an employee, a job that he has held for a considerable number of years. This means that a recipient of a large amount of redundancy pay will tend to be elderly and, as there is a strong association between age and unemployment duration, it will come as no surprise that men who had received large sums tended to experience long unemployment. In an attempt to take into account the age factor, the association between amount of redundancy pay and length of unemployment amongst the under 50s was examined. In one area, Coventry, there was a slight, but not statistically significant, association between high redundancy pay and low unemployment. This suggests that the good service records of recipients of high redundancy pay make them attractive to future employers, though in any case possession of a good record is correlated with other factors related to short unemployment, such as possession of a skill.

In general, however, as Table 9.2 shows, the numbers amongst the under 50s with redundancy payments of any substance were sufficiently low to render this a rather unlikely ' cause ' of prolonged unemployment. However, it must be said that, as with earnings-

Table 9.2   *Recipients of redundancy pay*

	Coventry	Numbers of men Hammersmith	Newcastle
Whole sample	93	35	39
Under 50s	36	15	17
and over £200 received	22	7	7

related supplement, an entirely satisfactory test of the impact of redundancy pay would only be possible if some men were quite arbitrarily deprived of a benefit to which they had a right in order to create an experimental situation!

VOLUNTARY LEAVING

A considerable number of men in the samples acknowledged that they had left their last job voluntarily. Most of these men said they left because their job was unsatisfactory. Thus in Coventry 44 (12 per cent of the whole sample) said this, while only 16 (4 per cent) said they had no specific reason for leaving. Equivalent figures for Hammersmith were 24 (11 per cent) and 15 (7 per cent), and for Newcastle 42 (11 per cent) and 21 (5 per cent). For the purpose of this discussion these two categories of 'voluntary leavers' have been amalgamated, so any observations must be subject to two reservations:

(i) Many of these men will have had what many people will regard as 'good' reasons for leaving their jobs.
(ii) The identification of a group whose initial unemployment may be described as 'voluntary' is not the same thing as identifying the voluntarily unemployed at later points in time.

It was found that voluntary leavers tended to experience less prolonged unemployment than other men. However, the explanation for this appeared to lie in the fact that there was a strong association between age and voluntary leaving; the young, who are less prone to long unemployment, being also much more likely to give up jobs. The latter relationship is shown very clearly in Table 9.3.

Table 9.3   *Voluntary leavers by age group*

| | | Percentages | |
	Coventry	Hammersmith	Newcastle
All groups	16	18	18
Under 25	29	46	28
25 – 49	18	23	22
Over 50	9	6	12

Table 9.4   *Characteristics of voluntary leavers*

		Percentages	
	Coventry	Hammersmith	Newcastle
Whole sample	16	18	17
Not disabled	25	24	22
Above minimum education	21	30	28
and non-manual worker	.. [a]	38	.. [a]
Unskilled	20	18	20
Criminal convictions	21	13	19
High personal disturbance score	17	21	18
Prepared to accept less than £20 a week	25	23	19
and under 50 and fit	29	37	28
and also unskilled	31	.. [a]	25

[a]Too few cases in sample.

Table 9.4 shows that voluntary leaving was also found to be associated with not being disabled and with having above minimum education. For the whole samples there was no clear association between voluntary leaving and any particular level of skill.

Clearly, then, it is possible to say, in general terms, that those who leave their jobs voluntarily tend to be individuals who can get other work fairly easily. The particularly strong association between voluntary leaving and being young suggested that there was a need to look at the relationship between voluntary leaving and prolonged unemployment within the under 50s. In doing this marital status was also taken into account, since it seemed likely to be significant too. The finding, when this was done, was that only in one case was there any clear association between voluntary leaving and unemployment duration. The one case of an association was amongst the single in Hammersmith, and this showed a statistically significant tendency for the voluntary leavers to have *shorter* unemployment than others.

Finally, the relationship between voluntary leaving and unemployment duration was examined for the skill groups among the married under 50s, and once again no association was found. These further tests, therefore, still leave the conclusion that voluntary leaving is largely a characteristic of the young, and that any tendency that might be predicted for the low skilled to throw up jobs readily does not show up in the statistical data, because it is the case that others, with skilled trades which are in demand also behave in this way when they are young.

MEN NOT SEEKING WORK

Clearly the most direct way of trying to secure evidence on voluntary unemployment is to ask people if they are seeking work. While it is acknowledged that interviewers on a survey sponsored by government departments were unlikely to secure honest answers from everyone to a question like this, it is nevertheless worthwhile to analyse the replies received.

In Coventry 314 men (84·4 per cent) said they were seeking work, and a further 29 (7·8 per cent) were only not seeking work because they were already re-employed by the time they were interviewed. In Hammersmith 167 (72·8 per cent) said they were seeking work and 32 (13·8 per cent) were back at work already. In Newcastle 311 (75·1 per cent) were seeking work and 35 (8·5 per cent) were back at work.

The reasons given by the other men who were not seeking work (excluding those already back at work) are set out in Table 9.5. In each area a substantial group are in one or other of the three categories – 'no possibility of suitable job', 'considers self retired' and

Table 9.5   *Reasons given for not seeking work*

	Coventry		Hammersmith		Newcastle	
	Nos	%[a]	Nos	%[a]	Nos	%[a]
Awaiting recall to previous job	—	—	1	0·4	1	0·2
No possibility of suitable job	7	1·9	5	2·2	10	2·4
Better off out of work	2	0·5	2	0·9	5	1·2
Cannot work because of family commitments	1	0·3	2	0·9	6	1·4
Considers self retired	8	2·2	3	1·3	6	1·4
Too ill or too old	3	0·8	—	—	10	2·4
Other reasons	7	1·9	18	7·9	29	7·0
Don't know	1	0·3	—	—	1	0·2

[a]Percentages of whole sample in that town.

'too ill or too old'. In Coventry 15 of the 18 in these categories were over 50, in Hammersmith 7 of the 8 were over 50, and in Newcastle 20 of the 26 were in this age group. So it is probable that a substantial group amongst those not seeking work had simply come to recognise that their chances of getting work were very slight.

It is unfortunate that, owing to a miscalculation at the coding stage, the 'other reasons' group is very large here. To rectify this, these men's questionnaires were examined. It was found that, apart from a mere handful of men who gave replies that indicated a rejection of the work ethos or of the 'capitalist system', three kinds of replies had been given by this group:

(i) I have found a job which I am to start shortly.
(ii) I have (or am about to) returned to or started fulltime studies.
(iii) I am temporarily sick.

THE MAIN CORRELATES OF LONG-TERM UNEMPLOYMENT

In the earlier discussion some popular hypotheses about voluntary unemployment have been discussed and only in one case, high benefits relative to past earnings, has it been possible to show any link between the causal 'factors' and prolonged unemployment. Furthermore, even in that one case it was suggested that other factors, associated with both low pay and prolonged unemployment, were perhaps of more importance. In this section brief reference will be made to the main correlates of long-term unemployment set out in *Men Out of Work*, in order to examine the contribution this evidence can make to the problem of distinguishing voluntary from involuntary unemployment.

To avoid a lengthy and perhaps tortuous description of the findings, Table 9.6 sets out the main results for each area, using asterisks to denote those findings that were statistically significant at at least the 5 per cent level. Unemployment duration was grouped into 'under six months', 'six months to a year' and 'over a year'. The independent variables also tended to be grouped to allow three or four possibilities.

In general these findings suggested that the factors most strongly associated with prolonged unemployment were those which commonsense judgements suggest are the most clear-cut 'causes' of involuntary unemployment. Three elementary logical points prevent us

INVOLUNTARY UNEMPLOYMENT

Table 9.6. *Statistical significance*[a] *of certain key variables in relation to unemployment duration*

	Coventry	Hammersmith	Newcastle
Age	*	*	*
Disability			
All ages	*	*	*
Ages 25 – 49	—	—	*
Suspected mental illness	—	—	*
Registered occupation			
All ages	*	—	*
Age 25 – 49	*	—	*
Illiteracy			
All ages	—	—	*
Age 25 – 49	—	—	—
Number of convictions	—	—	—
Imprisonment	*	—	—
Birthplace[b]	—	—	—
Number of children[c]	—	—	—
Willingness to move			
All ages	—	*	—
Age 25 – 49	—	*	—

[a]An asterisk denotes significance at the 5 per cent level on a χ^2 test.
[b]Birthplace in the New Commonwealth as against elsewhere.
[c]For married men aged 25–49 only.

arguing that the main *causes* of unemployment in Coventry, Hammersmith and Newcastle were *involuntary*:

(i) The nature of all the statistical associations is inevitably partial.

(ii) The links between these factors and the actual reasons why men fail to get work are unknown; we can only say, for example, that we know many employers are likely to reject elderly or unfit men when they are able to choose between aspiring employees.

(iii) Within any particular disadvantaged group many unemployed men do succeed in getting work relatively quickly; the existence of a statistical association does not prove that those amongst, for example, the over 50s who fail to obtain employment do not try as hard to find work as those who succeed.

Against the background of these general observations it is of value to look at the fairly marked difference in the pattern of associated variables between Hammersmith and Newcastle. The Newcastle pattern was extraordinarily clear. Indeed when we employed a computer program designed to sort out the impact of the major variables (the A.I.D. program),[5] the picture for Newcastle was as set out in Figure 9.1.

Against a background like this, whilst standing by the general logical points set out above, we should not be too critical of those who make simplistic judgements about the involuntary nature of the unemployment of an elderly, low skilled and unfit man in Newcastle.

As far as the Hammersmith findings were concerned, however, the position was much more complicated. The absence of significant statistical associations in Table 9.6 suggests that a data ordering technique like the A.I.D. program will not provide comparably neat charts, and indeed it was found that (a) an absence of widespread variations in unemployment length, and (b) the competing impact of a number of variables differing but slightly from each other in their predictive power, provided often confusing results once age had been taken into account. The question that must be asked, then, is does this situation, together with the fact that in Hammersmith alone a subjective variable 'willingness to move' was of significance, indicate that, for groups other than the elderly disabled, voluntary unemployment is a more salient 'cause' of prolonged unemployment in Hammersmith than in the other two areas.

In *Men Out of Work* we argued against this conclusion,[6] largely on the strength of the logical points set out above. Yet we can go further than that; clearly the correlates of prolonged unemployment are easy to sort out in an area like Newcastle. In Hammersmith, by contrast, jobs are easy to get and only a very small minority experience extreme amounts of unemployment. However, the low skilled men who did not, on the whole, suffer long-term unemployment in Hammersmith were found to have experienced frequent spells of unemployment in the recent past. At the same time another group, who oddly figured amongst the long-term unemployed in Newcastle but not in Hammersmith, those suspected (on the basis of a short pre-diagnostic questionnaire) of being mentally ill, were also found to be likely to have experienced frequent spells of unemployment in the latter area. It can be concluded that in Hammersmith clear associations between variables like these and unemployment length are absent because employers both take on and put off low skilled men with a minimum

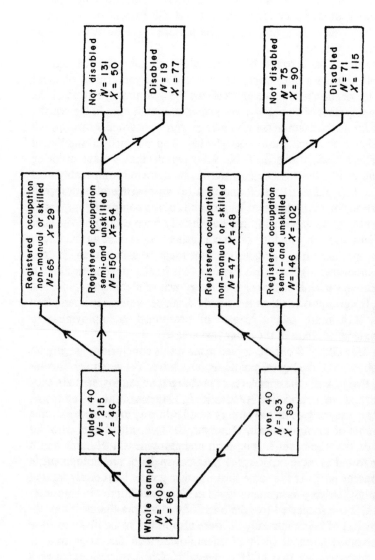

Figure 9.1. The sample of unemployed from Newcastle: results of the A.I.D. computer program

Source: Hill, Harrison, Sargeant and Talbot, *Men Out of Work*, Fig. 6.7, p. 123.

Note: N = no. of unemployed; X = mean unemployment duration in weeks.

of discrimination. A man with severe personal problems and no effective claim to skill may get casual work quite easily, whereas a qualified man with no discernible problems may find his own specific job market quite difficult, even in a general situation of low unemployment. The evidence on 'willingness to move' further supports this position. This variable was one of two which the A.I.D. analysis showed to be of marked significance in relation to unemployment length in Hammersmith alone. The other was birthplace – where the London born were found to be more prone to prolonged unemployment than those born elsewhere in Britain and abroad. It may be suggested that in Hammersmith, a borough with a large floating population, in which single people and rooming or lodging house residents are over-represented (relative to Britain as a whole), the most mobile will be a group of people who tend to be in various respects the least qualified. Hence mobility is another factor that may merely misleadingly counter-balance the impact of a factor like skill.

It is argued then that, while in the Newcastle case it was possible to come very close to being able to point out plausible correlates to involuntary unemployment, the failure to do this in Hammersmith can only be taken as an indicator of the greater complexity of the situation in that area and not as evidence that 'voluntary unemployment' is more salient there. Logically one would expect employers in a low-employment area to be more effective at discriminating against least favoured categories of workers; the Hammersmith employers do apparently reject the elderly and disabled as readily as employers elsewhere. However, the combination of absence of discrimination against the low skilled, with evidence of a very unstable employment pattern for this group, suggests that the reason for the absence of a strong association between skill and unemployment duration must be sought as much in the employment pattern of the area as in any behavioural difference which might be predicted to have an impact where unemployment is low.

UNEMPLOYMENT AMONGST THE UNSKILLED

A substantial proportion of the long-term unemployed are low skilled. It is widely believed that a high proportion of the unskilled are voluntarily unemployed, an impression which is reinforced by the tendency of the Supplementary Benefits Commission to concentrate its sanctions against the work-shy upon this group. This belief rests upon the fact that there are almost always, in any area, vacancies for the unskilled. Hence it is fallaciously assumed that any unskilled man can get a job. In fact it is rarely the case that the number of vacancies for unskilled men exceeds the number of unemployed men in that category, indeed the employment situation is very often markedly unfavourable to the low skilled person, For example, in Hammersmith, despite the fact that unemployment remained fairly low throughout the period 1968 to 1971, for heavy labourers the ratio of vacancies to men was never better than 1 : 35 and for light labourers never above 1 : 155.[7]

The difficulty to be faced, however, in studying the working of the labour market for low skilled men is that the situation is unlikely to be as undifferentiated as an examination of the crude figures on unemployment and vacancies suggests. Amongst the sub-sample of young long-term unemployed men from Coventry there were men whose only work experience was of low skilled factory work, who acknowledged to us that they were ignoring other opportunities and waiting for a chance to get back into the motor industry. At the same time there were other men, with similar characteristics, who apparently could not get 'good', high-wage paying employers to consider them, perhaps because of poor work or criminal records in the past. Yet when these men contemplated the other vacancies open to them they found that the wages were very low, offering in some cases less than their social security benefits. To a considerable extent, then, the men most ready to admit to being selective, and thus perhaps voluntarily unemployed for a while, were those who had the best job prospects within the sub-sample.

It was our impression that we failed to come to terms, in the quantitative survey reported in *Men Out of Work*, with many of the complexities of this part of the labour market; the combination of varying discrimination by 'good' employers with the poor prospects offered by other employers, which renders the employment situations of superficially very similar men so markedly different. There is a need for a study of the ways in which employers make choices, so that we have a much clearer idea of the extent to which experience, record, physique, literacy, and so on actually affect the prospects of low skilled men. We also need to know to what extent, in towns like Coventry for example, large employers operating fairly clear-cut selection criteria do contribute to the creation of two or more distinct labour markets for low skilled workers.[7]

CONCLUSIONS

In *Men Out of Work* we made, in the first chapter, the following observation on voluntary unemployment.

'The main difficulty in testing this "theory" (about voluntary unemployment) is that it is almost impossible to refute, since to do so it is necessary to prove that the men in question cannot behave in any other way than the way they do. Even where it seems possible to "explain" unemployment by reference to characteristics such as severe disability, it can always be argued that such people could find work if only they tried harder. What is required, therefore, in relation to any hypothesis about voluntary unemployment is a value judgement about the amount of effort individuals should make in order to overcome their disadvantages and handicaps.'[9]

This paper has tried to go beyond this negative standpoint, but has shown that the weaknesses in each of the arguments discussed tend in fact to bring us back to it. It seems very plausible that, scattered among the unemployed, perhaps distributed in a random way that cannot be related to any measurable characteristics, there are men who could try harder to get work. Yet we only seem to come close to discovering such men when we look at men who are in a very weak position in the labour market. The only one of the popular theories about 'voluntary' unemployment for which we found any evidence at all was the one suggesting that high social security levels relative to earnings deter men from seeking work.

As has been pointed out, the measures adopted by the social security authorities – the 'wage-stop' and 'four week rule'[10] – operated primarily against men whose only work prospects were of comparatively low-paid, low skilled work. The logic of using social security measures to combat voluntary unemployment means that coercion must be concentrated in this way. A formerly high-paid skilled worker cannot be wage-stopped, probably will have enough earnings-related benefit to avoid having to apply for means-tested benefits, may well have redundancy pay to further 'cushion' him when out of work, and is recognised by the Department of Employment as someone who is entitled to take his time to ensure he gets a new job that really suits him. If such a man takes twice as long as he 'needs' to get a new job, this probably only means his spell of unemployment is two months rather than one month. Similar selectivity on the part of a poorly qualified man may convert a spell of unemployment from months into years, in the course of which he will become an object of suspicion to prospective employers; he will have his own morale undermined and with it perhaps his will to overcome his handicaps and get work.

It may perhaps be the case that in recent years unemployed men have become more selective. It may also be true that improved financial provisions for the unemployed have contributed to this. Accordingly the easiest way to increase labour-market efficiency may be to reduce the extent of social security support for the unemployed, since the alternatives imply extension of training, rationalisation of employers' selection methods, and perhaps, above all, the elimination of low wages. But it must be recognised that adoption of such a simple approach means a direct attack not on the selective behaviour of the most privileged in the labour market, but upon those who get the worst deal in our Society, whether in or out of work.

NOTES

1 M. J. Hill, R. M. Harrison, A. V. Sargeant and V. Talbot, *Men Out of Work: A Study of Unemployment in Three English Towns*, Cambridge University Press, 1973.
2 See Olive Stevenson, *Claimant or Client? A Social Worker's View of the Supplementary Benefits Commission*, George Allen and Unwin, 1973.
3 Hill *et al.*, *Men Out of Work*, p. 80.
4 Ibid., p. 79.
5 J. A. Sonquist and J. N. Morgan, *The Detection of Interaction Effects*, University of Michigan Press, 1964. The use of this program in *Men Out of Work* is described there in Chapter 6.
6 Hill *et al.*, *Men Out of Work*, pp. 129–32.
7 This is based on some figures kindly supplied by the Statistics Branch of the Department of Employment.
8 I am grateful to Mr N. Bosanquet for introducing me to the American literature on this topic, and for lending me before publication a paper by himself and P. Doeringer, 'Is There a Dual Labour Market in Great Britain?' (*Economic Journal*, June 1973).
9 Hill *et al.*, *Men Out of Work*, p. 4.
10 See the Supplementary Benefits Commission's *Supplementary Benefits Handbook*, H.M.S.O., 1971. For discussion of, and in general an attempt to try to justify, the sanctions, see Department of Health and Social Security, *Report of the Committee on the Abuse of Social Security Benefits*, Cmnd 5228, H.M.S.O., 1973.

Chapter 10

The Duration of Unemployment and Job Search

COLIN LEICESTER

INTRODUCTION

The purpose of this paper is to describe an analysis of the flows on to and off the unemployment register, such a movement of labour being viewed as a process of job search. There are two reasons why this particular analysis seems both possible and desirable at the present time, one to do with economic facts and the other with economic theory.

The first is that, for Great Britain, a consistent and continuous time-series of both the on-flows and the off-flows of unemployment have been published for the period 1967 onwards.[1] The single most important feature of this new data is that the flows are large. Typically, for example, using the calendar quarter as the period of account, the flows on to the unemployment register for adult men have been around one and a half times or twice as large as the stocks of unemployed at either end of that 13-week interval. It is clear, therefore, that the register acts as a significant channel for the flows of workers moving through the British labour market. But, though the total on-flows and off-flows are large, it is equally clear that the duration of unemployment is longer at the present time than a decade ago. With the level of unemployment now higher compared with the flows, although a large number of people enter and leave the state of unemployment quite quickly, a smaller but growing proportion survive on the register and are remaining in that state for much longer. In the next section of this paper we define explicitly the parameters of such labour mobility and immobility, the rates of on-flow, the rates of survival and the rates of off-flow, for which this analysis attempts an explanation.

The second reason for this investigation is that recent contributions to the literature on the labour market appear to provide some kind of explanation of how these unemployment flows are generated.[2] The theory is usually couched in terms of a process of job search, that phrase being meant to describe workers who move either in search of work or in search of more advantageous work. In particular, if unemployed workers encounter unfilled jobs, the characteristics of the one are compared with the characteristics of the other, and the potential employer or potential employee may make a decision to recruit or be recruited. One such characteristic that may be considered is the wage that is offered and the wage likely to be accepted; other characteristics might be the age of the worker, the skill requirements of the type of work and so on. Whatever are the criteria by which such a matching is attempted, a necessary precondition for the process of job search to occur at all is that unemployed workers should meet unfilled vacancies. Such a meeting place in Britain is the employment exchange, one of whose main functions is to facilitate an interaction between a register of unemployment and a register of vacancies. It therefore seems natural to pay some attention to the area with which this paper is concerned; both because the developing theories of job search may shed light on how the unemployment register behaves, and because the way the unemployment register changes through time might confirm, or otherwise refute, the predictions of those theories.

Certain predilections of the present writer should be made explicit at the outset. One is that the mere existence of a job is viewed as being more basic to the process of job search than the characteristics of the job. This is not to imply that the latter, the details of available work, are irrelevant; it is simply to say that job-seekers are unable to evaluate the details of non-existent jobs. While the composition of unfilled vacancies is a subject for later research, the focal point of this analysis is the total of such vacancies. In particular, we have set up and tested a hypothesis based upon the changing size of the vacancy register and the changing size of the unemployment register, and in doing so we have the following thoughts about problems of statistical measurement in mind. The registered unemployed might indeed not be the full total of the people out of work and wishing to work, and the registered vacancies are clearly not all the jobs available in the labour market. But the official totals of unemployed and of vacancies are an accurate measurement of the size of the registers at the employment exchanges, and it is only the interaction of both, at the employment exchanges, with which this paper is concerned. How this interaction is hypothesised to occur, and in what manner such interaction affects the unemployment flows, is set out on pages 192-6 below.

The results of testing this relatively simple hypothesis by linear multiple regressions are presented on pages 196-200. The tests were carried out on data for men and women separately, in Great Britain, for the period 1967-73. The results are only preliminary, but they provide some confirmation for our starting point, namely the assumption that the unemployment and vacancy registers interact. They also provide some suggestive evidence for the following: that a cessation of unemployment, a leaving of the unemployment register, is not only determined by the number of jobs that are available, it is also apparently affected by the time it takes to complete the job search. Such a result connects in a most direct way the two concepts in the title of our paper, namely, that when the time to complete the job search lengthens the duration of unemployment will also lengthen. In fact, if entering the state of unemployment is viewed as the initial step in a process of job search, the two concepts are almost coterminous. These, and other implications of the analysis, are discussed in the concluding section of this paper.

THE FLOWS AND STOCKS OF UNEMPLOYMENT

It is useful to begin by setting out the relevant flows and stocks of the unemployment register within the kind of accounting framework proposed by Stone.[3] This is achieved in Tables 10.1-3. Table 10.1 defines the variables symbolically, Table 10.2 illustrates the framework in terms of (seasonally adjusted) data for men for the second quarter of 1968 and Table 10.3 restates those stocks and flows in terms of transition coefficients. (There is no special reason for choosing the second quarter of 1968, but it is not untypical.)

The nature of the framework may be described as follows. The columns refer to the start of the quarter, and the totals of those columns appear in the final row: these are, first, the total of people

188   INVOLUNTARY UNEMPLOYMENT

Table 10.1   *A symbolic accounting framework for the unemployment register*

	Unemployment categories						Closing totals (time t)
	1	2	3	4	5	6	
Off register	W_0	W_1	W_2	W_3	W_4	W_5	l
On register							
0–13 weeks	S_{01}	·	·	·	·	·	U_1
13–26 weeks	·	S_{12}	·	·	·	·	U_2
26–39 weeks	·	·	S_{23}	·	·	·	U_3
39–52 weeks	·	·	·	S_{34}	·	·	U_4
52 weeks +	·	·	·	·	S_{45}	S_{55}	U_5
Opening totals (time t–1)	r	U_1	U_2	U_3	U_4	U_5	·

Note: The six columns are titled as the corresponding rows.

registering as unemployed during the quarter, r; and, secondly, the opening stocks of unemployed categorised by duration of unemployment, U_j ($j = 1 \ldots 5$). The rows are dated at the end of the quarter, and the row totals appear in the final column: these are, on the one hand, the total number of people leaving the register, l, and, on the other, the closing stocks of unemployed, also categorised by duration of unemployment.

The main body of the symbolic framework contains flows of unemployed workers who transfer themselves from one of the accounts represented by a column into one of the accounts represented by a row over this particular interval of time. For example, those registering as unemployed, r, either survive on the register, S_{01}, to form the unemployed with duration 0–13 weeks, $U_1(t)$; or else they leave the register during the same interval in which they joined and form part of the leavers, W_0. Similarly, the opening stock of unemployed with duration 0–13 weeks, U_1 ($t - 1$), either survive on the register, S_{12}, to become the closing stock with duration 13–26 weeks, U_2 (t); or else they leave, W_1. And so on, for each of the other categories of duration. In addition, some people with a duration of unemployment greater than a year, $U_5(t - 1)$, survive on the register, S_{55}, to form part of the same category of duration at the end of the interval, $U_5(t)$.

The matrix is sparse and lower diagonal because the system is a strictly graded one; that is, those people starting off in any account only have two choices, of either passing on to the next account or leaving the system. In this sense the unemployment register is very similar to the array of stocks of the human population categorised by single years of age. Not surprisingly, the analogy between a population and the unemployment register is often invoked; those registering as unemployed are comparable to births, those leaving the register to deaths, and those remaining on the register are survivors. But certain marked differences between the human population and the unemployment register can be seen if we turn to the statistical magnitudes and the ratios between them, contained in the next two tables.

Table 10.2   *Flows and stocks of unemployed men in Great Britain, 1968 II*

	Thousands Unemployment categories						*Closing totals*
	1	*2*	*3*	*4*	*5*	*6*	
Off register	504·6	144·1	30·3	13·4	5·1	15·1	712·6
On register							
0–13 weeks	221·2	·	·	·	·	·	221·2
13–26 weeks	·	80·2	·	·	·	·	80·2
26–39 weeks	·	·	40·6	·	·	·	40·6
39–52 weeks	·	·	·	24·5	·	·	24·5
52 weeks +	·	·	·	·	20·1	59·0	79·1
Opening totals	725·8	224·3	70·9	37·9	25·2	74·1	·

Note: The data are seasonally adjusted. See also note to Table 10.1.

The data contained in Table 10.2 reveal the following features. The first, and most important, is that the total of on-flows per quarter (725,800) is greater than the total of the opening stocks (432,400) by almost a factor of 1·7. The second feature is that the majority of this on-flow (almost 70 per cent) leave the register within the same interval of time. This particular out-flow of unemployed (504,600) also forms the greater proportion of the total of leavers. Thus, in the second quarter of 1968, more unemployed men flowed on to the register and off it again than were already on the register at the start of the interval; furthermore, these ½ million adult males formed no part of either the opening or the closing stocks of unemployed men.

Table 10.3   *Transition rates for unemployed men in Great Britain,*
1968 II

	Proportions Unemployment categories					
	1	*2*	*3*	*4*	*5*	*6*
Off register	0·695	0·642	0·427	0·354	0·203	0·203
On register						
0–13 weeks	0·305	·	·	·	·	·
13–26 weeks	·	0·358	·	·	·	·
26–39 weeks	·	·	0·573	·	·	·
39–52 weeks	·	·	·	0·646	·	·
52 weeks +	·	·	·	·	0·797	0·797

Note: It was assumed that the rates were the same for those unemployed 39–52 weeks and for more than a year. See also note to Table 10.1.

Table 10.3 is a set of transition coefficients, obtained by dividing each column of Table 10.2 by its column total. A third feature of the unemployment register may be seen in a comparison between the leaving proportions (the first row of Table 10.3) and the opening totals of stocks and flows (the final row of Table 10.2). It is that the on-flow and the unemployed stocks categorised by duration are ranked in the same order as the leaving coefficients. This provides the sharpest contrast with the human population, for which, typically, mortality rates rise rather than decline with age.

This basic structure of the British unemployment register is, of course, well known, and was modelled by Fowler[4] and Weeden[5] as continuous distribution functions, using the log-normal and a general polynomial, respectively. The very marked skewness of the unemployment register categorised by duration led my colleague, Andrew Forbes, and myself to carry out some preliminary tests with the mixed exponential,[6] a study which continues at the Institute of Manpower Studies involving a test of a number of alternative functions. One idea shared with, but made more explicit in, the interesting and persuasive paper by Cripps and Tarling[7] deserves some discussion, since it may be relevant to some of the results presented later in this paper.

The previously accepted explanation of why the leaving rates should fall with increased duration of unemployment used to be, quite simply, that the latter determined the former. The longer a man is out of work the less likely is he actively to seek to supply his labour and the less attractive is he as a potential unit of productive labour. Hence, workers staying on the unemployment register a long time have a lower chance of leaving. The recent and more persuasive explanation is that the on-flow to the register is heterogeneous, consisting, to put the argument simply, of some workers with advantageous personal characteristics who can be re-employed quickly in a given job situation and of some other workers whose personal characteristics put their chance of re-employment low. Examples of such characteristics, which are independent of time spent on the unemployment register, would be differences in age and differentials of skill. Since the kind of transition rates shown in Table 10.3 are a weighted average of the different chances of re-employment, the average leaving rate of any category of duration will tend to be lower than that of an earlier category, because the more easily re-employed workers have already left.

It is plainly desirable that further attempts at modelling the structure of the leaving (or survival) rates use assumptions other than those of a stationary register. It is equally desirable that some investigation be attempted into the dynamics of the register – and by that is meant the changes over time of the on-flow rates, the survival rates and the leaving rates of the registered unemployed. Accordingly, we decided to test a hypothesis of the determinants of changes over time in the following.

The first and most important flow rate is that for the on-flow, defined for our purposes as:

$$r^* = \frac{r}{\Sigma U_j} \quad (j = 1 \ldots 5) \tag{A}$$

The second and third were leaving rates and survival rates, respectively, for the on-flow:

$$w_o^* = \frac{W_o}{r} \tag{B}$$

$$s_o^* = 1 - w_o^* \tag{C}$$

and similar rates for the existing stock at the start of a quarter:

$$\bar{w}^{*} = \frac{\Sigma W_j}{\Sigma U_j} \quad (j = 1 \ldots 5) \tag{D}$$

$$\bar{s}^{*} = 1 - \bar{w}^{*} \tag{E}$$

Finally, we examined the individual leaving and survival rates for the unemployed in different categories of duration:

$$w_j^{*} = \frac{W_j}{U_j} \quad (j = 1 \ldots 4) \tag{F}$$

$$s_j^{*} = 1 - w_j^{*} \tag{G}$$

There are only four pairs of such flow rates on the assumption that the unemployed of duration 39–52 weeks have the same transition rates as those unemployed for more than a year. These 13 flow rates were calculated for men and women separately in Great Britain quarterly from the start of 1967 to the end of 1973.[8] The stocks are dated in the first month of each quarter; the flows occur over the corresponding intervals. These flow rates were the dependent variables in a test of the following hypothesis.

SEARCH COMPLETION AND JOB PROSPECTS

In principle, everyone joining the unemployment register in Great Britain is looking for a job; that purpose is, officially, what the act of registering as unemployed is taken to imply. In practice, not all those registered as unemployed leave the register for gainful employment; some retire, others die and certain numbers leave the working population for various reasons, including leaving the country. Be that as it may, our basic hypothesis is that the total of unemployed interacts with the total of unfilled vacancies, and, as the manner of the interaction alters quarterly over time, so does the rate at which people leave the register change quarter by quarter. The hypothesis is presented in terms of the determinants of the leaving rate, but, by implication, since a leaving rate and the corresponding survival rate sum to unity, any factor raising a leaving rate lowers the corresponding survival rate. By a simple extension, the same ideas lead to a similar hypothesis for the rate of on-flow.

We begin by assuming that the probability of leaving the register can be represented by the leaving rate, w^*, and that this is the product of two other probabilities: first, the probability that a person will have completed his job search within a given period of time; and, second, the probability that at the end of his search a job is available for him. That is

$$w^* = P.Q \tag{H}$$

where P is the proportion of people on the register completing their search within a calendar quarter, and Q is the proportion who find at the end of their search that there is a job for them. The two elements of the hypothesis should be distinguished from one another. It is possible, for example, for two similar workers to inspect fully the same sample of unfilled vacancies, within which there is only one job suitable for both. In this case, $P = 1$, $Q = 0.5$. Alternatively, they may both be searching through the same sample of vacancies, within which there are two jobs of the right kind, one for each; however, only one of them finishes his search by the end of the period, perhaps because he is more efficient in conducting it. In this case, then, $P = 0.5$, and $Q = 1$. Both hypothetical situations will lead to only one person leaving the unemployment register; and the leaving rate, $w^* = 0.5$, is identical in both cases.

We proceed to discuss how the interaction between the unemployment and vacancy registers determines the proportion of job-seekers who will have completed their search, P. The underlying idea is suggested by Holt,[9] and may be explained in the following way. Suppose that the number of vacancies inspected by any one job-seeker is a constant proportion, f, of the total vacancies, V. Thus, if $f = 0.1$, and $V = 50$, each search would desirably comprise looking at five jobs. (If the size of the vacancy register doubled, each search would involve inspecting ten jobs.) This supposition of proportionality may be justified in these ways: a higher total of vacancies will lead the employment exchange to submit each unemployed worker to more of them, will lead the unemployed worker to look at more vacancies in order to exercise wider choice, and will increase the chance that the unemployed worker will find work more suitable, rather than less suitable, for him. If the number of job inspections that should be completed by each unemployed worker is equal to fV, then the total that all the unemployed workers need to carry out is equal to fUV. Thus, if $f = 0.1$, $U = 100$, and $V = 50$, a total of

194 INVOLUNTARY UNEMPLOYMENT

500 job inspections have to be completed if all those on the unemployment register are to complete their searches. Suppose, furthermore, that there is a limited number of such job inspections, g, that can be completed within a given period of time; either because the efficiency of job-seekers in carrying out their search is fixed, or because the capacity of the employment exchanges in matching the unemployment and vacancy registers cannot be changed rapidly. Then, the time that has to elapse for all the unemployed to complete all their job inspections is given by $(f/g)UV$. Thus, if the unit of time is a calendar quarter and $g = 250$, six months are required. Alternatively, the proportion of job searches completed within a calendar quarter is the reciprocal of that expression, namely, $(g/f)(UV)^{-1}$ or, in our numerical example, 0.5. Though some of the assumptions used above may be unduly restrictive, we would now write

$$X = \frac{1}{UV} \tag{I}$$

and propose that

$$P = aX^b \qquad (b > 0) \tag{J}$$

The positive exponent of X means that the higher the proportion of job searches completed, the higher the rate of leaving the unemployment register. But, since X is defined to be related to the reciprocal of the length of time spent on the job search, equation (J) also means the faster that job searches are completed, the higher the rate of leaving the register. This element of the hypothesis rests heavily on two ideas: on the efficiency of the worker in carrying out his search (or alternatively on the efficiency with which the unemployment and vacancy registers are matched), and on the suggestion that this matching of the registers can be represented by the reciprocal of the product of total vacancies and total unemployed.

The other element of the hypothesis can be more briefly described, and is also suggested by Holt and David.[10] This is that the job prospects for the unemployed engaged on searches are directly proportional to the relative number of unfilled vacancies; or rathe to the vacancy–unemployment ratio. That is, defining

$$Y = \frac{V}{U} \tag{K}$$

we shall propose that

$$Q = cY^d \quad (d > 0). \tag{L}$$

In other words, as the vacancy–unemployment ratio rises on the upswing of the cycle, the job prospects for those on the unemployment register improve; and conversely on the downswing.

Combining equations (H)–(L) yields the very simple hypothesis:

$$w^* = kX^bY^d$$

$$= k \left(\frac{1}{UV}\right)^b \cdot \left(\frac{V}{U}\right)^d \tag{M}$$

where $k = ac$. The two terms on the right-hand side of equation (M) represent the two ways in which interaction between the sizes of the unemployment and vacancy registers can occur. Clearly, that hypothesis can be restated so that the leaving rate is simply a function of total unemployed and total vacancies, but we hesitate to take this step, because unemployment and vacancies are highly correlated. The product moment correlation coefficient between X and Y, however, is $-0 \cdot 351$, which confirms that their movements are sufficiently unassociated. The quarterly series of X and Y were calculated from monthly observations on total unemployed and total vacancies in Great Britain, for men and women separately, from the same statistical source.[11]

Finally, a similar hypothesis for the survival rates

$$s^* = f(X, Y) \tag{N}$$

should be expected to have signs for its coefficients opposite to those of the hypothesis for leaving rates. And a hypothesis for the rate of on-flow

$$r^* = f(X, Y) \tag{O}$$

should have the same coefficient signs as the hypothesis for the leaving rates. This follows from the main assumption with which this paper began: namely, that, if job search takes place on the unemployment register, then the greater the expected chance of successful completion of the search the greater the numbers who will flow on to the register. Such reasoning on behalf of this hypothesis should not be taken to imply that all workers flowing on to the register are assumed to do so voluntarily, and that none of these flows are involuntary, for example as a result of layoffs.

THE TESTS OF THE HYPOTHESES

The 13 dependent variables used in our tests have already been described on pages 191 – 2, as have the two main independent variables, X and Y, in the preceding section. The tests whose results we shall describe in this section involved using a double logarithmic function connecting the variables in unadjusted form, together with three seasonal dummy variables. Before considering those results, some brief mention should be made of other tests whose results will not be quoted.

The algebraic formulation of relationships whose dependent variables pair-wise sum to unity should more strictly be an equation such as the linear logistic proposed by Cox.[12] This particular type of equation gives better parameter estimates but lends itself less easily to interpretation. Seasonally adjusting the data beforehand improved matters a little, as did disaggregating the national totals of unemployed and of vacancies by region, calculating X and Y regionally, and then averaging the results, and replacing the time-series of X and Y by distributed lag transforms removed some of the serial correlation among the residuals.

The results of testing the hypothesis in the form of log–linear equations are presented as Tables 10.4 and 10.5 for men and women respectively. Four general comments can be made. First, the fit is encouragingly good for the majority of the dependent variables and most of the coefficients for the independent variables are highly significant. The residual errors are highly auto-correlated, and there may be simultaneity bias in some of the equations estimated. Secondly, the constant term in many equations is statistically the most significant, and this may be taken to reflect the relative stability of the structure of the unemployment register, discussed earlier.

Thirdly, if X can be said to represent the propensity to complete job searches, and Y to represent job prospects for the job-seekers, then the impact of these two variables is the one anticipated by the hypothesis. As can be seen from rows 2 to 5 in Table 10.4, both variables have a positive impact on the leaving rate and a negative impact on the survival rate of both the new registrants and the exist-

Table 10.4 *Regression results for the on-flow, survival and off-flow equations: men, Great Britain, 1967–73*

dependent variable	Independent variables						$\bar{R}^2$	d-statistic
	log k	X	Y	z_1	z_2	z_3		
r^*	0·816 (22·4)	0·777 (25·2)	0·505 (24·7)	−0·022 (1·1)	−0·116 (5·6)	0·020 (1·0)	0·974	0·50
s_0^*	−1·472 (29·1)	−0·274 (6·4)	−0·395 (13·9)	−0·179 (6·3)	−0·141 (4·9)	−0·135 (4·7)	0·902	1·04
w_0^*	−0·201 (7·5)	0·144 (6·4)	0·220 (14·8)	0·098 (6·5)	0·074 (4·9)	0·074 (4·9)	0·911	1·08
$\bar{s}^*$	−0·745 (33·0)	−0·120 (6·3)	−0·135 (10·7)	−0·116 (9·2)	−0·172 (13·4)	−0·056 (4·4)	0·925	1·57
$\bar{w}^*$	−0·637 (23·6)	0·127 (5·5)	0·151 (9·9)	0·131 (8·6)	0·181 (11·8)	0·069 (4·5)	0·908	1·62
s_1^*	−1·352 (34·5)	0·022 (0·6)	−0·229 (10·4)	−0·181 (8·2)	−0·267 (12·0)	−0·135 (6·0)	0·921	1·55
s_2^*	−0·651 (17·9)	0·083 (2·7)	−0·067 (3·3)	−0·085 (4·1)	−0·248 (12·0)	−0·083 (4·0)	0·883	1·52
s_3^*	−0·469 (11·2)	0·140 (3·9)	−0·027 (1·2)	−0·046 (2·0)	−0·195 (8·2)	−0·098 (4·1)	0·802	1·02
s_4^*	−0·291 (11·4)	0·043 (2·0)	−0·032 (2·2)	−0·005 (0·3)	−0·049 (3·3)	0·002 (0·1)	0·523	0·76
w_1^*	−0·285 (11·7)	0·004 (0·2)	0·124 (9·1)	0·101 (7·4)	0·138 (9·9)	0·078 (5·6)	0·891	1·45
w_2^*	−0·754 (15·4)	−0·099 (2·4)	0·086 (3·1)	0·122 (4·4)	0·297 (10·7)	0·124 (4·4)	0·853	1·37
w_3^*	−1·030 (11·4)	−0·258 (3·4)	0·040 (0·8)	0·096 (1·9)	0·359 (7·0)	0·210 (4·1)	0·741	1·08
w_4^*	−1·349 (12·7)	−0·166 (1·8)	0·127 (2·1)	0·008 (0·1)	0·175 (2·9)	−0·008 (0·1)	0·468	0·79

Notes: (i) Both the dependent and the independent variables are expressed in logarithms.
(ii) t-ratios are shown in brackets.
(iii) z_1, z_2 and z_3 are seasonal dummy variables.

ing stock of unemployed. In economic terms, the mobility of unemployed men off the register is increased the shorter is the search time and the better the job prospects. Fourthly, very similar remarks can be made about the flows on to the register: if conditions alter so that more people can obtain jobs faster, the numbers registering as unemployed relative to the numbers already unemployed will rise. This remark applies equally to women as to men.

Certain interesting features can be observed in the results obtained

Table 10.5 *Regression results for the on-flow, survival and off-flow equations: women, Great Britain, 1967–73*

Dependent variable	Independent variables						$\bar{R}^2$	d-statistic
	log k	X	Y	z_1	z_2	z_3		
1 r^*	−0.677 (2.6)	0.708 (6.6)	0.504 (10.8)	0.056 (1.2)	−0.102 (2.2)	0.117 (2.5)	0.852	0.46
2 s_o^*	−1.398 (4.8)	−0.047 (0.4)	−0.417 (8.1)	−0.101 (2.0)	−0.066 (1.3)	−0.001 (0.1)	0.734	0.95
3 w_o^*	−0.298 (3.6)	0.018 (0.5)	0.127 (8.8)	0.030 (2.1)	0.016 (1.1)	0.002 (0.1)	0.763	0.94
4 $\bar{s}^*$	−0.998 (9.0)	0.022 (0.5)	−0.163 (8.4)	−0.020 (1.0)	−0.106 (5.4)	0.024 (1.2)	0.849	2.25
5 $\bar{w}^*$	−0.478 (6.3)	−0.008 (0.3)	0.108 (8.2)	0.015 (1.1)	0.065 (4.8)	−0.012 (0.9)	0.830	2.18
6 s_1^*	−1.726 (11.1)	0.163 (2.6)	−0.255 (9.4)	−0.062 (2.3)	−0.159 (5.7)	−0.065 (2.3)	0.882	2.14
7 s_2^*	−1.124 (11.3)	0.182 (4.5)	−0.100 (5.7)	−0.055 (3.2)	−0.197 (11.2)	−0.035 (2.0)	0.914	1.51
8 s_3^*	−1.112 (8.0)	0.251 (4.5)	−0.049 (2.0)	0.009 (0.4)	−0.179 (7.2)	−0.030 (1.2)	0.836	1.11
9 s_4^*	−0.740 (7.5)	0.163 (4.2)	−0.013 (0.8)	0.056 (3.2)	−0.017 (1.0)	0.067 (3.8)	0.672	0.75
10 w_1^*	−0.205 (3.5)	−0.044 (1.9)	0.092 (9.0)	0.025 (2.5)	0.055 (5.3)	0.026 (2.5)	0.864	2.28
11 w_2^*	−0.351 (3.5)	−0.148 (3.6)	0.097 (5.4)	0.056 (3.2)	0.171 (9.5)	0.038 (2.1)	0.885	1.56
12 w_3^*	−0.096 (0.4)	−0.346 (3.6)	0.077 (1.8)	−0.023 (0.6)	0.224 (5.2)	0.044 (1.0)	0.749	1.24
13 w_4^*	−0.137 (0.5)	−0.465 (3.9)	0.041 (0.8)	−0.173 (3.4)	0.033 (0.6)	−0.193 (3.7)	0.643	0.85

Notes: (i) Both the dependent and the independent variables are expressed in logarithms.
(ii) t-ratios are shown in brackets.
(iii) z_1, z_2 and z_3 are seasonal dummy variables.

for the unemployed with different durations on the register. One of these features is that, for men especially, the seasonal variation in the leaving and survival rates is higher for those with shorter duration. Another is that the impact of job opportunities, Y, diminishes as the duration lengthens. For example, the elasticity of the leaving rate with respect to job prospects for men unemployed 13–26 weeks (0·086) is significantly lower than for men unemployed 0–13 weeks (0·124), which in turn is below the coefficient for the on-flow (0·220).

Yet another result of testing the disaggregated leaving and survival rates is possibly the most intriguing of all, but here we may have to be speculative. This is that the impact of the variable representing search completion, X, changes its nature between one end of the register and the other. For men, the elasticity of the leaving rate for the on-flow with respect to this variable is significant and positive at $0 \cdot 144$; for the unemployed 0–13 weeks it is not significantly different from zero; and for those unemployed in the next three categories of duration it is significant and negative. One explanation offers itself and it has disturbing implications; it is that changes in the job-search time on the register discriminate between people who have been unemployed for different lengths of time. When the job-search time shortens, it raises the leaving rate for those newly arrived on the register and lowers the leaving rate for those who have been on it for some time. Conversely, when the required time for the job search lengthens, then, other things being equal, those with the longer duration of unemployment stand a relatively better chance of leaving the register than before. In other words, these results suggest that those people who are unemployed for a long time are also those people who take a while to complete any given job search. They are at a disadvantage when the search is short, because the unemployed who search more quickly will accept the going vacancies before they do. On the other hand, when the required time for search lengthens to something more appropriate to their pace of search, they will then stand a relatively better chance of leaving the register. The occasions when they have a relative advantage are also the occasions when the economy is running with high levels of unemployment or vacancies, or more probably both. All the remarks of this discussion apply to women as well as to men, and to women more than to men.

One final result deserves our attention. Though the coefficients estimated for the equations for women are usually different from those for men, we can see from the top lines in Tables 10.4 and 10.5 that the exponents of X and Y in the equations for the on-flow rate for the two sexes are very similar. Furthermore, their numerical values give rise to the statement that the difference between the exponents of X and Y is not very dissimilar from the sum of the two exponents minus unity. In other words, re-arranging the terms in U and V, we obtain the following:

$$r = k(UV)^{-h} \tag{P}$$

Thus, if r, the level of the on-flow for a period, stays constant, then the recorded levels of unemployment, U, and of vacancies, V, will plot an exact hyperbola in two-dimensional space. But on the occasions when the level of the on-flow falls, this UV curve will shift outwards from the origin; when the level of the on-flow rises the UV curve will move towards the origin. Accordingly, it may be argued that, if these two variables are related because the unemployment and vacancy registers interact but via a third variable, then to describe a shift outwards from the origin of the simple two-variable curve as 'a break in the relationship' may be positively misleading. Indeed, as we observed on another occasion,[13] the level of unemployment and of unfilled vacancies may be related by an interaction between the two registers at the employment exchanges, but linked this time by the flows of the vacancy register. That result is not incompatible with the one discussed in this paper.

CONCLUDING REMARKS

Our concluding remarks can be brief. The analysis described in this paper was conducted because it was thought that an explanation of the flow of unemployed workers on to, through and off the unemployment register was probably as important as a study of the level of unemployment itself. One feature of those flows (which are large) would underline this supposition: the number registering as unemployed who leave the register before the end of a calendar quarter is typically, in Great Britain, as large as the stocks at either end of that 13-week interval. These on-flows who then flow off are, of course, not counted in either stock.

The process of flowing on to and then off the unemployment register was modelled quite simply in terms of two factors: first, the probability of completing a job search within a given period of time, and second, the probability of there being a job available at the completion of the search. These two factors were statistically represented in terms of the sizes of the unemployment and the vacancy registers, because the explicit assumption being made is that the two registers interact, and are made to interact, as a result of the way employment exchanges operate. The results of testing this hypothesis are reasonably good, but possibly only tentative conclusions should be drawn at this stage in the research. The evidence, however, does suggest that the level of registered unemployment and the level of unfilled vacancies are inter-dependent.

The economic implications of the analysis described in this paper may possibly be these. If the absolute level of unemployment is to continue to remain high during most of the seventies compared with the sixties,then this factor alone would probably slow down the job search that is conducted via the unemployment register, which means that the average rate of flow of workers through it will be reduced. If, furthermore, the level of unemployment relative to the level of vacancies is also higher in this decade than in the last, this too will reduce the flow rate through the unemployment register. A reduction in the flow rate through the register is tantamount to an increase in the duration of unemployment.

Our attention, therefore, should focus on the workers who tend to have the longest spells of unemployment. Though the boundary between a tolerable spell of unemployment and an intolerable one is a difficult line to draw, once the line is drawn the magnitude of the problem can be known; not only how many workers spend too long out of work, but who they are and why they are found to be in this situation. If inefficiency in job search (taking too long to find a suitable job) is an explanation, as some of our results suggest, then an improvement in the allocative mechanism in the labour market might be the appropriate recommendation. The solution to increased immobility is of course improved mobility. We do not pretend that any of the facts are in any way known at the present time; but this kind of distinction, bringing to light such a problem and possibly prompting that type of solution, is decidedly more helpful than the Keynesian distinction between involuntary (meaning 'non-frictional') and frictional (meaning 'voluntary') unemployment. The kind of labour mobility analysed in this paper might involve a voluntary choice to engage in job search on the unemployment register, followed by an involuntary failure to leave it.

The statistical implications of the results of this analysis, preliminary though they may be, are relatively easy to propose; the execution of the proposals may be more difficult. We believe that a growing insight into the behaviour of unemployment and some attendant lessons for policy will be obtained by continued future research into the behaviour of flows in relation to the corresponding stocks of

202   INVOLUNTARY UNEMPLOYMENT

unemployed. This would seem to mean that any attempt to dis-
aggregate the national totals of on-flows and off-flows would be very
welcome. The most immediately obvious forms of disaggregation
would be by industry, region and occupation.

NOTES

1 *Department of Employment Gazette*, September 1972 and September 1973.
2 Especially, but not only, E. S. Phelps (ed.), *Micro-economic Foundations of Employment and Inflation Theory*, Norton, 1970.
3 And described, for example, in United Nations, Economic and Social Council, *An Integrated System of Demographic, Manpower and Social Statistics*, 1970.
4 Central Statistical Office, *Duration of Unemployment on the Register of Wholly Unemployed* by R. F. Fowler, H.M.S.O., 1968.
5 R. Weeden, 'Duration of Unemployment and Labour Turnover', (mimeographed, 1974).
6 *I.M.S. Monitor*, April 1973.
7 F. Cripps and R. Tarling, 'An Analysis of the Duration of Male Unemployment in Great Britain, 1932–73', *Economic Journal*, June 1974.
8 *Department of Employment Gazette* (various issues).
9 C. C. Holt, 'How Can the Philips Curve be Moved to Reduce both Inflation and Unemployment?' in Phelps (ed.), *Micro-economic Foundations of Employment and Inflation Theory*.
10 C. C. Holt and M. H. David, 'The Concept of Job Vacancies in a Dynamic Theory of the Labor Market' in National Bureau of Economic Research, *The Measurement and Interpretation of Job Vacancies*, Columbia University Press, 1966.
11 *Department of Employment Gazette* (monthly).
12 D. R. Cox, *Analysis of Binary Data*, Methuen, 1970.
13 C. Leicester, 'Vacancies and the Demand for Labour', *I.M.S. Monitor*, October 1973.

Chapter 11

Unemployment in London[1]

DAVID METCALF AND RAY RICHARDSON

Unemployment is (in our view correctly) normally held to be an important 'problem'. Unfortunately the data available to measure the extent of the problem are seriously deficient. In addition, the nature of 'the problem' is seldom spelled out clearly. The first two sections of this paper therefore make some suggestions concerning how the data might be improved and how the nature of the unemployment problem may be specified more clearly. It also contains a plea to discontinue the use of the value-ridden adjectives 'voluntary' and 'involuntary'.

To formulate sensible policies to mitigate the hardship associated with unemployment it is necessary to know how the unemployment is caused. In the third section we therefore analyse the causes of male unemployment in a specific area – the 32 London boroughs – in 1971. Although the dependent variable is the rate of unemployment, our discussion goes behind the information on rates and emphasises that the unemployment rate is the outcome of four probabilities:

(a) the probability of being laid-off, made redundant or dismissed (involuntary separations);
(b) the probability of quitting (voluntary separations);
(c) the probability of being offered a job;
(d) the probability of accepting an offer.

The first two elements determine the number of people entering the unemployed state and the last two the duration in that state. We believe that such a treatment is an important innovation in our understanding of the nature of unemployment.

THE MEASUREMENT OF UNEMPLOYMENT

Measured unemployment rates are very influential in determining governments' policies in many fields. For example, in 1971–2 the British government fundamentally altered its whole economic strategy largely in reaction to a rising level of registered unemployment. Similarly, governments have for many years justified enormous expenditures on industrial re-location principally by quoting the rates of registered unemployment across different regions. Within Greater London more than 30 districts have been designated priority areas, to a large extent because of their persistently high unemployment rates relative to those found elsewhere in the area. As a final example, there have been urgent calls from the Greater London Council for changes in central government policies in order to reduce the extent of the recent decline in London's population and employment levels; these representations have been based on the view that employment declines lead to 'hardship' for Londoners, quickly translated into higher unemployment. These and other variations by area and changes over time in registered unemployment rates have been dominating causes of government action; unemployment relativities, unlike pay relativities, have been a cause of concern for many years.

To assess whether government policies with respect to unemployment are appropriate, it is necessary to know, first, whether the available measures of unemployment accurately indicate those aspects of unemployment that need to be known before sensible policies can be formulated; and second, the sense in which unemployment is a problem. These two points are discussed in turn.

The perception people have of the phenomenon of unemployment is coloured both by the available information on unemployment and by the terminology used. For the United Kingdom the best readily available information on the extent of unemployment refers to males of particular ages broken down by area and unemployment duration. Even for these groups there is a real problem as to how accurately the periodic register captures the phenomenon, as the discrepancies between the censuses and the register underline. These discrepancies are greater for certain age groups, particularly the young and the old, and for certain areas, notably Greater London. They may also be greater for certain ethnic or race groups and for certain occupational or skill groups. Little work has been done on explaining the discrepancies, so their significance is not obvious. It is well known that the register measures female unemployment badly, particularly for married females, and this failure quite possibly affects government policy adversely.

In addition to the data mentioned above, there are disaggregations of the registered unemployed into industry and occupational groupings. A person's position in either of these disaggregations is usually determined by his job immediately prior to his current period of unemployment and so might be misleading for many purposes. More important than this problem, however, might be the lack of information relating either of these series, or one of skill composition on a different basis, to the other features of unemployment, like age, duration and region.

Other aspects of unemployment often escape even attempts at serious measurement in the United Kingdom, again to the possible detriment of effective policy formulation. First, there is very little evidence available on the life-cycle pattern of unemployment between individuals. An analogy may be made with the problem of inequality in the distribution of income; one's perception of this problem is likely to be faulty if one concentrates on the distribution of income in any calendar or tax year. The source of the error stems from the fact that the location of an individual in the income ranking varies from year to year, partly in a predictable way, partly randomly. Evidence on this point shows, from a longitudinal survey, that of those male manual workers who were in the lowest-paid tenth in 1970 only 46 per cent were in a similar position in both of the succeeding two years.[2] It would be very revealing to have similar information for the unemployed. Specifically, the following information would be useful:

(i) How many periods of unemployment can workers with specified characteristics expect to have over a number of years?

(ii) Are workers who are relatively frequently unemployed at one stage of their working life likely to be in a similar position at a different stage?

As part of this life-cycle view it would be useful to know something about the relation between a person's earnings (which represent, in part, under-employment caused by factors like short-time working or absenteeism) and his unemployment experience. To some extent the occupational disaggregations help, but earnings vary considerably between persons within any occupation and also a person's occupation changes over time. What is particularly important here is the extent to which the relatively low-paid have their difficulties compounded by a high probability of unemployment. To the extent that there are positive correlations between (a) low earnings potential and high unemployment probabilities in any one period, (b) low earnings potentials from one period to another and (c) high unemployment probabilities from one period to another, the problems raised by unemployment might be much more severe than is implied by the information which is typically available.

Further, it would be very useful to know much more about the family context of the unemployed. As far as the existing family context is concerned, one would like to know the relation between the incidence of male unemployment and both the number of dependants and the number of actual and potential supporting workers in the family. For example, the policy prescription would differ when the unemployment probability facing the husband was positively related to that facing the wife from when the relationship was an inverse one.

In many ways the *past* family context of the unemployed person is the most important piece of information of all, and it is one that has virtually been ignored. But if sensible unemployment policies are to be formulated, how is it possible to overlook the impact on the child's future probability of unemployment of such factors as the father's occupational or unemployment status, or the family's housing circumstance, or the parents' health record, or the mother's work pattern? The recent interest in the 'cycle of deprivation' reflects a new concern with these issues.

Finally, it would be desirable to know more about the unemployment experience of various ethnic and race groups. Data are regularly published on the number of unemployed non-white workers by region. It would seem appropriate to extend these reports to include information on occupation, duration and age, so as to facilitate sensible comparisons with white workers.

The last point to be discussed in this section concerns terminology, particularly the distinction that is drawn between 'voluntary' and 'involuntary' unemployment. It seems to us that there is a very strong case against using either of these adjectives because they can be so misleading. First, although this is not decisive, different analysts use the terms in different ways (see a number of papers in this volume). Secondly, whatever the definitions used, whether a person is unemployed voluntarily or not may depend on the point in the period of unemployment when the inquiry is made. For example, a man may become unemployed voluntarily when he quits his job in the confident expectation of better opportunities elsewhere; subsequently, he may be proved wrong, have no job offers at all and become involuntarily unemployed. Thirdly, and much the most important, the two terms have complicated value connotations.

It is hard to see what use the two terms can have in purely positive analysis. There is a use for them only in normative analysis, but there they tend to confuse rather than enlighten. For example, there is a strong implication in the literature that voluntary unemployment is the result of free choice, like a preference for apples over oranges. A frequent but erroneous corollary of this view is that there is no reason for the government to try to change the extent of such unemployment. This corollary might deserve support if it were true that unemployment is the outcome of judicious decisions on when and to what degree leisure rather than wage goods was to be enjoyed. When the argument is taken further, however, and the existence of vacancies (net or gross) is supposed to indicate that unemployment is voluntary, so that governments have no role to play in affecting the level and structure of unemployment, it loses appeal. Thus, there has been much work done recently on search unemployment – the process where a person has a subjective probability distribution of wage offers obtaining in the market and looks for a job that offers rewards at least equal to some point on that distribution. During the search process some offers may well be rejected, thereby justifying for many analysts the term 'voluntary unemployment'. However, when individuals take decisions that prolong their period of unemployment, it does not follow that the context within which they take those decisions cannot be improved by government action.

In their usage, 'voluntary' tends to be a code word denying the desirability of government action and 'involuntary' tends to be a code word supporting government action. When one attempts to give the terms an independent definition, however, this coding ceases to be right. If a man is voluntarily unemployed, he either does not want a job at all at that time, or he wants a job but has rejected all offers made up to that time as being unsuitable. A man who is involuntarily unemployed is one who would like a job and has looked for one, but has had no offer of one. Some qualifications are necessary for the latter definition. First, with heterogeneous labour an individual may have been applying 'inappropriately', that is for jobs for which he could not reasonably consider himself suitable. Secondly, a man may have been searching in the wrong area, so that had he moved he would have found a job. Thirdly, there is the problem that a man may not have received an offer because his reservation wage was thought to be too high. With these qualifications the number of unemployed persons to whom the label 'involuntary' can be attached is very small indeed. That fact does not deny the possibility of substantial efficiency and equity gains from government action seeking to change the extent of unemployment. More than anything else, the terms 'voluntary' and 'involuntary' seem in the context of unemployment to be tools of rhetoric, not of analysis.

IN WHAT SENSE IS UNEMPLOYMENT A PROBLEM?

It is widely held that unemployment is both a social and an economic problem. Presumably this means not merely that unemployment is regrettable, but also that its existence demonstrates that social and economic mechanisms have failed. In defining an economic problem, that is evaluating an economic system or phenomenon, use can be made of the notions of efficiency and equity.

Taking the former notion first, a situation is inefficient if there exists an attainable alternative situation from which those who gain in moving to the alternative can fully compensate those who lose and still be better off than before. In terms of unemployment an inefficient situation may have more or less total unemployment than an efficient one. This is obviously true if one is considering the traditional set of macro-economic goals, for example price inflation, and one has a model which demonstrates that alternative combinations of such goals are permanently attainable. It is also true even if one follows Friedman and talks of a natural equilibrium unemployment rate which is determined by various institutions.

An example of economic efficiency being associated with more unemployment concerns one of the possible arguments favouring a system of unemployment compensation; to the extent that such a system facilitates a judicious and efficient search for a good job, rather than a man being driven to accept an early and possibly socially unsatisfactory job offer, unemployment may be higher than it would be without such compensation. An example of economic efficiency being associated with less unemployment (or at least lower unemployment durations) concerns the current attempt to improve the efficiency of the employment exchanges by separating the payment of benefits from the job-finding function, establishing 'job shops' in the High Street and opening late at night.

In this connection it was something of a surprise that so little of the commentary on the substantial rise in unemployment after 1966 even considered the impact of earnings-related unemployment benefits and redundancy payments. It was, after all, one of the stated intentions of both pieces of legislation that measured unemployment rates should rise.

With reference to some set of values a situation may be said to be inequitable if there exists a preferred situation from which those who gain from the change could compensate those who lose. In terms of unemployment, certain regional policies might be defended not on the grounds that they reduce total unemployment or affect favourably other aggregates, but on the grounds that they share out the burdens of a given level of unemployment more evenly. For example, a policy might be thought to be successful if it raised unemployment in the South East by exactly the same amount as it reduced unemployment in Scotland, other aggregates remaining unchanged.

In labelling the phenomenon of unemployment as an 'economic problem', one must demonstrate that it implies either an inefficiency or an inequity. In formulating a policy to deal with the problem one must know the causes of the unemployment. We now consider this problem, focusing the discussion on explaining the variation in unemployment rates across London boroughs.

MALE UNEMPLOYMENT IN LONDON

An important feature of unemployment is the persistence of a settled geographic pattern of relative unemployment rates. This has, for example, been demonstrated for the British regions by Cheshire, who states that 'the relative position of regions has been remarkably stable for fifty years.'[3] Hall has reported a similar finding concerning the structure of unemployment amongst cities in the United States.[4] London boroughs are no exception; the Spearman rank correlation between male unemployment rates across the 32 London boroughs in 1966 and 1971 is 0·92 (t = 12·8 which is significant at the 1 per cent level).[5]

The structure of unemployment differentials in London boroughs in 1971 is similar for males and females (the simple correlation is 0·891), all females, married females and, more interesting, when the sick are excluded from the economically inactive. The Spearman rank correlation between the total male unemployment rate and the male unemployment rate when the sick are excluded is 0·937 (t = 34·1, significant at 1 per cent).

The exclusion of the sick from the economically inactive causes a similar proportionate reduction in unemployment (of around one-quarter) in each of the 32 boroughs. Thus the data suggest that the sick are not distributed equally within London. If two boroughs have identical populations, the borough with the higher unemployment rate also has the higher absolute number of sick people (for example, see Table 11.1). If the sick were distributed equally, the last column would be substantially larger for Merton than for Tower Hamlets, yet the reverse is true. This highlights the importance of examining a large number of hardship indicators when designing social policy.

Table 11.1. *Proportions of sick among the unemployed in two London boroughs: males, 1971*

	Male population	Unemployed (total)	Unemployed (excl. sick)	Sick/total unemployed
		(%)	(%)	(%)
Merton	84,205	3·50	2·76	21·2
Tower Hamlets	82,104	8·57	6·20	27·7

Source: Office of Population Censuses and Surveys, *Census 1971. England and Wales. County Reports: Greater London*, H.M.S.O., 1973.

When explaining geographic unemployment differentials it is important to isolate the characteristics of the area (such as the industry-mix) from the characteristics of the population. Cheshire finds that the pattern of regional unemployment differentials is *not* attributable to the different industrial structures; rather all industries in high-unemployment areas tend to have unemployment rates above United Kingdom average for those industries.[6] Whilst this might be attributable to the inferior economic quality of the population in high-unemployment regions (perhaps caused by over a century of net out-migration), Cheshire suggests that the explanation lies in the fact that unemployment rates are not industry-specific, and a high unemployment rate in (say) shipbuilding will tend to spread out over all the other industries in a depressed region. In the model that follows the importance of area characteristics and personal characteristics are examined with respect to unemployment in London.[7]

Differences in percentage unemployment arise from two sources: the probability of becoming unemployed and the duration of unemployment. Clearly, both will be determined by both demand and supply influences. More specifically, the percentage unemployment rate is determined by the four probabilities listed on page 203.

The variables which can be observed as measuring these theoretical determinants of unemployment can be divided into personal characteristics and area characteristics. The first include:

Age: Although it is often held that young and old workers suffer higher unemployment than prime-age workers, we make no such hypothesis here, *ceteris paribus*. Young workers have higher separation rates (especially voluntary quits) and lower unemployment duration than prime-age males, whilst older workers have lower separation rates but much higher unemployment duration.[8]

The dual labour-market hypothesis[9] asserts that young workers experience relatively high unemployment rates: for example Hall has suggested some teenagers in the United States exhibit 'pathological job instability' caused by them moving from one dead-end job to another and often experiencing unemployment between moves.[10] Our data provide a test of this hypothesis.

There is a problem in isolating the effect of age on unemployment, especially for old workers; if an old worker becomes unemployed (perhaps because he is made redundant) he may 'bump down' the skill ladder in an effort to secure employment.[11] The influence of age on unemployment may then be masked by the skill variable. This possibility is tested by excluding the skill variable in some of the regression equations.

Marital status: The conventional hypothesis that the marginal utility of income relative to leisure is higher for married than for unmarried men is adopted here. Married men are therefore less likely to become voluntarily unemployed, and the duration of any unemployment they experience will tend to be shorter. Further, on the demand side, it is possible (but unlikely?) that, *ceteris paribus*, the employer discriminates in favour of married workers (on equity grounds) when making hiring and firing decisions. It is expected therefore that marital status would be inversely related to unemployment.

Number of dependants: This variable exercises two conflicting influences on unemployment. On the one hand, identical arguments to those advanced for marital status work to reduce unemployment for individuals with a relatively high number of dependants. On the other hand, supplementary benefits are positively related to family size, which may result (from the supply side) in increased unemployment because the higher supplementary benefits lower the cost of becoming unemployed and of prolonged unemployment.

Immigrants: The influence of race on unemployment is complicated and may vary according to country of origin.[12] From the supply side it may be hypothesised that immigrants have migrated to improve their welfare; they will tend to work harder and are therefore less likely to be unemployed. Against this view, however, it is sometimes asserted that immigrants are lazy, and so are more likely to be voluntarily unemployed. Also, recent migrants might have poorly developed labour-market information networks[13] and might therefore have to spend relatively large amounts of time in labour-market search activity, although the poor information may lead to inferior jobs rather than overt unemployment.

Skill: Supply side influences will tend to cause unskilled workers to have relatively high unemployment rates. They may have poor information or may be inefficient at search. The dual labour-market hypothesis suggests that the unskilled, because their jobs are relatively boring, will tend to have higher quit rates, with job-changes frequently involving a bout of unemployment. The demand side arguments pull in the same direction: the well-known specific training arguments initiated by Oi[14] and the 'bumping down' the skill hierarchy hypothesis of Reder[15] both appear to have merit in explaining why the unskilled suffer higher unemployment rates than the skilled.

The second group of variables comprises characteristics of the area, which include:

The proportion of employment in manufacturing industry: Employment in manufacturing in London recently declined substantially.[16] An important question concerning this run-down in manufacturing is whether, as suggested by Eversley,[17] it resulted in considerable hardship (including higher unemployment), or whether it was primarily in response to people leaving first and jobs following them, as suggested by Foster and Richardson. A positive significant coefficient for the variable measuring the proportion of the labour force resident in a borough working in manufacturing in 1966 is consistent with Eversley's view being correct.

Redundancies:[18] It is important to know whether, *ceteris paribus*, areas which suffered a relatively high number of redundancies in the years immediately prior to 1971 also suffered higher unemployment in 1971. If they did, then action to reduce their labour supply (for example, by providing information) or to increase their demand for labour (for example, by relaxing zoning laws) may be necessary. Redundancies may also be positively associated with unemployment because of the existence of redundancy payments.[19]

The results of the regressions are presented in Table 11.2. Equations (1) and (2) indicate the importance of personal characteristics in explaining inter-borough differences in unemployment. The variables for marital status, dependants and the proportion of unskilled workers all have significant coefficients, and show that boroughs with a high proportion of unskilled, a large number of children in relation to male workers and a small proportion of married men will tend to have higher unemployment than boroughs with the opposite characteristics. The coefficient for the proportion unskilled indicates that, *ceteris paribus*, an increase of 4 percentage points in that proportion (for example from 9 to 13 per cent) raises the unemploy-

Table 11.2. *Regression results for equations explaining unemployment in 32 London boroughs: males, 1971*

Independent variables	Equation nos			Mean standard deviation
	(1)	(2)	(3)	
Percentage of male labour force:				
Aged 15–24	−0·108	−0·280	0·035	15·74
	(1·03)	(1·13)	(0·31)	(1·50)
Aged 54+	0·289	0·169	0·054	23·10
	(0·64)	(1·62)	(1·25)	(1·79)
Married	−0·281	−0·572	−0·217	66·39
	(6·13)	(6·37)	(3·48)	(6·45)
All persons aged 0–14 as a percentage of males 15–64	0·071	0·209	0·057	64·8 5
	(3·89)	(6·50)	(2·97)	(10·37)
Percentage of male labour force:				
New Commonwealth immigrants	−0·035	−0·079	−0·016	9·88
	(1·91)	(1·86)	(0·69)	(5·51)
Unskilled	0·249	·	0·257	8·82
	(11·10)		(10·27)	(3·94)
Employed in manufacturing, 1966	·	·	−0·018	·
			(1·07)	
Numbers of male redundancies:				
1966–9	·	·	−0·011	·
			(2·47)	
1970	·	·	0·045	·
			(2·28)	
Constant	17·934	30·444	12·006	
	(4·40)	(3·25)	(2·50)	
R^2	0·97	0·82	0·98	

Sources: Office of Population Censuses and Surveys, *Census 1971. England and Wales. County Reports: Greater London*; Greater London Council, *Annual Abstract of Greater London Statistics*, 1971, and special data supplied on skill and employment in manufacturing for 1966; Department of Employment, data on redundancies; London Boroughs' Association and Salvation Army, data from survey of hostel accommodation.

Notes: (i) The dependent variable is the unemployment rate for male residents in April 1971.
     (ii) The regressions are estimated by ordinary least squares and expected signs are negative for percentage married, positive for percentage unskilled (see text).
   (iii) t-ratios are shown in brackets.

ment rate by 1 percentage point (for example from 4 to 5 per cent). The hardship caused by the higher unemployment rate experienced by the unskilled will be compounded by the imperfect capital market – higher borrowing rates – that they face.

The sign on the variable for numbers of dependants hints that the influence of this factor in cheapening the cost of unemployment outweighs the influence which causes men with large families to 'need' to be in work. In view of the importance of this finding, for both social and economic policy, we experimented with an alternative definition of dependants to check the robustness of the result. The definition chosen was the proportion of a borough's population living in households with five or more people. If individuals with a relatively large number of dependants are really likely to have a higher propensity to be unemployed then the coefficient for this variable should have a significant positive sign. In the event, its coefficient whilst positive was non-significant ($t = 1 \cdot 27$), which suggests the result in the equations shown must be treated with caution.

The results with respect to age are as predicted, in that they suggest that, *ceteris paribus*, neither young nor old workers are more likely to be unemployed than prime-age males.

The results also suggest that, *ceteris paribus*, immigrants do not have a higher unemployment rate than people born in the United Kingdom. This important result is sustained when the variable is split into four categories according to area of origin (West Indies, Asia, Africa, Ireland) and each category is entered in equation (1) separately; in no case does the variable have a significant coefficient. This hints that, where labour-market discrimination exists, it occurs via lack of training opportunities for immigrants (to enable them to become skilled workers) rather than via hiring and firing policies within a given (for example, unskilled) grade of labour. Further, as immigrants are disproportionately unskilled ($r = +0 \cdot 37$), the unemployment experienced by immigrants is attributable to those factors which make them unskilled, such as discrimination in the education system, or a high rate of time preference, or wage discrimination causing the rate of return on training to be relatively low. Discrimination does not result in higher unemployment within a skill group.

The area characteristics are added in equation (3). They do not change the results found for the personal characteristics. Despite the run-down of manufacturing industry in London, there is no association between the proportion of a borough's labour force (by residence) working in manufacturing in 1966 and 1971 unemployment. This hints that the run-down in manufacturing employment did not cause hardship in those areas experiencing the decline.[20]

This result is supported by the fact that boroughs experiencing a large number of redundancies over the years 1966–9 have a relatively low unemployment rate in 1971. This could be attributable to a variety of factors, for example:

(i) New employers may move into a high redundancy area.
(ii) Redundant workers may move away (which could result in hardship).
(iii) Individuals made redundant during the period 1966–9 may have a lower propensity to quit in 1970 or 1971, possibly because their assets were exhausted whilst unemployed.
(iv) Individuals living in high redundancy boroughs may have a low propensity to quit.
(v) The Department of Employment might put more resources into an area of high redundancies to speed the search process.

This last point may be consistent with the dual labour-market hypothesis, in that firms operating in the so-called primary sector, with well developed internal labour markets, will tend to give the Department of Employment and their employees advance warning of forthcoming redundancies so that action may be taken to avert their consequences.

On the other hand, boroughs experiencing a relatively large number of redundancies in 1970 suffered relatively high unemployment in 1971.

Some extensions were also made to the basic model. When the proportion of the borough's labour force that is semi-skilled was added to the proportion unskilled the combined variable was positively and significantly associated with unemployment ($t = 4 \cdot 54$) in an equation similar to (1). But wealth, which influences unemployment from the supply side, had an ambiguous effect. On the one hand, the return from greater wealth reduces the cost of unemployment, but on the other hand it may enable the individual to buy more or higher quality information, get more contacts, engage in bribery, etc., which would tend to reduce unemployment. The proportion of the borough's population which lives in owner-occupied houses was used as a (poor) proxy for wealth. It was not significantly related to unemployment when added to equation (1), but this reflects problems of multicollinearity, as it is highly correlated with the proportion unskilled ($r = -0.80$) and with marital status ($r = +0.75$).

Area characteristics are given more prominence in explaining labour-market disadvantage by those who believe in the dual labour market or the radical paradigms than by those who accept the neo-classical explanations of disadvantage. Gordon suggests that a run-down area reflects the fact that individuals have no control over their own destiny, and he emphasises the problem of multiple disadvantage, incorporating such factors as poor transport, poor housing and poor information.[21] Given its diffuse nature, it is difficult to test this hypothesis. However, two proxies for the 'run-downness' of an area were added to equations (1) and (3) to provide a blunt test. These were (a) the number of hostel places per thousand of the borough's population and (b) the infant death rate (for legitimate, illegitimate and all infants).[22] These variables were never significantly related to unemployment. Whilst this should not lead us to reject entirely the importance of area characteristics in explaining unemployment, the result does suggest that explanations of labour-market disadvantage which are not based on conventional theory ought to be defined more rigorously to facilitate a fair test of their predictions.

CONCLUSIONS

The results suggest that male unemployment in London is primarily determined by certain individual characteristics, especially skill and marital status. Once these variables have been controlled for, race, age and area characteristics appear unrelated to unemployment.

It is necessary to consider why individuals with a high propensity to be unemployed live where they do (which, in broad terms, is in the inner boroughs). The answer is found by examining the differences between boroughs in housing stocks. Individuals who are unlikely to be unemployed live disproportionately in owner-occupied houses, and therefore boroughs with a high proportion of owner-occupied houses have low unemployment rates. Conversely, the unskilled tend to live in low-rent housing (between the percentage of public housing and the percentage unskilled $r = + 0.80$) and therefore boroughs with a high proportion of public housing suffer high unemployment rates. Inner city problems occur because individuals who suffer labour-market disadvantage live disproportionately in the inner city, because that is where the largest stock of cheap housing (especially public housing) is found. The problems are a function of the housing stock accumulated over the last 150 years. Further, the problems become circular, because boroughs whose residents tend to suffer labour-market disadvantage build a large amount of public housing in an effort to look after the welfare of their residents. This accounts for the observed temporal stability of the structure of unemployment within London.

In the United States inner city unemployment is usually attributable to employment suburbanisation, housing segregation, inadequate public transport systems, poor labour-market information and discrimination.[23] Our results suggest that the problem of labour-market disadvantage in London is caused, more narrowly, by the given housing stocks, rather than by all the factors listed by Gordon.

This paper has made a modest start on the analysis of the problem of labour-market disadvantage in urban areas. Much more needs to be done including:

(i) An analysis of the problem of multiple disadvantage to determine the extent to which unemployment, low pay, poor health, low participation rates, under-employment, poor information, poor housing, inferior local government services, etc. are interrelated.

(ii) An analysis of the problem of labour-market disadvantage which both takes account of the lifetime pattern of disadvantage (it is clearly more serious if the same individuals fare badly all their life than if the problems come only at particular times, such as at old age) and analyses disadvantage in a family context.

(iii) Unemployment *rates* must be broken down into numbers flowing on to the register (by analysing quit functions and layoff functions) and duration (by analysing the probability of getting a job, which in some large part will depend on vacancies). Sensible measures to reduce unemployment or alleviate its consequences are entirely different according to whether the problem is numbers or duration.

One way by which all the above aspects of unemployment could be examined is via a cohort analysis. All (or a sample of) the individuals coming on to the unemployment register on a particular day (or week) could be surveyed in regard to such factors as their personal and family characteristics, location and previous job history. They could then be followed for (say) about five years to get details of their labour-market experience, including bouts of unemployment and their duration, job aspirations, actual jobs, pay, skill, etc. Although this would be costly, our hunch is that the social rate of return on such a survey would, via the policy measures it would indicate to alleviate the problem of labour-market disadvantage, be handsome.

NOTES

1 We acknowledge with thanks the research assistance and comments of Carol O'Cleireacain and Hen-fong Hayllar, and helpful discussion with Christopher Foster and Steve Nickell. The evidence presented in the third section of the paper is drawn from a wider study of the London labour market financed by the Social Science Research Council.

2 *Department of Employment Gazette*, April 1973.

3 P. C. Cheshire, 'Regional Unemployment Differences in Great Britain' in N.I.E.S.R. *Regional Papers II*, Cambridge University Press, 1973, p. 1.

4 R. E. Hall, 'Why is the Unemployment Rate so High at Full Employment?', *Brookings Papers on Economic Activity*, no. 3, 1970.

5 It is interesting that the dispersion of unemployment across the 32 boroughs is very similar in the two years:

	Mean unemployment	Standard deviation	Coefficient of variation
1966	2·19	0·83	0·38
1971	4·72	1·73	0·37

6 'Regional Unemployment Differences in Great Britain', Chap. 1.

7 Labour is more mobile amongst boroughs within London than amongst regions of Britain and area characteristics might therefore be expected to be less important in explaining differences in unemployment within London. It would be interesting to carry out an intermediate level of analysis using cities as the unit of observation.

8 For evidence on duration of unemployment by age see F. Cripps and R. Tarling, 'An Analysis of the Duration of Male Unemployment in Great Britain, 1932–73', *Economic Journal*, June 1974.

9 D. M. Gordon, *Theories of Poverty and Underemployment: Orthodox, Radical and Dual Labor Market Perspectives*, D. C. Heath, 1972.

10 Hall, 'Why is the Unemployment Rate so High at Full Employment?'

11 M. Reder, 'The Theory of Occupational Wage Differentials', *American Economic Review*, December 1955.

12 The data used in the regressions refer to immigrants and therefore exclude non-whites born in Britain. Some tests were undertaken to see if immigrants

from Ireland experienced different unemployment rates from those from
Africa, Asia or West Indies.
13 A. Rees, 'Information Networks in Labor Markets', *American Economic
Review*, May 1966.
14 W. Y. Oi, 'Labor as a Quasi-fixed Factor', *Journal of Political Economy*,
December 1962.
15 'The Theory of Occupational Wage Differentials'.
16 C. Foster and R. Richardson, 'Employment Trends in London in the 1960s
and their Relevance to the Future' in D. Donnison and D. Eversley (eds),
London: *Urban Patterns, Problems and Policies*, Heinemann, 1973.
17 D. Eversley, 'Problems of Social Planning in Inner London' in Donnison and
Eversley (eds), London: *Urban Patterns, Problems and Policies*.
18 Redundancies refer to the redundancies in the borough, whilst the dependent
variable is unemployment by residence. Inclusion of redundancies therefore
does not cause estimation problems.
19 Although no such association was found by D. I. Mackay and G. L. Reid, see
'Redundancy, Unemployment and Manpower Policy', *Economic Journal*,
December 1972.
20 See the debate in Eversley, 'Problems of Social Planning in Inner London',
Foster and Richardson, 'Employment Trends in London in the 1960s and
their Relevance to the Future', and C. O'Cleireacain, 'Labour Market
Trends in London and the Rest of the South-East', *Urban Studies*, October
1974.
21 Gordon, *Theories of Poverty and Underemployment*.
22 These variables could also act as proxies for wealth. The hostel places variable
might be endogenous; hostel places are provided, in part, in response to
demand by disadvantaged individuals. The variable was entered both as a
dummy (with a value of unity when the ratio was > 1 and zero when < 1)
and as a continuous variable. Some alternative variables to represent 'run-
downness' might include the proportion of a borough's residents receiving
social security or family income supplement or rent rebates; or the proportion in multi-occupied houses or houses lacking specific basic amenities.
23 Gordon, *Theories of Poverty and Underemployment*, Chap. 1.

Chapter 12

Unemployment and the Social Structure[1]

ADRIAN SINFIELD

The analysis of unemployment as one measure of the state of society – one part of what used to be called 'the condition of the people' – remains undeveloped in Britain today. While the collection of statistics on unemployment as an instrument of economic and manpower analysis has been long established and its importance fully recognised, the data tell us very little about the significance of unemployment for society as opposed to the economy. Recent debates on the adequacy of the official statistics have been confined, as the terms of reference adopted by the Inter-Departmental Working Party indicate, to changes needed 'in order to provide a more accurate indication of the real level of unused labour resources in the economy'.[2]

Considerable limitations in the present data on unemployment become evident if one regards unemployment as one of those 'social costs and social insecurities which are the product of a rapidly changing industrial–urban society'.[3] How many are unemployed? and Who are the unemployed? become only the first of many questions. Just as important are answers to other questions, of which some we have only just started to ask and others have never really been pursued systematically. How is unemployment, and its costs, distributed throughout society? And to what extent or in what ways are these costs paid by individuals, families, communities, employers or the wider society? To what extent, and in what ways, does unemployment serve to maintain or reinforce the stratification of our still classbound society? And what changes have there been over time?

The answers to all these questions are central to the analysis of the social structure of any predominantly market society, and the aim of this paper is to discuss the available data and to suggest the data and research needed for further analysis. There are, of course, considerable problems related to the definition of unemployment and the methods of collecting the data which in Britain particularly affect the labour force status of many married women and retired people, but the paper will draw mainly on the Department of Employment statistics, which are the most detailed and comprehensive regularly available.[4]

This paper begins with an examination of the unequal incidence of unemployment and its implications for analysis, and considers the available evidence on the experience of being out of work and on the efficiency of the variety of income maintenance programmes in compensating the unemployed. The final sections discuss the significance of institutional changes in the labour market and attempt to distinguish four categories of job-changing, which may provide a guide for priorities in policies designed to tackle unemployment.

THE UNEQUAL INCIDENCE OF UNEMPLOYMENT

The unequal incidence of unemployment by occupation is one of those facts about society so well known that it is rarely discussed. 'Economists and public policy makers debate the question: how much unemployment can the country stand? Strictly speaking, it is not "the country" that is being asked to "stand unemployment". Unemployment does not, like . . . God's gentle rain, fall uniformly upon everyone . . . it strikes from underneath, and it strikes particularly at those at the bottom of our society.'[5]

The disproportionate share of unemployment has long been borne by the unskilled. Over half the unemployed men, and often more, have been registered for jobs as labourers in every year since occupational data were published in 1959. Bosanquet and Standing have calculated that in 1970 unskilled men were three, or possibly four, times as likely to be out of work as other men.[6] Their work, however, underlines the need for better and more regular analyses to provide a clearer picture of the class impact of unemployment.

There are, of course, fewer job opportunities available for the unskilled than for other workers. At best over the last 15 years, there have been only four times as many men registered for labourers' jobs as vacancies known to the exchange, while vacancies for others have actually exceeded the numbers out of work. In 1974 the ratio of unskilled men to job vacancies was 13 : 1 compared with a ratio of $1\frac{1}{2}$: 1 for the rest. And this very different job situation cannot be denied whatever the inadequacies or limitations of the vacancies data.[7]

The inequality of the unskilled man is increased in those parts of the country where unemployment is highest. In those regions the unskilled form a higher proportion of unemployed men, while the vacancies suitable for them comprise a smaller part of the opportunities available. In the Northern region, for example, it has not been unusual over the last decade for the labourers category to contain two-thirds of the unemployed men but only one-eleventh of the vacancies.

Unemployment is not of course confined to the unskilled or to manual workers; workers in clerical, administrative, professional and technical jobs comprise almost a fifth of all unemployed men, and their numbers of unemployed increased much faster than the average for all occupations between 1959 and 1972.[8]

This does not invalidate Liebow's point – the risk of unemployment is much greater for the unskilled. But occupational status is not the only factor influencing the incidence of unemployment. The older worker, the very young, the disabled, the immigrant, and those in depressed areas and declining industries are all more vulnerable to joblessness, and the combination of two or more of these characteristics considerably increases the risk. The older, unskilled man in the North East or Scotland, with developing bronchitis, is usually very well aware of his precarious security in the present situation.

The Acceptance of Association As Explanation. Any observer from another world would not fail to recognise that our society appears, by its actions, to accept some of these risks, while it attempts, more or less wholeheartedly, to reduce others. The regional imbalance of unemployment has received considerable attention, and there have been many different, though not very successful, efforts to reduce it. On the other hand, other risks seem to be so much part of the way we expect life to be that the opposite applies. Demands for government action to reduce unemployment are frequently supported by: 'It's not only the unskilled out of work; tradesmen are losing their jobs', or 'It's even hitting the family man now – not just the old.' The observer would note that in Britain it is more acceptable for the old or unskilled to be unemployed – our sense of what is proper and normal is less offended. This acceptance of certain inequalities in the distribution of unemployment as more 'natural' than others is very important for the analysis of the impact of unemployment, and carries considerable significance for the organisation and stratification of society. As society becomes increasingly complex, we become even more dependent upon statistical data for so many analyses and assessments. Yet any attempt to explain the current distribution of unemployment is frustrated by the fact that the unemployment data are not only inadequate in many respects; they may even be said to have a misleading effect on those who are supposed to use them, or one might have expected less indifference to the persistence, and even the increase, of some of the inequalities.

Perhaps the clearest example of this is the association of unemployment with age. Older workers are more likely to lose jobs and are particularly vulnerable to prolonged unemployment. The reduction of the long-term unemployment rate for men aged 55 years and over to that for men under 55 would reduce the extent of prolonged joblessness very considerably. In July 1966 this reduction would have approached 50 per cent, in 1969 and 1974 about 40 per cent (based on numbers out of work six months or more per 10,000 employees).

But the association of increasing age with very much higher rates of unemployment is not inevitable as many seem to regard it; it is not even common to market economies.[9] This obliges us to question the common view expressed by employers in Britain that older men are much less suitable, adaptable, fit, or generally able.

Unless men aged 55 and over in Britain differ in significant relevant characteristics from men of the same age in the United States, Italy or Sweden, or jobs actually require more of an older man in Britain than in these other countries, we must conclude that there is greater age discrimination in Britain, with employers, officials in private and public employment offices, and even workers and unemployed themselves having a lower estimation of the potential contribution of the older worker.

Analysis of discussions in the media and elsewhere, especially during the so-called 'shake-out', would, I think, show evidence of a general, and possibly increasing, acceptance that older men can be laid-off. One implication is that we are moving towards a more meritocratic, technically oriented society, in which a premium goes naturally to the better educated and better trained, with consequential benefits to the younger, more recently trained worker. 'A major new source of inequality and of poverty in society' can result from two apparently contradictory trends. 'On the one hand, the development of seniority rights in large organisations and the disproportionate increase of such organisations is strengthening the situation of earnings of some employed men in the older age-groups. ... On the other, redundancies from certain types of skilled jobs and the lagging of pay and conditions in the older industries . . . are tending to increase the proportion of older male workers occupying low-paid and insecure jobs.'[10]

New policies and attitudes lead to changes in the institutional structure of the labour market and in turn are reinforced over time by this structure. The emphasis on seniority for both promotion and layoff procedures in collective bargaining in the United States has had an influence, both direct and indirect, on the distribution of employment across the labour force, which probably does much to account in that country for the lower rates of unemployment among older men relative to all men. The very different development and extent of apprenticeship schemes, as well as the seniority procedures, may help to explain the much greater vulnerability to unemployment of young members of the labour force in the United States than in Britain.

The cause, therefore, of older workers' greater vulnerability to unemployment, and to prolonged unemployment particularly, is not simply their greater age – about which we can do nothing; it rests in policies, procedures and attitudes, which serve, whether deliberately or not, to favour younger workers. Such factors can be changed or modified so that the association between older men and unemployment is by no means as inevitable as many seem to regard it.

Age is, of course, not the only characteristic that may serve to mislead us about the causes of unemployment if we keep to simple measurement only. Such an example only underlines the need to explore the causes of particular distributions of unemployment among the labour force much further than we have done in the past.

The Power to Avoid Unemployment. Any analysis of the inequality of unemployment must also take into account the varying protection different workers have against it. Where there is less work, workers in some occupations are more likely to be hoarded, while those in other jobs may be paid off. Some professions and occupations have developed their own methods of ensuring security, for example, the tenure arrangements of university teachers. Obviously some workers have greater power than others; others have scarcity value. When there is a shortage of skilled men in certain trades and a surfeit of labourers, the latter recognise that they have much less freedom, and that they need to be more punctual and more deferential to the foreman. The work rhythm gives some workers more freedom than others; the merchant seaman who wishes to be at home when a child is born because there will be no-one else to look after the other children may have to jump ship, gaining a bad record with his employers as well as losing his entitlement to unemployment benefit. A shipyard labourer may be able to arrange with the foreman to be included in the next pay-off, without stigma and with a fair chance of recall. The teacher or lecturer out of term is likely to experience none of these restrictions. Within the firm, as Dorothy Wedderburn has shown, only those with higher status are entitled to personal leave and the freedom of arrangements this brings.[11]

Industrial needs or conventions also lead to different patterns of action when there is less work. In the car industry it is customary to cut overtime first, then to go on short-time, and only then to lay off workers. By contrast, in the shipbuilding and repair industries workers may in fact work more overtime in the final weeks of the job because of the massive payments the yard may have to make if the ship is delivered late. The worker in the car industry may have less chance of pay-off, but when it comes his resources may already be reduced, while the shipyard worker may finish with more wages in his pocket than he has had for some time.

These examples indicate that the unemployment figures are not, and have never been, a clear and unambiguous indication of the under-utilisation of labour – and this is quite apart from the extent of hidden unemployment that may occur as individuals stay outside the labour force. With the greater organisation and rationalisation in industry today, the better trade union organisation and many other factors, unemployment data probably relate less and less to the simple lack of demand for labour. We have come to regard unemployment 'as a kind of inevitable exhaust of our economic engine. We fail to see that it is also a social process powered by the values we hold and the choices we make.'[12]

Unemployment and Economic and Social Exclusion. These are long-term issues relating to the distribution of power in society that have long been neglected in any examination of the incidence of unemployment. Yet their relevance for understanding the differing extent of social and economic security possible for different groups in Britain today is in fact likely to be increasing. Writing in the depression years of the 1930s, G. A. Briefs 'singled out liability to unemployment or insecurity of tenure as the distinguishing feature of the proletarian estate.'[13] Since then the extent of unemployment has been reduced dramatically in market economies, but one might very well argue that its significance in separating groups within the labour force has not only persisted but increased.

Today, unemployment brings for most not only loss of current earnings but exclusion from a whole range of benefits and rights. As the significance of these additions to earnings has increased in both extent and value in recent years, the loss of a job gains further importance in dividing the secure from the insecure. It is not only that those receiving, or eligible for, most occupation-related benefits lose them on unemployment, but that these occupational benefits are not provided, or are much less available, for those in the jobs more liable to unemployment. When these benefits are increasing in range and value, the worker in such an insecure job loses out even if he does not in fact become unemployed. Many benefits or facilities are only available to workers who have been employed by a firm for a specific number of years and many of them increase in value with the length of unbroken employment. Company pensions and redundancy payments are both important examples, but the whole scale of private welfare benefits provided by employers has increased considerably in recent years.[14]

The rating of a worker's unemployment risk also affects his access to resources outside his work. One of the most common examples of this, which has gained significance in the tight and increasingly expensive housing market of recent years, is the building societies' treatment of working-class applicants, who may have high wages but little guarantee of long-term security in employment. By contrast, the young professionals, with low earnings but a high expectation of security and an incremental salary scale, may be more favourably regarded. Those with greater risk of unemployment may be cut off from the security and advantages – in our society both financial and social – of home ownership.

Although most of this is very well known, it is not linked to any discussion of the risk of unemployment and too little attention is given to the ways in which unemployment, and even the greater risk of unemployment, still function as a control over the stratification of society. Instead, there is more discussion of the supposed inflation of the official figures of unemployment by 'voluntary' unemployed, or by others regarded as unemployable or unsuitable for employment, and recurrent concern over welfare abuse and 'dole-dodging'.

There are debates about the reduction, persistence, or increase of poverty and inequality, but the major evidence remains based on weekly earnings and incomes. We all know that there is a great difference socially, economically and psychologically between the earner whose weekly £50 comes steadily and predictably year after year with a good chance of a regular increase, and the man whose £50 is dependent on all the fluctuations in his occupation and industry and in the economy, and whose increase depends not on time and the increment but on collective bargaining and negotiation. Simply to invite the reader to imagine a life history, a career, a geographical and social location, and a standard of living for two such men living in London should be enough to convince him that any measurement of income without evidence of its security and predictability can only be a very partial and limited indicator of the extent of economic as well as social inequality.

For many people these points lack weight because of the belief that in a full employment welfare state the burden of unemployment is both light and temporary. Even with 3 per cent unemployment, one is reminded, there is 97 per cent employment, whereas Beveridge thought he was being quite optimistic in basing his insurance plans on $8\frac{1}{2}$ per cent unemployment. And we now have an impressive range of insurance benefits – earnings-related supplements, supplementary allowances and redundancy payments, quite apart from the generous additional provision that many employers provide; all these are likely to be tax free, and there is also the possibility of income tax rebates. In such a situation the call for closer and more detailed measurement of the unequal incidence and distribution of unemployment loses force, except perhaps as the perennial special pleading of the social scientist for more data.

The following sections therefore explore the nature of unemployment for those individuals experiencing it and the performance of the variety of income maintenance programmes.

THE EXPERIENCE OF UNEMPLOYMENT

First of all, although Beveridge would have been pleased by the much lower level of unemployment after the war than before, he would have been quick to point out that Britain has not by any means met the requirements for 'full employment in a free society' which he set out in 1944. Full employment 'means having always more vacant jobs than unemployed men, not slightly fewer jobs. It means that the jobs are at fair wages, of such a kind and so located that the unemployed men can reasonably be expected to take them; it means, by consequence, that the normal lag between losing one job and finding another will be very short.'[15]

Thirty years later our measures of unemployment and employment cannot give us a precise picture of how well the current labour market meets these requirements. Even so, while the relation between total unemployment and total vacancies is not at all clear, the official figures have only overlapped once, briefly, since 1956, and the disparity has been much greater for the unskilled. The economic return and quality of the jobs available to the unemployed or job-changers is not known and there has generally been a failure to consider the nature of the job to which an unemployed worker returns.

Finally, while the Department of Employment now stresses the considerable turnover of unemployed, with between 250,000 and 350,000 adults joining the register every month, and a similar number leaving, for many the length of unemployment between jobs is considerable. The number of men out of work for more than six months has not fallen below 170,000 since January 1971 and was over 250,000 during 1972. In October 1974 the long-term unemployed formed 35 per cent of men out of work (1·3 per cent of male employees); the last time the proportion fell clearly below three out of ten was in January 1968.

The gravity of the problem of long-term unemployment in Britain has received very little attention, although the first article in the *Department of Employment Gazette* for many years to discuss the duration of unemployment does mention 'an underlying upward trend since the late 1950s in the duration of unemployment'.[16] An

analysis of ten O.E.C.D. member countries in the mid-1960s showed
that Britain had a very high rate of long-term unemployment in
relation to its low overall rate. In 1966 only Belgium and Ireland had
clearly higher levels of long-term unemployment, while Canada and
the United States, with much higher overall rates of unemployment,
were as low as Britain (expressed as a rate per thousand members of
the labour force).[17]

Since then long-term unemployment in Britain has risen. In mid-
1973, when unemployment in Britain stood at 2·4 per cent and in the
United States at 4·5 per cent (by each country's own definition), the
rate of long-term unemployment in the labour force was a little
higher in Britain than the United States. Even generous allowance for
differences in definition and measurement would not alter the basic
situation, that Britain has a much greater incidence of prolonged
joblessness in the working population in relation to its level of overall
unemployment.

The impact of unemployment in Britain therefore falls longer –
and, so one would expect, more heavily – on a greater proportion
of those who do become unemployed than in the United States and
many other western economies. The risk is worst for those already
most vulnerable to unemployment – the old, the disabled, the unskilled, those in the regions furthest from London, all in fact except
the very young worker. The non-manual unemployed from clerical,
administrative, professional and technical jobs come predominantly
from the older age groups and are particularly liable to long unemployment.

The Repeated Experience of Unemployment. The burden of being
out of work for any one member of the labour force may only be
partly measured by the length of his current spell of joblessness.
One of the greater omissions from the British data is the failure
to measure the repeated impact of unemployment on the same
individual and any dependants. British data on the duration of
the current spell of unemployment were by far the most detailed,
comprehensive and reliable of the ten O.E.C.D. member countries I
studied in the mid-1960s, but, together with most other countries,
there was very little (and no regular) data on the repeated experience
of unemployment. The few studies, however, do reveal the clear
importance of this factor.[18] Without such data, we may be lulled into

believing that short-term unemployment is relatively painless and not realise that for many it is only the visible part of a recurrent experience, which may gradually erode a worker's confidence and a family's resources.

The government's inquiries into the characteristics of the unemployed in 1961, 1964 and 1973 provide the most comprehensive data on the extent to which unemployment is repeated. In the latest survey in June 1973, 28 per cent of the unemployed had been out of work at least once before in the previous 12 months. If one excludes those out of work for the whole year, at least two-fifths of the men and one-third of the women had two or more spells of unemployment during that period.[19]

The scale of recurrent unemployment over time is shown by the PEP national survey – 51 per cent had been out of work at least once before in the previous five years.[20] The government's earlier survey of the characteristics of the unemployed found that two out of every three men unemployed in October 1964 had been out of work in at least one of the two 12-month periods before October 1963 as well, and more than two out of five men had been unemployed in both years. Excluding those out of work continuously for all three years, more than three out of five men had unemployment recorded in all three years.[21]

The cumulative impact of many spells of unemployment may be considerable, especially in areas hard hit by unemployment. In a small random sample survey of 92 unemployed men in North Shields in 1963–4, the distribution by duration was quite close to the national picture at the time. Yet over the previous five years an average of one year and five months had been spent 'signing on at the dole'. The total of the many different experiences of unemployment came to 28 per cent of the five years and as much as one-third of the time spent in the labour force, according to both the men's account and that of the local employment exchange.[22]

The risk of repeated unemployment is also much greater among particular groups. The Three Towns study shows that the long-term unemployed are likely to have had more unemployment in the past – a finding similar to national surveys in the United States.[23] A 'pattern of intermittent unemployment' was found to be characteristic of the experience of 105 unemployed youths in a city in the north of England in the early 1970s.[24] Data from the United States also indicate the

particular vulnerability of the low-paid worker to frequent unemployment, and there is a certain amount of scattered and often rather
impressionistic evidence in support of this in Britain.

Clearly there is enough evidence of the extent of repeated unemployment to warrant more effort being directed to measuring it
regularly and in greater detail. The fact that a significant proportion
of the unemployed are reappearing time and again in the statistics
must raise serious questions about the adequacy of terms such as
'frictional' or 'temporary' unemployment, and the analysis of current
duration alone for indicating the social impact of unemployment.

The Experience of Unemployment Over the Year. In addition to
better data on the recurrence of unemployment, we need a
clearer indication of the proportion of the labour force with
any unemployment over a period of time. Since the mid-1960s we
have moved to a higher level of unemployment – almost a doubling
of the basic trend of the first two post-war decades. Dorothy Wedderburn has stressed 'the growth of insecurity as a central feature of
workers' lives in contemporary Britain': in 1971 'possibly as many
as one in ten of the workforce learnt what it was like to lose a job'.[25]
But at present our measurement of unemployment is so limited that
we cannot say to what extent and in what ways insecurity has grown.

How much has the risk of unemployment increased across the
whole labour force? How much has the increase been concentrated
among certain groups who have experienced more and/or longer
periods out of work? These are central questions for any analysis of
unemployment and society, which would be answered, at least partially, by a measure of the proportion of the working population experiencing unemployment in the course of a year, similar to the
annual analysis in the United States. Over the last 15 years the annual
number of unemployed there – the average of the 12 monthly counts
– has been over 3 million, but the total number with any experience of
unemployment in the year has been around 13 million. This is about
one in eight of the labour force, a proportion some four times larger
than the average of the monthly counts. At the same time there have
been significant variations in the proportion with any unemployment
in the year at roughly similar levels of annual unemployment.
Analyses of this type, linked with better data on the occupational
incidence of unemployment, its duration and recurrence, would help

us to study much more precisely any changes in the distribution of unemployment across society.[26]

A major and valuable innovation beyond current American practice would be to collect data – in the General Household Survey, for example – on the amount of joblessness among the labour force members of a household in the course of a year.[27] Such evidence would be of considerable significance for assessing the impact of unemployment on different groups in society.

The Costs of Unemployment. The increased level of unemployment, and its greater duration, make it all the more important to measure the social and economic impact of joblessness on those experiencing it. In addition, the evidence of repeated unemployment underlines the need to study the burden of this over time and its effect on particularly vulnerable groups. Detailed analysis of the immediate effects, let alone any long-term ones, of being out of work for the individual and dependants is surprisingly limited; but there is general agreement any with the latest and most comprehensive survey by W. W. Daniel that the costs remain 'substantial for all groups'.[28]

The Three Towns survey found that 'the majority of the unemployed were living . . . on what can be described as no more than subsistence incomes . . . and a small group . . . fell seriously below the minimum levels prescribed by the Supplementary Benefits Commission.'[29] This conclusion deserves particular emphasis, given the considerable care 'not to exaggerate the numbers with incomes below supplementary benefits levels'[30] – what must appear from the view point of the unemployed as more than necessary caution. The safeguards taken to measure poverty 'in this very cautious and stringent way'[31] resulted in the exclusion of groups particularly prone to poverty, and yet in Coventry, Hammersmith and Newcastle 17–19 per cent of the households were getting more than £1 below their assessed supplementary benefits levels.[32]

Evidence of the generally low level of income of the majority of those unemployed for more than a few weeks is provided by the Family Expenditure Survey. In December 1972 some 120,000 heads of households who had been out of work at least three months were receiving incomes below their appropriate supplementary benefits level,[33] and this excluded the 220,000 recipients of supplementary benefits, whose standard of living will not have been very much higher.

Most surveys of the unemployed, however, have been confined to the redundant; and the government's own review of the effect of the Redundancy Payments Act concluded that 'generally speaking, redundant workers tend to lose income, pension rights, fringe benefits and job satisfaction as a consequence of changing jobs'.[34] The evidence of other studies indicates that there is less economic hardship for the redundant worker when the local demand for labour is high, although older and disabled workers are generally more likely to suffer income loss and longer unemployment. In areas of high unemployment these workers are still more vulnerable, and all those declared redundant seem less likely to return to work quickly and for as good or higher pay.[35] There is some suggestion that the redundant are liable to further unemployment but British studies have generally collected little data on later employment and unemployment experience.[36] American studies, however, have found this to be a particular hazard; especially when local labour demand is poor, the redundant worker may join those liable to recurrent unemployment.[37]

There are, however, some difficulties in comparing many of the redundancy studies with the Three Towns and North Shields surveys, for the former have tended to focus on the relative drop in income and to estimate the severity of financial hardship by the actual or percentage fall in resources. Such an approach tends to direct concern towards those who had the highest income in work, usually skilled, technical, or white-collar workers. The fact that lower-paid workers may be least able to cope with a reduction in their resources, however small, tends to have been overlooked. Unemployment may bring chronic poverty to an acute state, but the increase in measurable deprivation may be relatively small. There has also been a tendency to aggregate resources, and to neglect variation in the constancy and predictability of income and the effect of this added insecurity on the morale of the unemployed.

Finally, there is considerable variation in the detail with which the extent and nature of resources and hardship are measured and discussed; a review of the literature suggests that the greater the detail the more hardship is revealed. This in fact is not surprising; it is hard to measure the effects of unemployment on an individual and any dependants in one or even two interviews. In the North Shields study it was clear that men, and their families, played down the impact to a stranger while they remained out of work, but interviews after the return to work often revealed a much greater extent of insecurity, both economic and psychological.[38]

The North Shields study also suggested that more attention needs to be paid to distinct patterns in the variation of responses to questions about the impact of joblessness which, if undetected, may lead to conclusions particularly misleading for policy. The man suffering his first experience out of work, or the first for many years, presents a much sharper, much more detailed account of his experience of unemployment. This seemed particularly true of the redundant man in his first few months out of work; the sense of injustice and outrage was still raw, and there was often some eagerness to talk. By contrast, the man slowly becoming more vulnerable to frequent pay-offs – for example, the unskilled man in his forties – was very much more laconic; there was little new or different about this spell and if he returned to work he would be out again. The hardships were much more taken for granted and were rarely volunteered, particularly at the first interview. This also seemed to be characteristic of interviews with many of the long-term unemployed. Failure to detect these differences and to search for other indications than initially expressed attitudes may well lead to a distorted view of the burden and costs of unemployment.

In reviewing our knowledge of the impact of unemployment, it is necessary to emphasise the gaps, because they may well have serious implications for our understanding of the effects of being out of work on different groups in the labour force. Most of the studies have been confined to men made redundant and, although this is an important group, they are not likely to be a majority, even of unemployed men. The focus has tended to be on men with a few years' service at least – thus tending to exclude those liable to recurrent unemployment – and on men with skilled manual, technical and white-collar jobs in industry, and less on the unskilled and those outside manufacturing industry.

In addition, there appears to be a presumption of less need among women, despite their increased numbers in the labour force, the independent needs of the single woman, the importance of the married woman's wage for the whole family and, probably, a currently increasing proportion of women bringing up families by themselves. Even the studies which include women provide scant analysis of their position.[39] Youth too is neglected; the unemployed teenager has received less attention as a member of the labour force than as a 'social problem' in need of control or welfare.[40]

The lack of data on those who become unemployed in other ways than redundancy creates serious problems for both policy-making and its evaluation. The redundant man, more likely to be better paid and a union member, has for many reasons long been regarded as the most deserving of the unemployed, and his unemployment is more likely to be a public and political issue. These factors largely account for the fact that he is more likely to be the subject of a survey. It is not only technically easier to carry out such as study than one of a random population of people out of work in different ways, at different times and in different places, but it is also easier to obtain funds for the survey.

These comments are not by any means intended to diminish the importance of better knowledge of the experience and impact of redundancy, for there are an inadequate number of such studies too. The purpose is to draw attention to the partial picture of unemployment that is created. With very little data on the needs of other groups, the partial knowledge has the function of diminishing general understanding of the other unemployed, who have always tended to be seen as less deserving, while increasing public sympathy for the displaced worker. The history of policies for the unemployed in both Britain and the United States only serves to confirm these anxieties.

Income Maintenance for the Unemployed. Given the lack of adequate comprehensive data measuring the impact of unemployment amongst all the unemployed, examination of the data on the income maintenance schemes for the unemployed becomes even more important. It is surprising therefore that, with the exception of the Redundancy Payments Act, so little attention should have been given to this. The little information available is, when it is examined, not at all reassuring that the costs of unemployment are being efficiently or fairly picked up.

Well below half those registered as unemployed (44 per cent) have been drawing National Insurance unemployment benefit at the last four quarterly counts (ending February 1975). Just as many are receiving a supplementary allowance, almost a quarter of these in addition to the insurance benefit. Well over a fifth are not receiving either benefit, and to this group one might add the unknown number of people out of work but not registered as unemployed – on the basis of the General Household Survey in 1971 equivalent to one-third of the total registered.[41]

There has been a deterioration since the 1960s, but even so the figures have never been good. On average, little more than half the unemployed were receiving any National Insurance benefit at the quarterly counts from 1961 to 1970, and the official impression is that the picture had been much the same for many years before that. And an apparently unknown number are receiving reduced benefit. Even for men, the proportion receiving any insurance benefit at all was below three out of five before its recent decline, but women, single as well as married (many of whom do not pay the full insurance contribution), were less likely to be receiving benefit; and younger workers were worse off still.

This is not the place for a discussion of this failure of the National Insurance scheme, but, despite limited data, published and unpublished, one major factor is clearly the considerable extent of long-term unemployment. More than half the registered unemployed without National Insurance benefit have exhausted their full year's entitlement to benefit – for men the proportion has only twice been significantly below one-half since the figures for each May were first collected in 1961.

The rate of exhaustion is accelerated by the conjunction of repeated unemployment and the policy of linking in the same 'period of interruption of employment' any spells out of work separated by less than 13 weeks. For this reason, exhaustion of the full 12 months' benefit occurs on average less than nine months after the end of the last job; in Wales, Scotland, the North and the North West, the average benefit stops after six months.[42]

Earnings-related supplement can provide a substantial addition for the first six months, but less than one in five unemployed have been receiving it on the date of the May counts (nearly two in five of men with unemployment benefit). But, at best, less than half of those one might expect to be eligible seem to be receiving the supplement. One explanation could again be the combination of recent unemployment and the linking procedures. In addition, sickness or any other interruption of earnings in the previous tax year reduces the amount of the supplement, quite apart from the decline in its value as a result of inflation.[43]

In summary, those unemployed likely to have only very limited resources, that is those vulnerable to prolonged and/or recurrent unemployment, receive less protection from the National Insurance system. Similarly, the redundancy payments scheme provides no support to those with less than two years in a firm, and gives better benefits to those with longer service. These unemployed are therefore much more likely to have to apply for allowances from the Supplementary Benefits Commission because of the shortcomings and low basic benefits of National Insurance and their low or interrupted earnings in the past. Yet there is growing evidence that the proportion of unemployed eligible for a supplementary allowance but not receiving it is very large.[44]

In addition, over one in five men unemployed at the quarterly counts receive neither insurance benefit nor supplementary allowance and the proportion has not changed much since 1960. Among these in May 1973 were some 40,000 men – 8 per cent of all unemployed men – who had exhausted all their benefit but were not receiving supplementary allowance. Most were over 55 and some could be receiving occupational pensions or have wives in work, but still many would appear to have been eligible for benefit.[45]

The examination of income maintenance during unemployment is not, of course, enough. Any full analysis of the costs of unemployment needs to take into account the effect on others besides those actually unemployed. As well as those temporarily laid-off and expecting to be recalled and those working a shorter week, there are others whose overtime is reduced or stopped. While these indirect effects are not measured in such a way that one can see their impact on the social structure very clearly, the burden of any decrease in economic activity clearly falls on the working class. Those manual workers who have been able to obtain some protection for the security of their jobs may still have their earnings reduced by fewer hours of overtime or a cut-back to the guaranteed workweek.

RECURRENT UNEMPLOYMENT AND THE DUAL LABOUR MARKET

But, on the evidence so far available, the greatest costs would seem to be borne by the long-term unemployed and those recurrently out of work. While redundancy has received some consideration in the research, recurrent unemployment has been remarkably neglected. The next section, therefore, considers some suggestions that recurrent unemployment may be increasing, linked with the renewed debate about dual labour markets, particularly in the United States, which has produced much thought-provoking discussion in the last five years.

The basic issues were set out by Clark Kerr in two rather neglected papers in 1950 and 1954 when he discussed the trend in the United States 'unmistakably toward the institutional market'.[46] 'These institutional policies affect less importantly the number of jobs available and the adequacy of supply to match them than they do the selection of those workers to whom individual opportunities are open.' With remarkable foresight, he added that the institutional market 'is more likely to lack as a job distributing market than as a wage setting market, although it is the latter aspect which more often generates the greater concern'.[47]

There has been very little research in either Britain or the United States on the actual extent to which 'institutional rules . . . establish more boundaries between labor markets and make them more specific and harder to cross' as Clark Kerr claimed in 1954.[48] The impression is that these developments have occurred less in Britain, although some may have been established here for a longer time.[49]

But the recent development of internal labour markets, for example, appears to have reinforced some barriers to upward mobility. In the United States such changes have led to fresh debates about the extent to which dual or even tertiary labour markets have emerged, with a polarisation of the secure, stable and well paid sectors, and the insecure, poorly paid on the margins of the labour force.[50]

The very limited amount of research tends to support Kerr's hypothesis: 'the more secure are the "ins", the greater the penalty for being an "out" '.[51] In Britain, analysis of local labour markets provides evidence of these polarising factors excluding women from the securer and better-rewarded jobs;[52] and there has been some discussion of the youth labour market with its greater insecurity and poorer returns.[53]

Although some discussion has failed to distinguish between the extent to which the working of any secondary or irregular economy is itself helping to create a marginal underclass of workers, and the extent to which irregular and unstable jobs are rather a product of, and largely determined by, the general economy, there has been

slowly increasing recognition of the need to examine more carefully
those factors on the demand side of the market which help to maintain poor jobs with poor pay and have the effect of restricting certain
groups of workers to an insecure succession of jobs, deficient both in
immediate rewards and in long-term opportunities.

In a recent study of unemployed youth, it was concluded that
'frequent job changing seems to be essentially accepted by both
employers and employees . . . neither side expects employment to be
a permanent thing. Both sides need to show only a minimal commitment to a particular employment. . . . The pattern has benefits for
[both groups].'[54] The tactic of frequent job-changing may serve to
ease the boredom and constraints of the many dead-end jobs available to unskilled youth, but with high or increasing unemployment,
such 'games turn deadly'.[55]

An American study concluded that 'low wage employers have few
incentives to create a stable work force'.[56] In addition, larger companies may well come to depend on a supply of low skilled, marginal
workers. The combination of persistently high rates of unemployment and marked racial inequalities and discrimination may well lead
to greater polarisation in the United States. But in Europe there is
also some evidence that immigrant workers in particular may become
locked into a ' "transient underclass", which turns out to be not so
transient after all'.[57] A recent study of immigrant workers and the
class structure in Western Europe found that 'virtually every advanced capitalist country has a lower stratum, distinguished by race,
nationality, or other special characteristics, which carries out the
worst jobs and has the least desirable social conditions.'[58]

These developments are seen by some analysts as a 'natural'
outcome of the present state of capitalist societies. Just as it is
argued that more redundancies may be expected with increasing
technological change, proponents of the dual labour market see its
growth as 'likely to be closely connected with planning for increased
productivity characteristic of neo-capitalism, both in macro-economic terms and on the level of the individual corporation'.[59] The
need for long-term planning of the vital labour supply combines
with trade union pressures to bring in measures promoting the
welfare and loyalty of workers. 'Since this inevitability raises labour
costs, employers may be expected to attempt to isolate secondary
occupations in such a way as to complement their long-term labour

investment with a pool of highly "disposable" labour, in which a marked degree of labour turnover may be tolerated or even encouraged.'[60] This would mean an increase in recurrent unemployment concentrated among particular groups of workers.

The nature and extent of these developments are not at all clear at present, as we lack data that are both sufficiently comprehensive and sufficiently detailed to enable the different elements to be identified and traced. A central issue, of course, is whether there is a sharp division between separate labour markets, or whether it is more realistic to speak of a continuum. Further research seems particularly likely to increase our understanding of the nature and function of unemployment in Society, and this is especially important if any effort is to be made to reduce its impact and to compensate more fully the social costs that otherwise remain as private loss.

UNEMPLOYMENT AND POLICY

These analyses have important implications for economic and social policy. The main force of the argument is to shift the focus of discussion away from gross aggregate unemployment levels to a more detailed analysis of the different components of the total. This can only be illustrated briefly here. If the working of a market economy is seen to depend upon a certain level of job-changing, the diagram indicates how one may, theoretically at least, distinguish four types of job-changing, some of which may result in unemployment. In each case a plus sign (+) indicates a net benefit and a minus sign (−) a net cost.

	A	B	C	D
To the nation	+	+	−	−
To the individual	+	−	+	−

Category A includes the worker who moves of his own choice to a better job, and from an industry with redundancies to a growing industry with benefits to the nation, or a new entrant to the labour force going to such a job. Any period of unemployment would be brief, without any significant reduction in the individual's resources. Category B still involves a shift to a growing industry from a declining one, but the job would provide less reward or less security to the worker; or it would provide much the same return, but at the cost of a long and poorly compensated period out of work, or of a loss of important social relationships. Category C contains workers moving quickly, or with a very brief period of well-compensated unemployment, to a better job, but the move would be against the generally desired shift from declining to growing industries. Category D comprises the long-term unemployed, whether or not they are well-compensated (the cost being either social or private), the frequent job-changers, bringing no benefit to themselves or the economy, again whether or not they are well-compensated, and those who remain out of the labour force although they need a job.

Obviously the crude categorisation leaves many questions unresolved – particularly I think in categories B and C – but its use here is simply illustrative. A major objective of any mix of policies should, at the very least, be to reduce the amount of unemployment in category D and ensure that, if unemployment is necessary, it should be of category A. There would of course be considerable difficulties in measuring the amount of unemployment in each category with any degree of precision. Still, even the briefest analysis suggests that very little of the job-changing accompanied by unemployment in recent years is likely to fall into category A. Only one of the 92 unemployed interviewed in North Shields in 1963–4 would clearly have qualified for category A and the great majority fell equally clearly into category D.[61] The typical pattern of intermittent unemployment for youths interviewed in a northern city in the early 1970s is almost stereotypically D.[62]

This approach places a premium on policies to reduce the amount, length and recurrence of unemployment. It directs attention to securing the resources of those experiencing unemployment, not only in terms of better benefits and compensation but also by devising means to secure the additional benefits, such as pensions and other future resources, which are increasingly linked to particular jobs or employers. But in a market economy a certain level of unemployment has been regarded as essential for a variety of purposes, including the reduction of inflationary pressures, especially those resulting from wage demands or the simple growth of employment. Economic journalists have referred to views said to be current in Whitehall, particularly in the last Conservative government, on the use of unemployment to restrain trade unions from strikes and other industrial action.

Ironically this resurrection of unemployment as a class weapon 'in the national interest' may well lead to a more searching analysis of the political sociology of unemployment. Such a scrutiny would have to pay attention to any government's willingness to permit or maintain a higher level of unemployment than in the past, and then relate this to its attitude to increasing public debate about 'dole-dodging'. In the past such concern seems to have risen with low unemployment, the implication being that those remaining out of work were more likely to be doing so by choice; in recent years this concern has continued or even risen amid high or rising unemployment. Public concern over rising or high unemployment is likely to be moderated by the suggestion that much, or an increasing part, of this is not beyond the control of the individual. So the ways in which the issue of 'dole-dodging' is presented and promoted, and the part, conscious or unconscious, played in this by a whole range of groups, including politicians, civil servants and social scientists, warrants particular research.

*   *   *   *

If there has been any strength in the arguments of this paper, then unemployment is distinguished as one of the most important areas 'where the attempt of men consciously to control their own destinies clashes with social arrangements'.[63]

The arguments for the necessity of unemployment must be strong for a democratic society to accept knowingly such a price. The basic thesis of this paper has been that the full social effect of this unemployment is not recognised; in part because the burden falls unequally and as a private cost on the poorer and weaker sections of society, in part too because current measurement with its technical economic discussion, unaccompanied by any measurement of the social impact, has the effect of concealing the social significance of unemployment. The inequality and misery it creates could well lead us, if it were better understood, to ask whether the price of retaining our current social arrangements is worth paying.

NOTES

1 In preparing this paper I have been able to drawn on unpublished data and tables provided by the Department of Employment and the Department of Health and Social Security, and I would like to acknowledge their help in making these available. I also want to thank Mr Alan Walker and Mr Stephen

Winyard for giving their time to prepare some of the calculations, and those who gave me comments on the first draft, although I am, of course, entirely responsible for the use to which they have been put and for any errors or omissions.

2 Department of Employment, *Unemployment Statistics: Report of an Inter-Departmental Working Party*, Cmnd 5157, H.M.S.O., 1972, para. 1.2. For a valuable summary of the available data, see *Department of Employment Gazette*, March 1975, pp. 179–83.

3 R. M. Titmuss, *Commitment to Welfare*, George Allen & Unwin, 1968, p. 133. See also K. W. Kapp, *Social Costs of Business Enterprise*, Asia Publishing House, 1963, p. 203.

4 See A. R. Thatcher, Chapter 4 in this volume; Department of Employment, *Unemployment Statistics: Report of an Inter-Departmental Working Party*, United States President's Committee to Appraise Employment and Unemployment Statistics, *Measuring Employment and Unemployment*, U.S. Government Printing Office, 1962; N. Bosanquet and G. Standing, 'Government and Unemployment, 1966–1970: A Study of Policy and Evidence', *British Journal of Industrial Relations*, July 1972.

5 Elliot Liebow, 'No Man Can Live with the Terrible Knowledge that He is Not Needed', *New York Times Magazine*, 5th April 1970.

6 Bosanquet and Standing, 'Government and Unemployment, 1966–1970: A Study of Policy and Evidence'.

7 For a brief discussion, see *Department of Employment Gazette*, March 1974, pp. 222–7.

8 *Department of Employment Gazette*, March 1973, Table 3, p. 254.

9 See, for example, Constance Sorrentino, 'Unemployment in the United States and Seven Foreign Countries', *Monthly Labor Review*, September 1970, p. 17, where only Japan and West Germany have much the same differential as the United Kingdom.

10 P. Townsend, 'The Older Worker in the United Kingdom' in *Elderly People Living in Europe*, International Centre for Social Gerontology, 1972, p. 194.

11 Dorothy Wedderburn, 'Inequality at Work' in P. Townsend and N. Bosanquet (eds), *Labour and Inequality*, Fabian Society, 1972.

12 Liebow, 'No Man Can Live with the Terrible Knowledge that He is Not Needed'.

13 David Lockwood, *The Blackcoated Worker*, George Allen & Unwin, 1958, p. 55, referring to *The Proletariat*, 1937.

14 Department of Employment and Productivity, *Labour Costs in Great Britain in 1964*, H.M.S.O., 1968; Industrial Society, *The £.s.d. of Welfare in Industry*, 1958 and *Costs of Personnel Services and Administration, 1968*; A. Sinfield, 'Industrial Welfare in the United Kingdom' (report to the United Nations, 1970).

15 W. H. Beveridge, *Full Employment in a Free Society*, George Allen & Unwin, 1944, p. 18.

16 *Department of Employment Gazette*, February 1973, p. 111.

17 O.E.C.D. Directorate of Manpower and Social Affairs, *The Long-term Unemployed* by Adrian Sinfield, 1968, p. 26.

18 O.E.C.D., *The Long-term Unemployed*, pp. 44–6.

19 *Department of Employment Gazette*, March 1974, p. 216.

20 W. W. Daniel, *A National Survey of the Unemployed*, Political and Economic Planning, 1974, p. 16.

21 Unpublished data from the inquiry of 1964. For data on unemployment over a whole working career, see M. J. Hill, 'Unstable Employment in the Histories of Unemployed Men', *I.M.S. Monitor*, December 1974.
22 Adrian Sinfield, 'Poor and Out of Work in Shields: A Summary Report' in P. Townsend (ed.), *The Concept of Poverty*, Heinemann, 1970.
23 M. J. Hill, R. M. Harrison, A. V. Sargeant and V. Talbot, *Men Out of Work: A Study of Unemployment in Three English Towns*, Cambridge University Press, 1973, p. 72.
24 D. Phillips, 'Young and Unemployed in a Northern City' in D. Weir (ed.), *Men and Work in Modern Britain*, Fontana, 1973, p. 413.
25 D. Wedderburn, 'Working and Not Working' in Weir (ed.), *Men and Work in Modern Britain*, p. 420.
26 Hyman Kaitz, 'The Duration of Unemployment', *Proceedings of the American Statistical Association, 1972* and 'Unemployment Issues – Unemployment Flows' (unpublished, 1974).
27 This question has been added to the General Household Survey from July 1974 onwards.
28 *A National Survey of the Unemployed*, p. 149.
29 Hill *et al.*, *Men Out of Work*, p. 139.
30 Ibid., p. 83.
31 Ibid., p. 84.
32 Ibid., p. 85.
33 *Hansard, Written Answers to Questions*, 20th May 1974, cols 45–8.
34 Department of Employment, *Effects of the Redundancy Payments Act. A Survey carried out in 1969 for the Department of Employment* by S. R. Parker *et al.*, H.M.S.O., 1971, p. 7.
35 Dorothy Wedderburn, *White Collar Redundancy: A Case Study*, Cambridge University Press, 1964, *Redundancy and the Railwaymen*, Cambridge University Press, 1965 and 'Inequality at Work' in Townsend and Bosanquet (eds), *Labour and Inequality*; J. W. House and E. M. Knight, *Pit Closure and the Community: Report to the Ministry of Labour*, University of Newcastle, 1967; E. M. Knight, *Men Leaving Mining, West Cumberland 1966–67: Report to the Ministry of Labour*, University of Newcastle, 1968; B. M. Thomas, 'Redundancy among Aircraft Workers: the Fragmentation of a Work Community' (report to the Social Science Research Council, 1972); R. Martin and R. H. Fryer, *Redundancy and Paternalist Capitalism*, George Allen & Unwin, 1973.
36 But see for support, Department of Employment, *Effects of the Redundancy Payments Act*.
37 For a discussion of some of the data, see O.E.C.D., *The Long-term Unemployed*, p. 42.
38 Sinfield, 'Poor and Out of Work in Shields', pp. 227–30; also Dennis Marsden and Euan Duff, *Workless*, Penguin, 1975.
39 For example, Daniel, *A National Survey of the Unemployed*; Department of Employment, *Effects of the Redundancy Payments Act*.
40 But see Phillips, 'Young and Unemployed in a Northern City'; Michael Carter, *Into Work*, Penguin, 1966 and, for references to other surveys, A. Sinfield, 'Shortcomings in the Functioning of the Labour Market' (paper presented to an O.E.C.D. Regional Seminar on Youth Unemployment, 1970).
41 Office of Population Censuses and Surveys, *General Household Survey: Introductory Report*, H.M.S.O., 1973, p. 207.

246   INVOLUNTARY UNEMPLOYMENT

42 My estimate, based on data for May 1973.

43 For a more detailed analysis, see Adrian Sinfield, 'Unemployment Compensation and Employment Security' (paper presented to a Fabian Society seminar, 1972).

44 As many as one in three of those out of work for at least three months in December 1972 (my calculation based on *Hansard, Written Answers to Questions*, 20th May 1974, cols *45–8*). See also Frank Field, *Unemployment: the Facts*, Child Poverty Action Group, 1975.

45 Some support for this view is provided by the 1973 inquiry (*Department of Employment Gazette*, March 1974, p. 220, Table 8). The majority of them would appear to be very poorly off, with little hope of the little known but generous service contracts that some directors and senior executives have been able to obtain, guaranteeing annual salaries for many years, whether employment with the company continues or not (see Sinfield, 'Unemployment Compensation and Employment Security').

46 Clark Kerr, 'Labor Markets: Their Character and Consequences', *American Economic Association Papers and Proceedings*, May 1950, p. 291.

47 Ibid., pp. 290–1.

48 Clark Kerr, 'The Balkanization of Labor Markets' in Massachusetts Institute of Technology, *Labor Mobility and Economic Opportunity*, Chapman and Hall, 1954, p. 109.

49 See, for example, E. P. Thompson and Eileen Yeo, *The Unknown Mayhew*, Merlin Press, 1971, p. 71, on Mayhew's distinction between 'honourable' and 'dishonourable' trades.

50 See particularly, L. A. Ferman, 'The Irregular Economy: Informal Work Patterns in the Ghetto' (mimeographed, 1967): B. Bluestone, 'The Tripartite Economy: Labor Markets and the Working Poor', *Poverty and Human Resources Abstracts*, July/August 1970; P. B. Doeringer and M. Piore, *Internal Labor Markets and Manpower Analysis*, D. C. Heath, 1971; D. M. Gordon, *Theories of Poverty and Underemployment: Orthodox, Radical and Dual Labor Market Perspectives*, D. C. Heath, 1972.

51 Kerr, 'The Balkanization of Labor Markets', p. 105.

52 R. D. Barron and G. M. Norris, 'Sexual Divisions and the Dual Labour Market' (paper presented to the British Sociological Association Conference, April 1974).

53 N. Bosanquet and P. Doeringer, 'Is There a Dual Labour Market in Great Britain?', *Economic Journal*, June 1973; N. Bosanquet, *Race and Employment in Britain*, Runnymede Trust, 1973.

54 Phillips, 'Young and Unemployed in a Northern City', pp. 413 and 417.

55 Ibid., p. 416.

56 P. B. Doeringer, *Program to Employ the Disadvantaged*, Prentice-Hall, 1969, p. 16.

57 Anthony Giddens, *The Class Structure of the Advanced Societies*, Hutchinson, 1973, p. 220.

58 S. Castles and G. Kosack, *Immigrant Workers and Class Structure in Western Europe*, Oxford University Press, 1973, p. 2.

59 Giddens, *The Class Structure of the Advanced Societies*, p. 220.

60 Ibid.

61 Sinfield, 'Poor and Out of Work in Shields'.

62 Phillips, 'Young and Unemployed in a Northern City'.

63 Richard Hyman, *Strikes*, Fontana, 1972, p. 10.

Part IV

ECONOMIC POLICY AND UNEMPLOYMENT

Chapter 13

Full Employment Policy: a Reappraisal[1]

S. BRITTAN

THE RECORD

This is a particularly appropriate year for a conference of this kind, as it sees the 30th anniversary (in May) of the publication by the coalition government of the White Paper, *Employment Policy*.[2] For the first time in our history a British government accepted as one of its 'primary aims and responsibilities' the maintenance of a 'high and stable level of employment'.

How successfully have the aims been achieved? Judging the period as a whole, the answer is: far more successfully than any would have dared hope at the time. Yet, if one examines developments within these 30 years, the degree of success has tended to decline with time if measured by the conventional indicators, and the costs and difficulties of that success have tended to increase.

The record from the beginning of the present series of unemployment figures in July 1948 to the end of 1973 is shown in Table 13.1. It is illustrated in slightly different form, and for a somewhat shorter period in a Department of Employment chart reproduced as Figure 13.1. Rough estimates of unemployment as far back as the mid-19th century were given in a chart in the White Paper,[3] from which several points are immediately apparent. The post-war record is an enormous improvement on inter-war experience, when unemployment ranged from 10 to well over 20 per cent. Nevertheless, within a broad range of what might be regarded by historical standards as reasonably full employment, the tendency has been for unemployment percentages to move upwards. If we concentrate on peaks, the upward movement is a gradual one until the sudden jump in the cycle of 1968–72. If we

250   INVOLUNTARY UNEMPLOYMENT

Table 13.1. *Troughs and peaks in unemployment rates^a for Great
Britain since July 1948*

	Percentages	
	Trough	Peak
June 1951	1·0	
November 1952		1·7
December 1957	0·9	
November 1958		2·1
March 1961	1·3	
March 1963		2·4
March 1966	1·2	
June 1968		2·4
May 1969	2·2	
March 1972		3·9
December 1973	2·1	

Source: Department of Employment.
^aWholly unemployed excluding school-leavers and adult students (seasonally
adjusted) as a proportion of total employed.

look at troughs, we notice a just discernible upward creep until 1966
and then a noticeable leap to 1969. In summary, unemployment was
gradually climbing in the 1950s and 1960s and seems to have made a
quantum jump from about 1966–8.

The evidence of a gradual long-term upward creep in measured
unemployment levels and intensities is by no means confined to the
United Kingdom; it is apparent in most industrial countries. The
O.E.C.D. has estimated that, at the end of 1972, the unemployment
rate in a sample of advanced industrial countries was about one
percentage point above the rate prevailing at a similar stage of the
previous business cycle.[4] In some places this can be traced at least
partially to changes in the composition of the labour force, greater
structural problems, or the increased availability of benefits (as in
Canada and the Netherlands). Another more tentative possibility
mentioned by O.E.C.D. is that the 'acceleration of wages' (presumably real wages) 'encouraged the substitution of capital for labour'.
Experience in the Netherlands is said to be consistent with a substitution of capital for labour over the previous cycle, or with a shortage
of capital relative to the available labour supply. A similar possibility
is entertained, although with more scepticism, for the United
Kingdom.

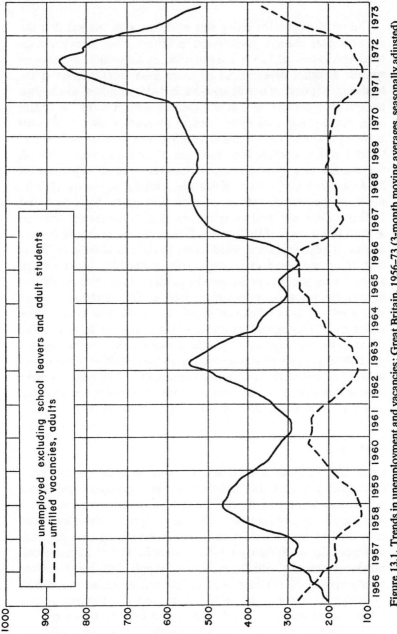

Figure 13.1. Trends in unemployment and vacancies: Great Britain, 1956–73 (3-month moving averages, seasonally adjusted)
Source: *Department of Employment Gazette*, December 1973.

The main reason for citing this evidence is to suggest that the recent secular unemployment trend in Britain is not merely a parochial phenomenon, but is symptomatic of something more widespread. Another development of more than local interest is the tendency, not only of unemployment, but also of prices, to rise over periods long enough to iron out cyclical influences. In the British case, retail prices rose by an annual average of over 5 per cent between 1948 and 1953, a phase covering both the Korean War and the removal of wartime food subsidies. Over the 14 years 1953–67, the average rate of price increase hovered around an average of $3\frac{1}{2}$–4 per cent per annum. Since then, taking the years 1967–73 together, the average rate of inflation shot up to 7 per cent, and British readers will need no reminding that it was accelerating fast in the last few years of this period. This escalation cannot be blamed on the oil-price explosion, which came too late to affect the calculation. Nor can it be explained away by the 1967 and 1972 devaluations, as there were also very pronounced escalations in the rate of inflation in countries whose currencies appreciated or did not change (and we thus need not pursue the question of what made these devaluations necessary). The popular scapegoat of the sharp rise in commodity prices in 1972–3 is not a sufficient explanation either, as the earnings per unit of primary producers are themselves sensitive to the rise of money incomes in the industrial countries. O.E.C.D. statistics make it clear that the 1972–3 upsurge of commodity prices was preceded by a long-term acceleration of industrial unit labour costs.

EXPLANATIONS

Confirmed institutionalists have, of course, been delighted to draw the conclusion that the behaviour of money-wages – and hence prices – has nothing to do with the state of the labour market. This would make the labour market of the last few years truly unique, both compared to other markets and compared to other periods. Such assertions derive (a) from a too hasty identification of official unemployment statistics with the balance of supply and demand in the labour market and (b) from neglect of the *ceteris paribus* clause in all properly formulated statements of the relation between money prices, on the one hand, and demand and supply, on the other.

The real difficulty has not been in explaining the tendency for unemployment statistics to rise while wage–price inflation has been accelerating, but to discriminate between a number of plausible explanations. The following are the three most credible hypotheses:

(i) Unemployment statistics have changed their significance as a labour-market indicator, so that a jobless rate of x per cent in 1973 did not have the same significance as in 1963 or in 1953.

(ii) Lower post-war levels of unemployment were associated with a degree of shortage of labour likely to cause an accelerating inflation once 'money illusion' was shed and people began to bargain and make contracts in real terms. This has now happened.

(iii) A greater use by unions of their monopoly power has raised the minimum sustainable rate of unemployment and/or worsened the inflationary implications of any given unemployment rate.

These hypotheses are not incompatible, and my own view is that they need to be taken together to explain what has been happening. If this is thought to be backing all the horses in sight, I can only reply that there are too many horses in the field, all alive and kicking.

But there is one hypothesis which I would rule out of court: that is that unemployment rose because of a lack of governmental zeal in stimulating aggregate demand sufficiently. Although there were occasional 'stops', imposed because of fears about sterling and the balance of payments, these were reversed once symptoms of recession appeared. The policy record up to 1973 showed on balance an increased rather than a diminished readiness to give employment priority in fiscal and monetary policy. One sign of this was that the last vestigial inhibitions about maintaining exchange parities or balancing the budget were shed in the course of the 1960s and early 1970s. There was also an increased readiness to shore up loss-making industries and firms to prevent micro-unemployment, and an increased amount of regional aid. Of course the stimuli were regarded by some as inadequate. If anyone believes that a still larger growth in the money supply and in public sector borrowing would have enabled the United Kingdom to regain and maintain the 1 per cent unemployment rate of the best years of the early 1950s, the proposition is unfalsifiable; but unlike some unfalsifiable theories, I am unable to take this one seriously.

INVOLUNTARY UNEMPLOYMENT

UNEMPLOYMENT AS AN INDICATOR

The least disputable of the three hypotheses is that unemployment changed its significance as a labour-market indicator between the early 1960s and the early 1970s. This was very apparent in 1973, when the total of wholly unemployed averaged 2·7 per cent, or 2·6 per cent excluding school-leavers and students. Such percentages would have signified a major recession a decade previously. Yet, quite early on in the year, the economy ran into labour shortages and supply bottlenecks. The Confederation of British Industry reported a level of capacity operations equivalent to the previous period of peak 'overheating' in 1964–5, and the level of unfilled vacancies for the year as a whole was by far the highest ever recorded.

The change in the relation of registered vacancies to registered unemployment was a genuine one. The view that it largely reflects an improvement in the official employment services has been effectively rebutted for the period in question both by the paper earlier in this volume by J. K. Bowers[5] and by the Department of Employment's own explanations of the nature and timing of its reforms. A special study carried out for the Department in September 1973 of 34 companies in seven areas,[6] biased towards those of above average unemployment, showed that 'companies in general undoubtedly believed that there was a labour shortage', which was becoming more severe. Moreover the Department of Employment data on vacancies substantially under-estimated the vacancies in the companies concerned – only some 32 per cent of the latter being notified to employment exchanges.

Why should a given state of the labour market have become associated with a higher unemployment percentage? There is much anecdotal evidence that a higher proportion of the unemployment was of a semi-voluntary nature. The most obvious causes of an increase in such unemployment – whether devoted to 'job search', leisure, or an indeterminate mixture of the two – were the introduction of redundancy payments in December 1965 and the earnings-related supplement to unemployment benefit in October 1966. These extra benefits make it easier for an unemployed worker to spend longer searching for a good job offer than before, and this increased search activity may well be socially desirable, despite its effect on the unemployment totals. Professor Martin Feldstein has cited a study suggesting that each £1 added to weekly unemployment benefits (in pounds of constant value) tends to increase the length of unemployment by half a week.[7]

Suggestions of this kind have generated an astonishing amount of hostility. While I would not claim that the influence of redundancy pay and earnings-related unemployment benefit has been conclusively established, much of the evidence cited on the other side does not withstand critical scrutiny. It is, for example, no refutation whatever to cite survey data, such as that described by Michael Hill in this volume, showing that men receiving the earnings-related supplement do not stay out of work longer than those who do. As Hill himself stresses, people are not entitled to the supplement for the sort of reasons, such as very low earnings or irregular employment, which also make them unattractive to prospective employers. A cross-section study cannot show the effects over time of the introduction of new benefits for comparable groups of people.[8]

The most plausible conclusion is that of Cheshire: that if the new benefits made a difference 'they did not do so all at once, but over a period of years; also they operated either at rather different rates in different regions, or to the accompaniment of influences peculiar to particular regions that in varying degrees masked or accentuated their effects.'[9]

The above interpretation is reinforced when it is remembered that earnings-related benefit and redundancy pay have not been the only subsidies to job search or voluntary unemployment between jobs. At least as important has probably been the increase in standard social security benefits. This could help to explain the increase in medium- and long-term jobless, who are unlikely to be affected by any form of severance pay. The supplementary benefit level for a three-child family in 1967–70 was officially estimated to represent about 68 per cent of the average disposable income while at work (and net of housing costs) of male manual employees. This represents a notable increase compared with 1954–60, when supplementary benefits represented only about 55 per cent of average earnings.[10] Again, the improvements were thoroughly justified, but it would be contrary to all experience if this did not reduce the initiative to seek work of those with limited earning prospects. As the Fisher Committee remarked: 'It is undeniable that for some unskilled men, particularly those with families, the financial incentive to work rather than to rely on benefits is slight.'[11] A related influence, higher up the skill ladder, has probably been the increased involvement of manual workers with a cumulative P.A.Y.E. system, which provides a cushion of repayments for those who lose or leave their jobs.

One should not avoid mentioning those falsely claiming to be unemployed. The Fisher Committee was satisfied that 'non-disclosure of regular and substantial earnings' occurred to a substantial extent.[12] The Committee gave a whole list of occupations, ranging alphabetically from building site work to window cleaning, which offered most scope for 'concealed self employment or working without a card'. For such fraudulent claims to make a difference to the interpretation of the unemployment trend, it is of course necessary that their number should have increased. There are many reasons to suspect that it has, the most notable of which has been the rise of the 'lump' of self-employed builders contracting to large concerns.[13] No doubt the original motive to keep quiet about employment arose from the desire to avoid income tax, National Insurance contributions and (in the employers' case) S.E.T. But once this happened, there was a strong temptation to claim some dole into the bargain. John Wood has put the number of 'falsely unemployed' at about 100,000. The figure can, of course, be no more than an informed guess, based partly on the fact that around this number were unemployed in construction alone during the period 1970–3, even when labour was notoriously scarce in that industry. It would be simply ostrich-like to treat as non-existent a phenomenon which is common knowledge merely because a good statistical estimate does not exist.

The reasons so far suggested for the changing significance of registered unemployment come from the supply side of the labour market. But there have almost certainly been influences on the demand side as well. Registered unemployment is, as Jim Taylor points out in Chapter 8, only a part of the reserve of unused, or under-used labour available in a normal peacetime economy.[14] A better approximation is to say that this reserve consists of registered unemployed, unregistered unemployed and nominally employed (but actually hoarded) labour. If labour hoarding in times of recession has declined, one would expect to see more violent cyclical swings in registered unemployment for a given amplitude of fluctuation in output, and there was evidence of this both in the 1971–2 recession and in the 1972–3 upswing. Moreover, if there is now less hoarding in a recession and no more in a boom period than in the past, there will be less hoarding over the average of the cycle. Thus any particular degree of slack in the labour market will be associated with more registered unemployed than in the past.[15]

There remains the question whether there have been shifts of a structural kind, making it more difficult to match the available supply of labour to the demand; the National Institute has made considerable efforts to find such shifts, but has been unable to discover them. It might be possible to treat the shift against manufacturing in the 1972–3 upswing, mentioned by Bowers, as such a structural change. The biggest shifts of a structural kind may well, however, have not been in geographical or industrial composition, but in the mix of skills required, which may have changed more rapidly than in the past. This is suggested by the increase in older and long-term unemployed as a proportion of the registered jobless; and it is supported by Jim Taylor's calculation in Chapter 8 that 'frictional' unemployment rose from around zero in the second half of the 1950s to around 2 per cent in 1972.

A VIEW OF THE LABOUR MARKET

Despite the many possible reasons for the changed significance of registered unemployment as a labour-market indicator, I doubt very much if the secular upward movement shown by the figures is *all* a statistical illusion. There is also the evidence from other countries (although their unemployment statistics too have been subject in varying degrees to distortions similar to those which have affected the British ones). Above all there is the combination of the increase in both unemployment and inflation rates to explain. No-one would, I imagine, try to do so by claiming that the true secular trend of unemployment has actually been downwards.

If one is to come to grips with this conjunction of events, it is necessary to move away from discussion of particular statistical indicators, and to put forward some provisional overall view of the labour market and its relation to unemployment and inflation. It does not help to say that the problem of rising rates of both unemployment and inflation is an international one, as this tells us nothing about causation. What is sometimes meant by saying this is that the problem of increasing rates of inflation is due largely to the international financial mechanism and has little to do with labour markets. To explain fully why this is unconvincing would be to take one too far outside the scope of this paper (and this volume). The role of the international financial system has, in my view, been mainly a permissive one, allowing internally generated inflationary impulses to work themselves out without too much external constraint; and, to the extent that inflation rates in different countries have been harmonised directly rather than via exchange rates, it is the less inflationary countries that have adjusted upwards rather than the other way round.

If the labour market is indeed central to the understanding of 'stagflation', where better to begin than with an analysis of 'involuntary unemployment'? Lord Kahn's fascinating paper reveals the paradox that, despite the central role of 'involuntary unemployment' in the structure of the *General Theory*, the concept was hardly discussed by Keynes' associates at Cambridge and played no role in his own analysis of actual problems. The categories Keynes actually used in, for example, a 1942 Treasury Paper, were (a) the 'unemployables', (b) the seasonally out of work, (c) transitional unemployment and (d) structural and regional unemployment. The remainder he ascribed to 'a deficiency in the aggregate demand for labour'.[16]

The distinction between voluntary and involuntary unemployment is a 'micro' concept, applicable to the individual, and is a matter of degree. Keynes' 'involuntary unemployment' is far better labelled 'demand deficiency unemployment'. He quite clearly had in mind the kind of unemployment that could be cured by what he called in his 1937 *Times* article 'a general stimulus at the centre'. Presumably, the reason for his earlier insistence on the term 'involuntary unemployment' was to emphasise that demand deficiency could be an equilibrium condition – a doctrinal point which, to put it mildly, no longer seems very pressing.

It seems entirely consistent with Keynes' own approach to policy, as cited in Lord Kahn's paper, to insist that there is something like a minimum rate or range of unemployment, which cannot be permanently reduced by stimulating total demand and which must be treated by other methods.

There are, of course, numerous alternative ways of subdividing non-demand deficiency unemployment. But we face the problem which has turned up in several papers in this volume that, whatever categories we use, their size varies with the overall state of the economy. The number of people experiencing unemployment of the transitional (or search), structural and regional varieties, and even the 'unemployables' and the 'falsely unemployed', moves up and down with the trade cycle.

We can break out of this circle if we say that demand deficiency is absent when unemployment has been brought down to the minimum level that is sustainable by monetary and fiscal policy (supported if necessary by exchange rate policy). Of course every variety of unemployment can be brought down during a boom, but this may well be a temporary improvement bought at the expense of abnormally severe levels during the next downturn.[17]

Such a definition of demand deficiency is helpful in its own right; it also makes sense of Keynes' repeated estimate of 800,000 or 6–7 per cent as the normal level of unemployment for which to plan (which would be well over a million with today's labour force and on today's definitions) and his advice in 1937, when unemployment was still over 10 per cent, not to stimulate the economy further but to rely on *ad hoc* measures for the 'distressed regions'.

Seen in this light, Keynes' idea of the level of unemployment which would exist without demand deficiency seems astonishingly similar to Milton Friedman's 'natural' rate of unemployment.[18] I do not wish to overdo the comparison. Friedman sees the economy as essentially self-adjusting if only politicians would put it on an automatic pilot and then leave it alone, while Keynes saw it as inherently unstable and in constant need of deliberate adjustment. But there is a similarity on the goal of the adjustment process.

It is unfortunate, however, that the minimum sustainable unemployment rate should have been labelled by Friedman the 'natural' rate, as there is nothing natural (let alone optimal) about it. It will depend on the efficiency of labour exchanges and other employment agencies, the pace of change in skills demanded, the availability of re-training facilities and the use made of them. It will depend on the geographical balance between areas where work is available and where the unemployed live, and on the willingness of the unemployed to move to different, lower-paid or geographically distant jobs. It will also depend, as explained in the next sections, on the extent of union power and the uses made of it. Thus the minimum sustainable rate is not given in heaven and can be influenced by

260   INVOLUNTARY UNEMPLOYMENT

labour-market policies. The point is that it cannot be changed simply
by injecting more spending power into the economy.

The original Phillips curve, which suggested a trade-off between
unemployment and the rate of increase of money-wages, took no
account of the effect of changing price expectations. But it is, of
course, likely that both workers and employers will take rising prices
more and more into account in their bargaining as time goes on. An
unemployment percentage which might have led to a 5 per cent
annual increase in money-wages in conditions of price stability will,
once expectations have been adjusted, lead to an 8 per cent increase
when prices are rising by 3 per cent. But that, of course, is not the
end of the story. An 8 per cent increase in wages is seen to be more
inflationary than a 5 per cent one and thus expectations of a still
more rapid rise in prices and wage settlements become embedded in
the system.

Such reasoning suggests that there is a family of short-term Phillips
curves corresponding to different rates of inflation. If an attempt is
made to push unemployment below the sustainable minimum, we
shall, on this view, obtain not just inflation, but accelerating inflation.
The best known attempt to formulate this picture is the vertical long-
run Phillips curve associated with Friedman and Phelps. This
assumes there is one rate of unemployment (everything else being
equal), associated not necessarily with price stability but with any
constant rate of inflation. The long-run effect of expansionary monetary or fiscal policies is thus almost entirely on the price level and not
on the level of output or employment.

This analysis points in the right direction. The real surprise is not
that the original sloping Phillips curve should have collapsed in the
face of rising inflation in the late 1960s, but that it should have
performed so well for as long as it did. Why, it may be asked,
were we able to combine a rate of inflation averaging 3–4 per
cent with exceptionally low unemployment for so long? It can
either be argued that union leaders refrained from exercising their
full market power, or that they or others were fooled for a long
time by money illusion and accepted wage increases without applying
a full inflationary discount. The two factors were, of course, inter-
connected. The compromise lasted as long as it did after the second
world war partly because various groups, such as those living on fixed
incomes, white-collar workers, professional groups and the lower

paid, either failed to organise, or (as in the case of holders of fixed interest paper) allowed themselves to be deceived. Once these other groups began to realise what was happening and acted in self-defence, the situation became explosive.

Nevertheless, a simple vertical long-run Phillips curve, although an improvement on its predecessor, does not in my view capture all the major forces at work. In the first place, it is only necessary to assume that the long-run Phillips curve is steeper than the short-term one to generate the policy dilemmas and events of recent years. It is not necessary to assume that it is strictly vertical. Even on the steeper assumption, a large part of the effects of a demand boost which takes unemployment much below the minimum range is temporary, and the authorities then have to choose between allowing unemployment to rise again and witnessing an accelerating rate of inflation. It is only possible to deny that there is a long-run Phillips curve steeper than the short-run one if either it is denied that the state of the labour market has any effect on wages, or it is believed that workers are fooled indefinitely by higher money-wage increases which are eroded by inflation. Both assertions border on the fantastic.

Secondly, there is a sense in which Friedman and Phelps understate their own case. The Phillips curve, long-run or short-run, is simply a relation between unemployment and wages, with time not appearing as an explicit variable. If unemployment is held down at a level which generates accelerating inflation, may not the rate of acceleration itself be projected into the future, and even the rate of acceleration of the acceleration?

Thirdly, and most important of all, there is an asymmetry between reactions to demand stimulation and to demand restriction. While a boost to demand when unemployment is already as low as feasible will, in current conditions, push up the rate of inflation fairly quickly, the main effect of demand restraints is likely to be an increase in unemployment above the sustainable minimum. Any effect in reducing the rate of inflation is likely to be slow and modest. Thus, it is tempting to say that, for practical purposes, there is a minimum rate of inflation as well as of unemployment.

For some time I have been accustomed to formalise the picture in the L-shaped long-run Phillips curve (PP') shown in Figure 13.2, in which W is the rate of increase of money-wages, U the unemployment rate and the point X the current position of the economy. (It is

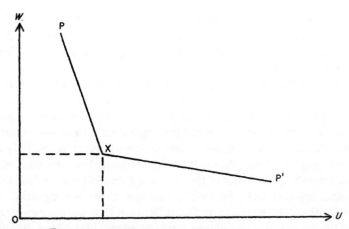

Figure 13.2. The L-shaped Phillips curve
Note: W = percentage increase in money-wages; U = unemployment rate.

possible to substitute for unemployment any other variable believed to be a better labour-market indicator. Alternatively, the diagram can be taken to refer to a hypothetical period during which registered unemployment retains its reliability as a measure). Points on the near-horizontal stretch of the curve to the right of X represent positions of demand deficiency. If we are starting at X, the main effect of restrictive demand policies will be to produce unemployment above the feasible minimum, with little beneficial effect on inflation. The main effect of boosting demand, on the other hand, will be to increase the rate of wage-inflation, with very little lasting benefit to employment.

It is often said that the influence on inflationary pressure of the rate of change of unemployment is more important than its absolute level, and also that a lower unemployment rate could be sustained if it were approached more gradually than in the past. Both these contentions are convincing, at least within a certain range. But their practical value is not very great unless there is any reason to think that the authorities are likely to find a way of managing demand in the labour market in a less jerky way than in the past. This is not all. For, however important the speed and amplitude of the oscillations, the level of unemployment around which the fluctuations are taking place must surely make some difference. The unemployment variable in Figure 13.2 can, if desired, be regarded as showing the effects of unemployment fluctuating around different average levels.

There are obviously problems about the construction. The downward rigidity of the rate of increase of money-wages means that the sharp corner at X will itself shift upwards if inflationary policies are being pursued. Moreover, if we are not economic determinists and allow the politics of government–union relations to affect the issue, the movements of X can be quite violent and sudden. The minimum unemployment rate also shifts with structural and institutional changes in the labour market, and with changes in union power and policy. A long-run curve which can itself shift quickly in the short run is not the most comfortable of constructions. It is not possible to get away from it entirely, but for some purposes, it is possible to simplify the problem. This can be done by laying down rules for the behaviour of the system *so long as it operates below the sustainable minimum unemployment point or range.*

(i) If aggregate demand is restrained sufficiently to stabilise (not eliminate) wage-inflation, unemployment will increase.
(ii) If demand is managed in such a way as to hold the level of unemployment constant, wages (and hence prices) will increase indefinitely, and at an accelerating rate.

If employment targets have been over-ambitious (in relation to other policies and the institutional structure) then one would expect either (a) an acceleration of price-inflation, or (b) a retreat towards higher levels of unemployment, or (c) a mixture of the two. We have, of course, had (c).

The process is illustrated in Figure 13.3. We start at point A, with the authorities alarmed by the effects of inflation (quite probably in the guise of a balance of payments problem). They tighten up enough to stabilise the rate of increase of money-wages and unemployment increases to point B. At this point they take fright and decide to stabilise unemployment instead,[19] and the rate of wage increases starts rising again to point C, where halting the acceleration of the inflation again acquires priority.

As far as unemployment is concerned, there is an end to the secular rise if and when a point on the long-run Phillips curve is reached (D on the diagram). But this is not necessarily the limit to inflationary escalation. The authorities will not know when they have hit the long-run Phillips curve; nor will economists be able to tell them,

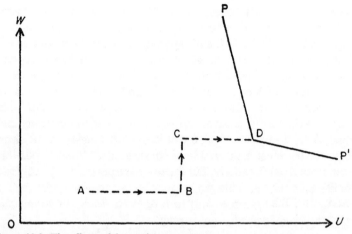

Figure 13.3. The effects of demand management
Note: W = percentage increase in money-wages; U = unemployment rate.

because they do not know where it is, even if they believe it exists. But what will be apparent to them is that unemployment at D is embarrassingly high by past standards. They will, therefore, be tempted to boost employment, which they will be able to do for a while, at the expense of a still faster rate of inflation. Thus by a series of zig-zag movements, they will be climbing upwards along the long-term Phillips curve to ever higher rates of inflation. There will be a sort of perverse learning process here, as people become accustomed to faster rates of inflation and eventually become prepared to tolerate rates of monetary depreciation which would have been 'politically impossible' to contemplate in the initial stages.

The one crumb of comfort is the finding that, once a Latin American state of very rapid and volatile inflation is reached, the end results of demand stimulation are so well known and so quickly discounted that their entire effect is on the rate of inflation and there is not even a temporary boost to real output and employment.[20]

The alternative to letting the Latin American solution take its course is to recognise that the unemployment percentage cannot be determined at a pre-ordained level by demand management policies, and that targets which remain unchanged for long periods are to be avoided. The shift of the pendulum, from the view at the end of the second world war that a 3 per cent unemployment target was

Utopian, to the view of the early 1960s that such a percentage reflected intolerable recession, and the beginning of a new shift back again, are evidence enough of the guesswork on which most such targets rest.

EFFECTS OF UNION POWER

Many economists who would be sympathetic to a good deal of what was said on labour markets in the preceding section would strenuously deny that trade unions have much to do either with inflation or with unemployment. Union monopoly power is, as has already been emphasised, by no means the only reason why slacker labour markets were combined in recent years with accelerating inflation. But, at the risk of alienating all schools of thought, it is necessary to fit unions into the analysis if we are to play more than intellectual parlour games.

Those highly reputable economists who have denied the relevance of the unions seem to be treating them as analogous to straightforward cases of corporate monopoly. In a system containing corporate monopolies, less will be produced of the monopolised products and more will be produced of other products than would be the case if competition prevailed throughout; and the prices of monopolised products will be higher *relative to other prices* than they would otherwise be. But this will not affect the general price-level, which is determined by monetary influences and the money-using habits of the community. A given distribution of monopoly power cannot, it is said, by itself be the cause of a continuing inflationary process.

The flaw in the argument is that there is an important way in which union power differs from corporate monopoly. A firm with market power will hold its output below competitive levels for the sake of higher prices. But it will not, from time to time, withdraw the whole of its output from the market, until representatives of the public sign an agreement to pay more. This is a quasi-political or threat power, which cannot be treated by the theory of single firm monopoly.

This kind of quasi-political blackmail power is clearly very unequally distributed among unionised workers. It is possible to imagine some sort of quasi-equilibrium, under which the relative shares of different groups were proportional to their threat power. It would be a very precarious, shifting and strife-torn equilibrium, as the degree of threat power is not entirely given by technological considerations, but varies with the degree of organisation (for example, action to prevent the movement of coal), the level of strike funds, the preparedness of the public authorities in terms of stock levels, availability of imports and so on. Those on the losing end of such a quasi-equilibrium at any one time might well find means of strengthening their own bargaining position. Even the teachers might be able to 'hold the nation to ransom' if they could accumulate sufficient strike funds to stay out of work for say a year. The more powerful unions in such a quasi-equilibrium need not be deterred by the fear of pricing *their* members out of a job, as they could always insist on 'no redundancies' as part of a settlement, even if this involved public subsidies or other protective measures.

Let us look at the whole economy, in which this threat is exercised at many key points. The quasi-equilibrium just discussed then involves a constant upward drift in the level of money-wage settlements. The trade union movement as a whole can force the monetary and fiscal authorities to choose between financing an inflationary level of wage settlements and facing a major increase in unemployment. This power is reinforced by the fact that each group of union negotiators knows that all other groups are also pushing for wage increases and the risk of its being left behind by the others is greater than the risk of the authorities refusing to finance the result. The employers on the other side of the table know this too. (In principle, monopolistic companies acting with the same tacit mixture of collusion and rivalry could present the authorities with the same awkward choice. But as a matter of fact there has been no profit-push inflation of this kind, at least in the United Kingdom and the United States; and the share of net profit margins, after providing for tax and depreciation, is so small in relation to wages that it is inherently much less likely to be important.)

There have been numerous proposals, dating back in embryo to the 1944 White Paper, that demand management should seek to stabilise the growth of expenditure in money terms in line with the growth of productive potential. In that case the unions would know that the faster money-wages rose the less jobs there would be. The same logic is inherent in the principle of a fixed annual target for the growth of the money supply, and lay behind Peter Thorneycroft's pronouncements as Chancellor in the short period between his measures of September 1957 and his resignation over 'little local difficulties' early the following January.

The trouble with such policies is that they have only deterrent value; they might work if they carried credibility, but would collapse if the threat had to be used. To take by no means fanciful illustrative figures; let us imagine that a limit of 10 per cent per annum is set to the growth of nominal income and expenditure, but wage settlements, in conjunction with normal pricing procedures, require a growth of 20 per cent if unemployment is to be held constant and output to grow by a normal amount. What then is to be done? A reduction in output of nearly 10 per cent at the end of a single year of the policy, with whatever rise in unemployment goes with it, will almost always appear too large a price to pay. The monetary and fiscal targets will therefore be the main ones to give way, and participants in wage bargaining are well aware of this probability. The odds are that the employment targets will also give way slightly too, as the authorities are unlikely to abdicate all control over the inflationary process. They may well, however, be only half conscious of what they are doing, and may suppose that they are acting only because of the balance of payments.

In terms of Figure 13.2, the corner point X will drift upwards. In this situation the long-term rate of inflation could be almost anything, without any breach in monetarist, let alone Keynesian, views of causality. The one safe prediction is that the inflation will tend to get faster over the years, although this phenomenon can take an astonishingly long time to develop before eventually gathering momentum.

The conclusion seems to me irresistible that the unions, both collectively and individually, have not in the past made use of their full potential power, but have tended to make increasing use of it in recent years. The constraints have been a mixture of moral inhibitions, political fears and (in the early stages) lack of knowledge. The formulation of a strategy containing the right mixture of firmness, conciliation and sheer bluff to cope with this power is a matter for statesmanship (or, if one prefers, low cunning) to which economics, or any other formal analysis, has comparatively little to contribute. Contrary to what some economists suppose, organised groups do not always use their full power to achieve their own way; and one of the chief tasks of government is to prevent them from doing so. If recognition of such points leaves a great deal to the accidents of history and personality, and introduces a large range of unpredictability into the system, then this is just hard luck on would-be social 'scientists'.

Many of those who are delighted to recognise (and exaggerate) the points made in the last paragraph fall for a myth of their own, namely that of a deal or pact between the government and the union leaders.[21] It is true that the latter do not collectively stand to gain much, if anything, from an accelerating inflation. But the trouble with the suggestion, apart from all the many other difficulties, is that each individual union leader has very little incentive to observe it. Most of the gains from price stability and fuller employment spill over to members of other unions and the general public, while the costs of settling for less than he could obtain are highly concentrated among his own members. (This is no more than to say that price stability is a public good, which by definition will not be provided by the forces of self-interest.) The British trade union movement has that combination of strong monopoly power among its units, coupled with weak centralised power, most calculated to make an incomes pact fail. As Sir Alec Cairncross has pointed out,[22] about half the increase in wages results from agreements at plant level, outside the scope of national pacts. But plant level agreements are also affected by union monopoly power, as any employer who tries to bid for cheaper non-union labour soon discovers.

It is often argued that unions and their members would become less self-regarding in their aims if governments pursued 'social justice' or 'fairness'. At its most primitive level such thinking assumes that social justice and fairness are natural qualities, such as redness or hardness, which are either present or not. The critical furore raised by Professor John Rawls' attempt to formulate principles for social justice, on which people might rationally agree if they had no idea of their own place in Society, should be sufficient warning to the unwary.[23] Rawls himself agrees that, even if his principles are accepted, there is much room for disagreement about the range of social and economic inequalities they actually justify.

John Goldthorpe has stressed that there is little consensus on what *ought* to determine relative income levels. 'Given the diversity of moral positions that are tenable in the existing state of public opinion, virtually any occupational group seeking a pay increase can find some legitimisation for its case.'[24] But I cannot accept his contention that a 'social' incomes policy, consciously tailored to egalitarian objectives, would help to create the missing consensus.

Why should one suppose that the adoption of any target reduction of inequality (however defined), or of the share of property incomes, would induce greater restraints in union wage-push? The more that policy concentrates on eliminating disparities and differentials, the greater the sense of outrage likely to be engendered by those that remain. Moreover, the smaller the financial contrast between the mass of wage and salary earners and the wealthy minority, the greater the attention that is likely to be paid to relativities among workers. As it is, 90 per cent of consumer spending comes from wages, salaries and welfare payments,[25] and the annual wage round is to a large extent a contest between different groups of workers for relative shares. It is one of the defects of a formal incomes policy, with its norms, criteria, exceptions and regulatory Board, that each group becomes much more keenly aware of what other groups are obtaining, and this increases rather than diminishes the ferocity of the struggle.

The most realistic conclusion, I am afraid, is that of Cairncross, who fears that there may be no escape 'from a long struggle between the Government and individual unions, with the Government seeking to impose its will, the unions resisting, and success alternating with failure as opinion veers this way and that and the unions seek confrontation or see nothing to lose by it'. In this struggle public opinion has its importance; and a shrewd government will attack the scapegoats of the moment, whether by being seen to be hurting 'property speculators', or by underpaying Ministers and M.P.s. This is a matter of keeping up with the media in attacking those targets that happen to be most visible, and should not be confused with the outcome of any moral logic or coherent distributional strategy.

DEMAND MANAGEMENT

Whatever the success of direct measures for dealing with union power, any achievements in this field would be undermined by over-ambitious demand management policies designed to keep unemployment below the minimum sustainable rate. Even if the unions were to vanish from the face of the earth, such policies would lead to accelerating inflation with little or no permanent gain to employment. In the real world they still produce accelerating inflation, however firm any apparent 'incomes policy', through their effect on wage-drift and all the dimensions of the labour contract by which, in practice, the pay of workers in short supply can be bid up, irrespective of any official regulations or agreements. Even if some form of incomes policy is possible in the right labour-market environment, it is almost certainly unfeasible, even as a short-term emergency device, when labour is so scarce across the board that provision cannot be made for wage or price increases to remedy shortages in specific areas on the grounds that this would open the floodgates everywhere else.

How then can we calculate the minimum sustainable unemployment percentage, or – to put the same thing in another language – the maximum feasible 'pressure of demand'? The answer is that we have no means of knowing in advance what is in any case a changing level, and the only way to find out is by experience, being careful to avoid predetermined targets.

The existence of union power does, however, introduce an important complication both for analysis and for policy. If the union element were unimportant, the appropriate policy would be to lay down a long-term target for the growth of money expenditure and incomes, along the lines discussed on page 266 above, not too different from recent averages although perhaps altering slowly, to be achieved by fiscal and monetary means. The relative importance of the two means (to the extent they can be separated) is a technical side issue that does not affect the main argument. The question of whether to maintain a steady pace of advance or to vary the pace around the long-term average for fine-tuning purposes is also not crucial. The central point is that we would then discover the minimum sustainable unemployment rate, without the need to guess it in advance.

But, once union power is allowed to be an important element, such a simple procedure no longer suffices. If the authorities persist with a predetermined limit to the growth of aggregate money expenditure in the face of, say, a wage explosion, such as that of 1969–71 in the United Kingdom, or of 1968 in France, the economy is liable to find itself stranded on the near-horizontal stretch of Figure 13.2. In other words it would be suffering from demand deficiency unemployment, even though the rate of inflation might be high and rising.

There is no watertight solution to this dilemma in terms of either policy or analysis. The best rule-of-thumb guidance would be to have long-term guidelines for the growth of money expenditure; to try to maintain them, but be prepared to make partial adjustments in the face of changes in union wage-push. To put it another way: accept that we are on a 'labour standard', but adopt a long-term fiscal and monetary policy of 'leaning against the wind'. In determining financial policy under such a regime it is important to be on the look-out for symptoms of overheating, which is likely to shift the rate of wage-inflation to ever higher levels.

The avoidance of overheating must mean labour surpluses in some activities and areas to offset shortages in others. The appropriate balance between the shortages and the surpluses is, moreover, not one of exact arithmetical offsetting, but must depend on the flexibility of different sections of the labour market and the willingness of unions to see changes in market conditions reflected in changes in traditional relativities These points are frequently overlooked in policy debates, where it is too often supposed that the absence of universal labour shortage is sufficient to refute the existence of over-heating. The behaviour of the current account overseas balance is also important with a floating exchange rate, not for its own sake but as a sign of overheating – or, in the terminology of this paper, that the economy is being run at an unsustainably high pressure of demand for labour (and/or of plant-capacity). This is the germ of truth behind the link between the overseas balance and domestic financial policy on which the New Cambridge School insists.

If the above approach does not lead to satisfactory levels of employment, something further should undoubtedly be done. That something does not lie, however, in larger budget deficits or money creation, but in measures to improve the workings of the labour market. These range from the regional, labour mobility and re-training policies advocated in the 1944 White Paper, but still not adequately implemented, to some mixture of strategies for both weakening the monopoly power of unions and persuading them to make less use of them.

It cannot be sufficiently emphasised that a lessened pre-occupation with target unemployment rates, so far from being a hard-hearted economic approach, would make it easier to achieve some important social objectives. Take for example the proposal to abolish the wage-stop, which limits social security payments to a person's normal earnings when employed. Some 50,000 working families were below the supplementary benefit level in 1972 and, judging by the experiences of earlier years, perhaps 250,000 were no more than £2 above it. There can be little doubt that the abolition of the wage-stop would be a disincentive to work for some of the 300,000 concerned (and, to the extent that it caused employers to raise wages, would reduce the amount of work on offer). One may believe that the social gain would be worth the loss of output. But those of us who take this view should recognise that, like other worthwhile reforms (such as the earnings-related unemployment benefits discussed earlier), it is likely to raise the percentage of registered unemployed. An uncritical pre-occupation with minimising the unemployment statistics is as much the enemy of enlightened social measures as of sound economic policy.

It is often argued that the major social problems are presented by the long-term unemployed, and this is true. But the statistics of long-term unemployment represent only the tip of an iceberg. The most important variables determining unemployment duration are age, skill and health. Appearance on the unemployment register is only one episode in a pattern of life, in which low pay, lack of skills, high sickness rates, job uncertainty and poverty in old age all go together. Many of these people in their younger days drift in and out of dead-end jobs and for a lot of the time do not appear even among the short-term unemployed or constitute a high proportion of their number.[26]

It would be surprising if this lack of skills or adaptability to working life could be cured by financial manipulation by the Chancellor of the Exchequer or the Governor of the Bank of England. Workers in the field often point out that it is much easier to find jobs for hard-core cases when the general level of demand and activity is high. But this is not a very helpful observation if such levels of demand are not sustainable and have to be balanced by periods of abnormally low demand. Stop–go policies are hardly the key to the problem of poverty. The basic contention of the demand expansionist school is that, if there are labour shortages, employers will not ask too many questions about whom they engage. But labour shortages are fundamentally, like other shortages, the result of under-pricing and, even with statutory Pay Boards, such under-pricing is a transitory phenomenon.

REAL WAGES AND EMPLOYMENT

So far the examination of the influence of unions has been conducted mainly in terms of their effects on the aggregate level of money-wages; their effect on average real wages has been deliberately left undefined. This is because of the considerable evidence that the inverse relationship between real wages and employment, which was common ground to Keynes and his opponents when Chapter 2 of the *General Theory* was being written, does not apply during the course of short-term business cycle fluctuations.

Keynes envisaged the possibility of dropping this relationship in a 1939 article.[27] Subsequent theoretical works by writers using a neo-classical framework have shown that no specific assumptions about the relationship between money-wage and price changes is required to generate cyclical fluctuations in employment. It is sufficient that wages and prices should not move so flexibly as to clear all markets instantaneously.[28]

But if we consider a longer period, in which businesses have time to adapt techniques and organisation to relative factor prices, the inverse relation comes back into its own. If trade unions succeed in pushing up real, and not just money, wages in a specific industry to a level higher than they would otherwise be, the effect will be to reduce the level of employment on offer. This will happen both because there will be a switch of final demand away from the products of that industry because of their higher relative prices, and because it will pay the employers concerned to use more capital-intensive, labour-saving methods.[29]

If trade unions succeed in the long run in raising real wages, not merely in one industry but across the board, above the competitive level, then one would expect to see an induced labour-saving bias in new investment. A time might therefore come in which there would eventually not be the capacity to keep the labour force employed. In terms of Figure 13.2, the minimum sustainable level of unemployment would have moved to the right. To call this unemployment 'voluntary', as one would have to according to the terminology of Chapter 2 of the *General Theory*, is misleading. For there is nothing that any individual worker could do to offset the effects of union policies on his employment opportunities. The unemployed do not always have a union to take their interests into account. One should remember that the main effect of higher real wages enforced by union power is not to create pools of unemployment attached to particular industries, but to reduce the level of recruitment below what it would be otherwise. It is not surprising that unions should be more interested in higher wages than in maintaining full employment.

The kind of unemployment here envisaged is a kind of high level under-development, where there is not enough capital, business organisation and other complementary factors of production to employ at conventional real wages all those seeking employment. This is reminiscent both of earlier epochs in Western economies, before they achieved maturity, and of the contemporary situation in the developing world.

The prospect of this long-term Keynesian unemployment is put forward as a speculative one, largely because it is not certain whether the unions are powerful enough or pervasive enough to raise real wages across the board sufficiently for this to happen. But it is certainly a possibility. Signs of it were detected in the O.E.C.D. survey already mentioned.[30] Union over-pricing of jobs could also be a contributory factor to the dual labour market said to exist by some sociologists, according to which the labour market has two sections – a majority sector with reasonably steady employment at or above the national average wage, and a depressed minority sector where workers drift into and out of employment at a 'poverty level' of earnings.

The inverse relationship between real wages and employment can, under certain conditions, manifest itself in a more short-run context. If there is a sudden acceleration in the rate of money-wage increases out of line with past experience, employers may become less confident about passing these increases on in prices, perhaps because they are less sure about what is happening to their competitors and how they will react. Thus an increase in real wages due to a sudden wage explosion can lead to a profit squeeze, an attack on overmanning and a consequent shake-out of labour, which more than outweighs in its effect on employment the higher consumption of those remaining in employment. This is what appears to have happened in the United Kingdom recession of 1971–2.[31]

It should be noted that, in this short-period context, trade unions collectively would have no difficulty (if they so wished) in reducing the rate of increase of real wages so that this unemployment did not occur. All they would need to do is to settle for a lower rate of increase of money-wages. Provided that the authorities did not reduce the growth of the money supply *pari passu*, this would lead to the required moderation in the growth of real wages and an expansion in output and activity. There would be little danger of the process being frustrated by a 'liquidity trap', as in inflationary conditions it is all too easy to discourage people from holding cash by producing negative real rates of interest.

The inverse relation between real wages and the quantity of labour of different aptitudes required is, of course, an argument against minimum wage laws and policies of priority for the lower paid, which – for all their apparent warm-heartedness – prevent the marginal, fringe or disadvantaged worker from pricing himself into a job. But there is also a more positive approach. This is to help such people to acquire attitudes or qualifications which will raise the market value of their skills so that they can be employed at better wages.

One may not be over-sanguine about the success of such measures, some of which may involve, unless the greatest tact is used, interference with people who are happier left alone. There is no space at the end of this overlong paper to analyse the pros and cons of the proposal by some American economists for wage subsidies for disadvantaged workers,[32] nor of my own view that advanced industrial societies are on the verge of being able to afford a modest minimum social dividend for all, whether at work or not. People would then have the choice of opting out altogether – at a price – and this would cut the ground from the whole argument about scroungers and shirkers.[33] The wage-subsidy type of proposal would reduce the unemployment statistics; the social dividend type of scheme would increase them. The point here is that this should not be the decisive consideration in either case.

CONCLUSION

The moral of this paper can be briefly stated. Much of the post-war discussion about the 'pressure of demand' or 'target level of unemployment' at which to run the economy[34] is a dangerous diversion. For although perverse monetary and fiscal policy can make unemployment unnecessarily high, we do not possess the power to choose any desired level of unemployment at will and maintain it by demand management. Other methods of approach must be tried if unemployment is persistently excessive. The attempt to manage demand to secure a wishful and predetermined unemployment percentage will not succeed in its object, but risks setting off an accelerating inflation – and would do so even if the trade unions did not exist.

The popular view that unions can be an independent cause of inflation is indirectly justified, but what is less generally realised is that they can directly cause an increase in the minimum sustainable level of unemployment. The ability of either a 'social contract' or a long-term statutory incomes policy to do much about either of these effects, in a Society preserving civil liberties, is open to severe doubt. But the attempt to move in such directions may nevertheless have highly undesirable side effects. It will in fact not be easy to reduce either union monopoly power, or the willingness of unions to use such power, in a Society retaining free institutions. But the least that can be done is to avoid compounding our problems by wrong-headed demand management policies in a vain pursuit of levels of employment not in fact obtainable by these means.

A shift from the *simpliste* approach to full employment is in any case likely. The only question is whether we make a conscious move to more fundamental economic and social objectives, or whether we are to remain so attached to once-radical orthodoxies that we are swept along by events, impotently protesting all the while.

NOTES

1 This paper was written before I had the opportunity of seeing an analysis of United States experience with many striking parallels: E. S. Phelps, 'Economic Policy and Unemployment in the 1960s', *The Public Interest*, Winter 1974.
2 Cmd 6527, H.M.S.O., 1944.
3 Ibid., Appendix I, p. 29.
4 O.E.C.D., *Economic Outlook*, December 1973, pp. 32–3. The countries in the sample are Belgium, Canada, Finland, France, the Netherlands, the United Kingdom and the United States.
5 Chapter 6 above.
6 *Department of Employment Gazette*, March 1974.
7 M. Feldstein, 'The Economics of the New Unemployment', *The Public Interest*, Fall 1973, p. 39.
8 Chapter 9 above, see p. 173 in particular.
9 P. C. Cheshire, 'Regional Unemployment Differences in Great Britain' in N.I.E.S.R. *Regional Papers II*, Cambridge University Press, 1973, Chap. 3.
10 Department of Health and Social Security, *Two-Parent Families: A Study of*

their Resources and Needs in 1968, 1969 and 1970 by J. R. Howe, H.M.S.O., 1971.
11 Department of Health and Social Security, *Report of the Committee on the Abuse of Social Security Benefits*, Cmnd 5228, H.M.S.O., 1973, para. 240.
12 Ibid., para. 492.
13 See the quotation from the Labour M.P. Eric Heffer cited in J. B. Wood, *How Much Unemployment?*, Institute of Economic Affairs, 1972, p. 59. New measures proposed in 1974 may or may not be successful in reducing the 'lump'.
14 It is of course absurd to suppose that an economy can be managed without any reserves of labour any more than without any stocks of goods and raw materials. To claim otherwise is not to help the human beings involved, but to make a mockery of them for ideological purposes.
15 The shift in unused labour from firms' books to the unemployment register is, of course, likely to counteract some of the supply side influences discussed in previous paragraphs.
16 Chapter 1, p. 29.
17 This is a different concept of demand deficiency to the one in Jim Taylor's paper, but I think my differences with him on this score are largely linguistic.
18 See M. Friedman, *The Optimum Quantity of Money and Other Essays*, Macmillan, 1969.
19 For the sake of simplicity we overlook the fact that the authorities nearly always overshoot the mark and end up with unemployment to the right of B; thus they end up trying to reduce and not merely stabilise unemployment. Inclusion of these complications would strengthen the argument of the text.
20 See R. E. Lucas, 'Some International Evidence on Output–Inflation Trade-offs', *American Economic Review*, June 1973.
21 These paragraphs were drafted well before the election of 28th February 1974 was announced.
22 Sir Alec Cairncross, 'Incomes Policy: Retrospect and Prospect', *The Three Banks Review*, December 1973.
23 J. Rawls, *A Theory of Justice*, Oxford University Press, 1972.
24 J. Goldthorpe, 'Political Consensus, Social Inequality and Pay Policy', *New Society*, 10th January 1974.
25 Cairncross, 'Incomes Policy'.
26 See, for instance, the paper by Hill, Chapter 9 above.
27 J. M. Keynes, 'Relative Movements of Real Wages and Output', *Economic Journal*, March 1939, conveniently reprinted as Appendix 3 to Volume VII of the new Royal Economic Society edition of Keynes' writings.
28 For example, D. Patinkin, *Money, Interest and Prices: An Integration of Monetary and Value Theory* (2nd ed.), Harper and Row, 1965, Chap. 13; D. E. W. Laidler, 'Simultaneous Fluctuations in Prices and Output' and 'A Monetarist Model', University of Manchester Discussion Papers, 1972; B. Chiplin and P. J. Sloane, 'Real and Money Wages Revisited', *Applied Economics*, December 1973.
29 There is also the recondite point that it may be rational for a worker in a unionised industry to accept a wage policy involving increased liability to unemployment if this increases his lifetime income expectation. This unemployment may in some sense be said to be 'voluntary'.
30 O.E.C.D. *Economic Outlook*, December 1973, pp. 32–3.

31 See S. Brittan, *Capitalism and the Permissive Society*, Macmillan, 1973, pp. 186–9.
32 See Feldstein, 'The Economics of the New Unemployment' and L. C. Thurow's reply to R. A. Posner on 'Economic Justice and the Economist', both in *The Public Interest*, Fall 1973.
33 Brittan, *Capitalism and the Permissive Society*, p. 223 *et seq*.
34 I have myself participated in this.

Chapter 14

The Target Rate of Unemployment[1]

F. T. BLACKABY

INTRODUCTION

In the last two decades there has been a quiet 'Tinbergian' revolution in the theory and analysis of macro-economic policy. It is now normal to analyse it in terms of a number of different objectives of policy and of the instruments available to reach those objectives. Policymakers now talk the same language – about the objectives of inflation, economic growth and full employment.

The change has been for the better. The concept of 'aggregate welfare', for all the mass of literature about it, never came anywhere near the concerns of the actual economic policymaker. One could not expect a Chancellor concerned with the construction of a budget to see much relevance in discussions of the problems of inter-personal comparisons of utility. The idea of 'management by objectives' has the attraction of realism. So we find this framework of thought has been used increasingly in the last two decades. Budget speeches usually have a passage in which Chancellors pay a kind of ceremonial homage to the four standard objectives of demand management policy.

For an 'objective–instrument' model of economic policy two of the things needed are, first, a list of objectives and, secondly, a method of quantifying the achievement of those objectives. The policymaker needs to know what it is he is trying to do and whether or not he has succeeded in doing it. Various lists of objectives have been put forward from time to time; one thing they have in common is that all of them without exception include full employment. Further, they are virtually unanimous in suggesting that the unemployment percentage is the best indicator for measuring the achieve-

ment of that objective. There are plenty of differences of opinion
about other objectives – should an adequate balance of payments
or the promotion of the international division of labour be considered as objectives in their own right, or only as intermediate
variables? There is no disagreement between the various lists about
full employment; as an objective of economic policy, it has won
universal recognition.

This paper is about unemployment in this role – as a target
indicator for the full employment objective of economic policy. First,
there is a short section on past targets – the implicit and explicit
quantifications of the target which British governments have set in
the past. The main part of the paper is about what the target ought
to be; it attempts to set out all the considerations – both economic
and social – which the policymakers should have in mind in setting
the target figures.

The main conclusion is that it is doubtful whether the *de facto*
upward shift in the unemployment target in the mid-sixties was
justified in the event. The review of the costs and benefits suggests
that it would be better to go back to the pre-1967 target figure of
1½ per cent.

WHAT TARGETS HAVE BEEN SET?

Before considering the evidence about the targets, a word about the
figures. In looking at targets over time we have to be sure that we
are using the same definition; and the definition which policymakers
probably had in mind changed slightly over the last ten or fifteen
years. In the early sixties, the most commonly quoted figure included
the temporarily stopped, school-leavers and adult students, but it
excluded Northern Ireland. Now, the most commonly quoted figure
excludes the temporarily stopped, school-leavers and adult students,
but it includes Northern Ireland. On balance, the figures on the new
definition are slightly lower than the figures on the old definition. If,
for example, we go back to the first plan, which was published in
February 1963,[2] the unemployment percentage given there for 1962
is 2·2 per cent. On the present prevalent definition it would be 2·0 per
cent. It is a point to watch in comparing past and present targets. All
the rates quoted in this paper are on the present prevalent definition
except where otherwise stated.

Evidence about past targets is twofold. First, there were many occasions when the government took reflationary measures – often rather urgently – because it thought that unemployment was too high. This provides us with a set of markers for an upper limit to unemployment. We can say fairly categorically that at those points of time the government took the view that unemployment ought to be lower than the observed figure. That is one set of pieces of evidence about past targets. The second set is provided by the three plans published by the National Economic Development Office and by the Department of Economic Affairs.[3]

First, the set of triggers for reflationary action. In the winter of 1958-9, the unemployment percentage on present day definitions reached a figure (seasonally adjusted) of 2·2 per cent. In absolute terms and unadjusted seasonally, it was the figure of half a million which then caught the headlines and helped to impel the government towards its fairly massive easing of credit restrictions, which set off the 1959 boom. The next trigger was at the end of 1962: then, as in 1958, it was the winter peak figure which caught public attention; governments are not normally impelled to reflationary action by anything that happens to unemployment in the summer. In the winter of 1962-3 the trigger was slightly higher than in 1958, but not much higher; the highest percentage reached on present definitions was 2·5 in the first quarter of 1963. We then have the major shift: the third indubitable case when a high level of unemployment triggered off reflationary action was in the winter of 1971-2, but this time the figure rose to the very much higher level of 3·9 per cent; that was in the first quarter of 1972.

In all cases one could say that the trigger for reflationary action was somewhere below the highest quarterly percentage reached; assuming that governments were not equipped with a correct set of unemployment forecasts in which they confidently believed, this assumption is almost certainly correct. We could probably say that the set of trigger figures in 1958, 1962 and 1971 were 2·0, 2·2 and 3·6 per cent respectively. Those are the three markers we can deduce from occasions on which there is no reasonable doubt that the government decided to reflate the economy because of the high level of unemployment. Quite clearly there is a major shift between the early 1960s and the early 1970s.

A second set of evidence is from the various plans. It is interesting that none of the three plans explicitly mentions a target unemployment figure, but in two of the three the target figure can be inferred without much difficulty.

In the first plan published in February 1963,[4] there is only one statement about the general level of unemployment: 'It is assumed for the purpose of this report that unemployment will be reduced substantially below the level of 1962.' The level of 1962, on present definitions, was 2·0 per cent. It is fairly clear that the report had in mind, as a target, a return at least to the unemployment percentage of 1961, which – again on present definitions – was 1·5 per cent, for it projected an increase in employment between 1961 and 1966 which was slightly higher than the estimated increase in the labour force. The implied target rate in 1963 was thus fairly clearly an unemployment percentage of 1·5 per cent.

The same target figure emerges from the *National Plan*, published in September 1965.[5] Here the relevant passage reads: 'With effective policies to increase employment opportunities in the less prosperous regions, it should be possible to reduce the numbers unemployed by some 50,000 during the plan period.' Such a reduction would bring the unemployment percentage, again on present definitions, down from 1·7 per cent on average in 1964 to just below 1·5 per cent.

The third implied unemployment target is given in *The Task Ahead*, published in 1969,[6] where it says: 'A reduction from the 1968 level of unemployment is an important aim of Government policy.' (Unemployment in 1968 was 2·4 per cent on present definitions.) Because of the slack in the economy, this assessment assumed that from 1968 to 1972 total output could rise some $3\frac{1}{4}$ per cent a year compared with an increase in productive potential of 2·9 per cent a year. This, again, implies a target rate of unemployment at the end of the period of around 1·6 per cent.

What can be inferred from this asserted evidence? First, one or two qualifications. A government is not monolithic; among individual policymakers and among departments there were almost certainly significant differences of opinion about the desirable unemployment figure. This qualification applied particularly to the figures which can be inferred from the plans. The dominant economic policy-making department, the Treasury, never had much enthusiasm for any of them, and there was probably a good deal of Treasury scepticism about the implied unemployment targets.

However, the observation of the points at which governments took reflationary action provides hard evidence. There is little doubt that in the early sixties the government considered that a rate of 2–2½ per cent was too high; the target rate was therefore probably not much higher than 1½ per cent as implied by the first plan. There is also probably not much reason to question the 1½ per cent in the *National Plan* published in 1965; certainly in its early years the Labour government was not persuaded of the need for a higher level of unemployment.

The target implied by *The Task Ahead* in 1969 is more questionable. This document was put out by a department which was just about to disappear entirely; and clearly the reduction of unemployment was not considered at the time to be an overriding objective, since the figure stayed at 2·4–2·5 per cent all the way from the middle of 1967 right up to the election in the middle of 1970.

Finally, we have the very high trigger figure of winter 1971. It is quite clear that the target figure had by then shifted substantially.

To some extent, therefore, the discussion in the rest of this paper can be put in this form. Should policymakers be advised to accept the substantial shift in the unemployment target which took place during the 1960s? I think there is no doubt that at present the general view of commentators on economic affairs is that they should. If we take as this general view an average of the opinions expressed at the end of 1973 in leaders in *The Times*, *Financial Times* and *Guardian*, plus an average of the views expressed by Mr Brittan, Mr Jay, Mr Harris and Miss Cairncross, then I think that their collective view comes down in favour of considering 2½ per cent unemployment – which ten years ago was a certain trigger for reflationary action – to be taken now as a trigger, if anything for deflation. Once it was considered to be an indicator of deficient demand; now it is considered an indicator of excess demand. Was this shift justified?

POSSIBLE REASONS FOR THE SHIFT

Before going on to an analysis of the costs and benefits derived from the two different levels of unemployment, it is perhaps useful to attempt a classification of the possible reasons for the fairly clear shift in the target figure. We can classify the possible reasons in the following way. First, the trade-offs – assuming that they exist – may have changed; that is, the cost in terms of other objectives of maintaining a given level of unemployment may be much higher than it used to be. This is the heading under which one would include the idea that in some way the relationship between unemployment and the pressure of demand has changed. Secondly, there is a possibility that, although the trade-offs with other objectives may not have changed, knowledge of these trade-offs may have increased; there may be more evidence now than there was ten years ago of the deleterious consequences of a low level of unemployment. Thirdly, one must put as a separate possibility that, although in fact there has been no change in trade-offs, and although there may be no firmly established increase in knowledge of deleterious consequences, none the less the views of policymakers about these things may have shifted. Given the uncertainty of our knowledge about the working of the economic system, it is perfectly possible for a shift of view of this kind to occur without any new evidence. The fourth possibility is that the relative valuation put on this particular objective is lower than it used to be. Which combination of objectives is chosen depends not just on possibility functions – the feasibility of particular combinations of objectives. The choice also depends on the preference functions of the policymakers; the possibility functions may be the same, but the preference functions may have changed. Which of these has happened?

The argument, widely put forward in the last few years, that unemployment is not what it was and that its relationship to the pressure of demand has changed has not stood up well under analysis. It rested on a comparison between the movement of unemployment figures and unfilled vacancy figures. Given that the vacancy figures depended on voluntary notifications, this was always rather a slender pillar on which to build an important argument – particularly since only a small proportion of vacancies are notified, so that there is plenty of scope for the relationship between unemployment and vacancies to shift as employers make more use of the Department of Employment's facilities. They may well be doing this, as the Department attempts to change the image of the old labour exchange to the new 'job shop'. A comparison of both unemployment and vacancy series with other indicators of the pressure of demand suggests that it is the vacancy series which is out of line.[7] Further, neither of the reasons put forward for a different pattern of unemployment behaviour has found any empirical support. The suggestions have been that, because of redundancy payments and earnings-related benefits, those who lose jobs allow themselves a longer period to find new ones. These suggestions tended to be put forward with some confidence, although there was no evidence for them. Recent surveys of the unemployed support neither hypothesis. On an age-standardised basis, those receiving redundancy payments find jobs more quickly than those who do not; and there seems some tendency for those not receiving earnings-related benefits to remain unemployed longer than those who do.[8]

It cannot be argued that there is firmer knowledge of the unfortunate consequences of low unemployment now than there was ten years ago; that is, one cannot say that knowledge of trade-offs has increased, rather the contrary. It is argued below that it is now uncertain whether a trade-off between unemployment and earnings increases exists within the range of politically possible unemployment levels.

It probably is true that politicians put a lower value on this objective than they did. They have found that higher unemployment is less of a political liability than they thought. Put crudely, the unemployed do not themselves have many votes, and the employed are not particularly concerned about the unemployed. The unemployed are almost wholly ineffective as a pressure group. Raising the level of unemployment is no longer considered to be electoral suicide.

Finally, it does seem that there has been a shift of view among many commentators on the economic scene and possibly among civil servants. Among the civil servants there are probably those who argued for raising the level of unemployment during the sixties; they may feel that this was an achievement of some kind which they are unwilling to let go. The commentators have made a good deal of shortages occurring towards the end of 1973 – though these were probably more a consequence of a sharp upturn following a long period of stagnation rather than of the pressure of demand itself; that is they were the consequence of the rate of change rather than of the level. In any case, the ability of the economy to survive the shortages imposed by the three-day week suggests that before then the difficulties must have been essentially marginal.

286

CONSIDERATIONS IN CHOOSING A TARGET FIGURE

So much for the evidence on what the target rate of unemployment has in fact been in the last 15 years, and the possible reasons for the shift. Now for the second question. Let us imagine a Prime Minister or a Chancellor of the Exchequer who asks for a brief which sets out the considerations he should have in mind in choosing a long-term target rate now for the next five years. What material should go into that brief?

I think the business-like way to go about the preparation of such a brief would be to try to set out as systematically as possible the evidence on the claimed benefits and costs, both economic and social, of the higher and the lower unemployment figures; and then to present a summing up which attempts to weigh this evidence. That is what this paper will now try to do.

There is one statistical point of some relevance throughout. We do now have two reasonably long periods with different general levels of unemployment. From 1950 to the mid-1960s there was an average level of around 1½ per cent. From the beginning of 1967 to the present day we have had over seven years in which the unemployment percentage has been 2 per cent or higher in every quarter; and from mid-1967 we have had 6½ years in which it has been 2·4 per cent or higher. That is quite a long time. It is fair to say that if a shift upwards in the general level of unemployment of this order of magnitude were a dominant or major force in the economy, leading to significant changes in its pattern of behaviour, one would have expected to see some signs of such changes breaking through by now.

THE CLAIMED BENEFITS FROM HIGHER UNEMPLOYMENT

The big argument for higher unemployment has, of course, always been that higher unemployment means a lower rate of price increase. Where does that argument stand now?

We all know that the old simple relationship has gone. In 1967 Professor Paish could write: 'On the basis of Professor Phillips' estimates, the level of unemployment which is compatible with a rate of wage increase no higher than the rise in output per head is thus probably rather more than 2 per cent, but almost certainly less than 2½ per cent. If we put it at 2¼ per cent, or a little less, we shall probably not be very far out.'[9]

I think it is important to remember how much we were promised, and by how many people, from a little rise in unemployment. Professor Paish is quoted because he was explicit; but there were many others, both inside and outside government service, who firmly believed not only that our price problem but that our balance of payments problem also would disappear like mist in the morning sun if only politicians would abandon their foolish adherence to absolutely full employment. Here at least is one conclusion which we can draw: the upward move in the level of unemployment from 1½ to 2½ per cent has not been dominant here.

The main attempt to salvage the relationship is, of course, by the introduction of expectations. The relationship between increases in earnings and the level of unemployment has been moved up somewhere into the stratosphere by expectations. One of the difficulties with this view is that those who put it forward have no idea where the relationship has got to. Professor Laidler, speaking at a conference in February 1971, said 'I do not think we can yet say anything very precise about the quantitative nature [of the policy trade-off between unemployment and earnings] other than to note that the experience of both Britain and the United States over the last few years suggests that, if unemployment rates are to be kept from rising any higher than they are at present, then the timetable for significantly reducing the rate of inflation must be conceived of in terms of years rather than months.'[10] When he was speaking the seasonally adjusted unemployment rate was 2·9 per cent; the passage indicates that in his view this would be high enough to bring down the rate of inflation very slowly. Thereafter the rate rose sharply up to 3·9 per cent; it did rise 'higher than at present'; it still had no visible effect in reducing the inflation rate. Those who held this view, therefore, have to say to the politician: 'If you continue to raise the level of unemployment, at some point, we don't know where, the rate of rise in earnings will begin to moderate. You will then have to keep unemployment at this unknown point for an unknown period of time, and you will then be able to bring it down again to an unknown figure.'

We know nothing about the shape of this alleged expectations-determined Phillips curve. It could well be that within the ranges of unemployment which are politically possible – say from 1½ to 4 per cent – the relationship is now a straight line, and it only begins to curve down at higher figures. Certainly one can accept the proposition that somewhere, at some point, there is a level of unemployment which would break the rise in earnings. It is perfectly sensible to believe this, and at the same time to believe that the movement of unemployment within the range from 1½ to 4 per cent will have little if any effect.

It is perhaps worth adding a reminder that one can take the view that expectations – or past price rises – have shifted up trade union demands over the past decade, without believing that there is an expectations-determined Phillips curve. The obverse relationship between unemployment and wage rates could also be explained by trade union behaviour – in that they pushed hard for increases when the going was good, and cannily bided their time for a little when the going was bad. But if this was the explanation, it did not follow that they would bide their time right through a long bad period.

This view was expressed, in a succinct way and in a secular context, by Professor Phelps Brown:

'Up to World War I, collective bargaining was concerned with particular industries and localities, with each bargain largely independent of the others. After World War II, the annual wage round began, in which the settlements no longer depended on the economic prospects of the individual industry, but on what others got. However, the consensus of expectations followed the cycle of the economic situation. Now the consensus is self-propelled, not anchored to economic indicators. . . . This is my analysis explaining the wage explosion.'[11]

In the examination of the evidence for the connection between unemployment and inflation, one ought to glance also at the evidence from international comparisons. If there were a general tendency for countries with low unemployment percentages to have higher rates of price-inflation, then this would be evidence of a kind. Briefly, there is no observable relationship.

At this point, let us introduce a new complication. Let us assume that the politician who asks what his target level of unemployment should be adds that throughout the five years he expects that there will be an incomes policy of some sort – either statutory or voluntary. Does this make a difference to the answer? I think it probably does. The purpose of an incomes policy is to moderate wage claims. It is likely to be more successful with fuller employment for a number of reasons. First, the official trade union leadership will be more willing tacitly to go along with it. Secondly, with fuller employment the pressure on trade union leaders from below will be less, since a larger number of households will have an additional income coming in. Thirdly, when there is significant unemployment, the trade unions argue that it is their duty to increase effective demand by raising wages; they are certainly not convinced that this is an ineffective method. It is interesting that one of the few sets of equations which attempt to explain the movement of earnings since 1969 and which produces a reasonable fit to the experience of the last three years is one in which the *fall* in employment since 1966 is a factor leading to a faster rise in money-wages.[12]

It may well be that, with an incomes policy of either kind, the effect of different levels of unemployment between the normal ranges is on balance neutral. With full employment, on the one hand trade unions may be willing to accept slightly lower figures in their negotiated wage bargains because they are less under pressure from the rank and file, on the other hand there may be more leakage outside the negotiated sector. There is no evidence on which to base an assertion that one effect is likely to be larger than the other. So, under an incomes policy regime there seems to be no strong evidence for saying that the average rise in money earnings would be significantly less with $3\frac{1}{2}$ per cent unemployment than with $2\frac{1}{2}$ per cent, or with $2\frac{1}{2}$ per cent unemployment than with $1\frac{1}{2}$ per cent. The evidence for these effects is now lacking, and the normal rule must apply that one does not assume effects in the absence of evidence.

So much for the effect of unemployment on prices. The next point to consider is the effect on the balance of payments. A number of complications arise when one attempts to answer this question. First of all, low unemployment can of course be caused, partly or wholly, by an export boom. Secondly, econometric examination of the evidence of the last 20 years has only indicated the possible effects of changes in the pressure of demand, not the effects of running the economy at a different pressure for any length of time.

On the import side, some studies have found a pressure of demand effect, others have not. However, in all cases the pressure term, where significant, measures the effect of a change from high to low unemployment. As one study comments: 'Do the estimated effects give any indication of the likely effects on imports of running the economy at any given constant level of capacity utilization over a longish period? It seems doubtful whether they do and best to regard them as merely summarizing the effects of variations in capacity utilization over the period analysed.'[13] On the export side, only fairly small and uncertain effects have been found in econometric studies using quarterly or annual data.[14] As with imports, however, these results give us no clue as to the effect of running the economy for long periods at a relatively high level of demand pressure. There is nothing in international experience to suggest that countries with low unemployment percentages are less successful in world trade in manufactures than those with higher percentages; the two most successful countries, West Germany and Japan, have, on an internationally comparable basis, had a much lower unemployment percentage than either Britain or the United States, both of whom have been relatively unsuccessful in world trade.

So here again, on the effect on the balance of payments of running the economy with a lower level of unemployment, we must return a non-proven verdict.

These are the two main benefits claimed for running the economy with a higher level of unemployment. There are others on which there is less literature. There is the argument that as unemployment rises labour discipline improves. There is the argument that with low unemployment there are widespread shortages and inefficiencies in the economy; in particular, that there is insufficient labour to man the public services. Thirdly, partly linked to the argument of the shortages connected with low unemployment, it has been argued that large firms are only willing to undertake substantial new investment projects when there is some margin of spare capacity in the economy; if they are undertaken when unemployment is low, then the new projects become a nightmare of shortages and delays.

The argument on labour discipline seems a rather old-fashioned one. Possibly with massive unemployment over a long period of time labour discipline might be improved, but it is doubtful whether it changes much as between $1\frac{1}{2}$ and 4 per cent. If it did, then possibly one might have found some evidence in a smaller number of new claims for sickness benefit; figures for the high unemployment period do not seem to show this. In any case, the threat of unemployment is not now regarded as the optimal method of improving workers' performance. There are examples of the contrary effect: at Upper Clyde

Shipbuilders, for example, when the workforce thought that they would be unemployed when the ship was finished, they let the work drag on as long as possible. On the point about lengthening delivery dates and public sector labour shortages, here again most of the observations concern the effect of a change in unemployment levels. In 1972 and 1973 for example, output in this country began to rise sharply after a very long period in which it had risen only slowly, and also after a long period – from late 1966 onwards – in which employment had been falling. It is not surprising that delivery dates lengthened; nor is it surprising that employers should complain that they were unable to find 'suitable' employees, since they had become accustomed during the previous five or six years to reject those they considered marginal. Certainly it would take time for the British economy to adjust itself again to a lower level of unemployment; but it is not very sensible to argue that it is in some way impossible to run it at that lower level, since it was in fact run at that lower level for about 20 years. Finally, there is no evidence in the figures that firms were more willing to undertake major new investment projects when there was widespread spare capacity and short order books; the evidence is rather the other way.

ECONOMIC AND SOCIAL COSTS AND BENEFITS OF LOW UNEMPLOYMENT

The main *economic* argument put forward by those who put the case for running the economy at a low level of unemployment is the argument that this serves as a stimulus to investment. There are fairly obvious *a priori* reasons for thinking that this might be so. Firms, like other institutions, are reluctant to change; they need some force to impel them to adopt new methods which require less labour. This force is provided when they are unable to get the labour which they need for continuing their existing methods of production. The higher the demand for labour the greater the stimulus to labour-saving investment.

Any stimulus to manufacturing investment is, of course, important for the balance of payments as well. In the medium term, export success probably depends more on private industry's investment policy than on short-term management (or on exchange rate changes, for that matter). The German success in maintaining their share in world trade in manufactures and the long-term upward trend in the Japanese share are not well explained by their exchange rate or demand management policies; they are better explained by substantial investment projects undertaken with the world market in mind. However, the econometric exercises which relate manufacturing investment to some indicator of 'capacity' do not prove the point. They have the same defects from this point of view as the analyses which use capacity indicators in helping to explain import and export trends. The relationships are essentially with *changes* in capacity utilisation; they do not answer questions about the effects of long periods in which the economy was operating close to capacity, or conversely.

There is also the argument that, with full employment, there is less likely to be opposition from organised labour to new investment in any particular plant which reduces the demand for labour in that plant. It is very hard to know precisely how important this is. Perhaps it is of some interest to cite an actual example in Newton Abbot, where the Claimants' Union was successful in persuading 70 workers at the local power station not to accept a national productivity deal. This incident is reported as follows:

'This is . . . what happened in Newton Abbot quite recently. The seventy workers at the power station were offered a £5 per week pay rise early last year as part of a national productivity deal which would have reduced the number of jobs at the station by twelve. They were promised that there would be no immediate redundancies, but that reductions in the workforce would eventually be made through early retirements and natural wastage. However, the men realised that, even if their own immediate prospects were not threatened by this productivity deal, the interests of twelve other unemployed people waiting for a vacancy in just such a job were very much at stake. They therefore decided to turn down the whole deal, and forego the payrise for the sake of protecting the jobs that would otherwise have disappeared, adding to the long-term unemployment problems of everyone in the area.

However, neither the management nor the union in the power industry were prepared to accept this isolated act of defiance, and a further campaign was launched to try to persuade the Newton Abbot workers to accept the productivity deal. Expensive management consultants were engaged by the Board to spend weeks interviewing the men to get them to change their minds. By December the matter was coming to a head again, but the power station workers found that on this occasion they were not without support. The Claimants' Union had been carrying out a leaflet campaign of its own against productivity deals, pointing out their causation of unemployment. Only a few weeks before the power station workers' decision was to be made, many such leaflets had been distributed at workplaces in the area, and they had all therefore had the opportunity of reading of the backing that we were giving them in their stand.

It was thus that a very surprised management consultant learnt from the workers when he outlined the productivity scheme to them that the Union was against it. When he assured them that their Union had fully endorsed the proposed deal he was again contradicted. When he asked what Union's statements they were referring to, he was told the Claimants' Union. At the decision, only three workers voted to accept the productivity deal, and the consultants returned to London, no doubt wondering who on earth the Union which had so inconveniently intervened might be'.[15]

One counter-argument on productivity is that, as the economy moves towards full employment, firms are forced to engage workers with lower productivity; they have to recruit untrained workers and train them, take on people with relatively poor sickness records and find jobs for those aged over 55. At the same time, with full employment, labour is more mobile and there is a more rapid turnover, particularly of unskilled workers. All this might reduce productivity for a time. But, again, if there is such a change, it is a once-for-all change accompanying the shift to lower unemployment, and it stops once the new level of unemployment is reached.

The evidence from the two periods with different levels of unemployment suggests that none of these factors has been dominant in determining the productivity trend. There are different versions of this trend, but none of them suggest that the move to a new higher level of unemployment after 1967 was a dominant factor.

SOCIAL COSTS

I want now to turn to the social costs of a high unemployment rate. Some people take the view that there is nothing to be said about this.

All an economist can do is to indicate the consequences to other objectives which he believes would follow from setting certain unemployment targets. The judgement of the value of having, say, 400,000 rather than 500,000 unemployed is a matter for the politicians, and the economist has nothing to contribute.

I do not agree that there is nothing to be said. First of all, the aim of this paper is to set out *all* the considerations which the policymaker should have in mind in choosing an unemployment target; there is no restriction that the considerations should be economic. Secondly, I think a humane politician can perfectly well ask whether unemployment is a serious social problem or not. This is not a meaningless question, for there is relevant evidence. There are alternative pictures of the nature of unemployment which make a great deal of difference to the assessment, as I hope to show. That is, there is information and there are figures which the policymaker should have when he comes to assess the social cost of unemployment.

Economists have traditionally fought shy of questions of this kind. For all their concern about welfare in the abstract, they have been very reluctant to get to grips with any actual welfare question in detail. They are certainly willing to concede that the object of economic activity is connected with human satisfactions, but basically that is as far as they are willing to go. If you ask whether an additional whisky and soda for a film star at Claridge's adds less or more to the sum total of human satisfactions than an additional bottle of milk for an undernourished family in Wigan, the reply is that there is no way of knowing. I am not suggesting that one can in fact turn the figures of unemployment into quanta of dissatisfaction, though I think it would be useful at some time to try. I am suggesting that there are alternative pictures of the nature of unemployment, some of which imply that it matters very little and others that it matters a great deal more; that there is evidence on the basis of which one can judge which of these pictures is nearer to the truth; and that this inquiry into the nature of unemployment is an essential part of the briefing of any policymaker who has to make a decision about his target rate.

Here is one picture of the unemployed which I think is the one in the minds of many of those who advocate keeping a 2½ per cent – or indeed a higher – target. The vast bulk of the unemployed consist of people who are only temporarily inconvenienced by losing one job; while they are looking for another job their income is reasonably well maintained with the help of earnings-related benefit and they find another job without too much trouble. At the bottom of the un-employment pile there is a collection of people of whom some are virtually incapable of employment and some are work-shy layabouts. Even if they got jobs their incomes would be little more than they are under social security, and in any case they are basically unenthusiastic about working. They are essentially drop-outs; the best thing to do is to make sure they do not starve and leave it at that.

If this is a correct picture of the unemployed, then the social cost of unemployment is not very high. If the average level is reduced, the only gain would be that the transitory unemployed would find another job in five days instead of six, and the bottom stratum might be tempted, rather unwillingly, into some kind of employment, which would give neither them nor their employers much satisfaction. If this is the correct picture of the unemployed, then one would only have to show fairly small net economic benefits to offset the social cost of raising unemployment.

I think that this picture of the unemployed, which is now very widely held, is not a correct picture; there is reasonably firm evidence to suggest that it is wrong. And if it is wrong, it follows that the weight of social cost in the decision about an unemployment target is heavy.

First of all, at any one time it is not true to say that the bulk of the standing army of unemployed consists of people rapidly changing from job to job and consequently suffering little inconvenience. Of those registered as unemployed now, over half will have been unem-ployed for over eight weeks. That is, a target rate of unemployment of $2\frac{1}{2}$ per cent will mean that there will normally be some 300,000 persons in this category – that of those unemployed for more than eight weeks. Being unemployed for more than eight weeks is some-thing more than a temporary inconvenience.

However, a more important point is that at the moment one-quarter of the standing army of the unemployed, that is 150,000 persons, has been unemployed for more than a year. Now, it is true that if unemployment continues at $2\frac{1}{2}$ per cent for some time this figure will come down – probably to around 100,000; duration is relatively high in a period when unemployment is falling. On the other hand, the simple figures of those unemployed over 52 weeks understates the size of the problem of the long-term unemployed. We know from other sources that a number of people have relatively long spells of unemployment, broken by occasional short periods in essentially temporary jobs. So, as a rough measure of long-term unemployment, 150,000 is probably not a bad figure. It is a crucial question to establish whether these 150,000 are unemployable or work-shy; for if they are neither then this is a substantial social cost.

Post-war studies of the unemployed are few and far between. It tended to be widely assumed that the problem of unemployment did not exist and therefore there was nothing to study. However, in the last few years some material has been forthcoming, and this section draws on it.[16]

First of all, are these long-term unemployed essentially work-shy layabouts? Neither of the surveys support this view. Mr Sinfield comments: 'The evidence so far has shown that the stereotype of the work-shy layabout is not an accurate picture of the long-term unemployed.' The survey of unemployment in three English towns comments: 'There seems to be no evidence from this survey to substantiate the view that many men remain unemployed because it is more lucrative than working. It is very doubtful that more than a very small number of men fall into this category.' In this survey the plausible hypothesis was advanced that those with longer periods of unemployment might be less willing to look for work than those with shorter periods of unemployment. The questions asked to test whether this was so concerned the number of methods which the respondents used to look for work. The mean score of job-seeking methods used was as high for those who had been unemployed for 78 to 103 weeks as it was for those who had been unemployed less than 25 weeks. To quote the conclusion of the survey: 'There is little evidence to suggest that the average number of techniques used diminishes as unemployment in the current spell increases and hence little to suggest that men unemployed for a long period of time were less diligent in looking for work.'[17] It would not have been surprising if those who had been unemployed for more than a year had indicated to the interviewers that they had more or less given up looking; indeed this was what the interviewers expected. In fact, the surveys suggest that those unemployed for a year or more were still looking for work as hard as ever.

The 'work-shy layabout' stereotype for the long-term unemployed seems not to be supported by such evidence as there is – that is, evidence from surveys systematically conducted. The evidence on the other side seems basically anecdotal. The next question is whether the 'unemployable' stereotype is correct. There is a short answer here: there is no reason to think that the 150,000 long-term unemployed which we have now are unemployable, because their equivalents in the 1950s were found employment. In the mid-fifties the number of those who had been unemployed for over a year came down at one point to 20,000. This is, I think, a fairly conclusive demonstration that the term 'unemployable, is a relative term; if the demand for labour is low they will not be employed, but if the demand for labour is high then they will find jobs. One can certainly agree that the long-term unemployed are those whom employers will reject if they get the chance; most employers would probably like, if they could, to employ exclusively able-bodied persons between the ages of 25 and 40. As the demand for labour rises, so they will cease to declare people redundant at the age of 50 and 55.

The same message – that the concept of 'unemployability' varies with the demand for labour – emerges if one looks at the unemployment rates for those on the register of disabled persons. The level of unemployment for this group is substantially higher than the national unemployment rate; when the national unemployment rate for men was $1\frac{1}{2}$ per cent, the rate for men who were registered disabled was 6 per cent. The point is that the rate for the registered disabled has moved up and down precisely in the same way as the total unemployment rate, so that, when in 1972 the national unemployment rate for men reached nearly 5 per cent, the rate for those who were registered as disabled reached 15 per cent. Quite clearly the extent to which the registered disabled are considered 'unemployable' depends precisely on the general pressure of demand for labour. Further, the relationship suggests very strongly – a point which will be developed later – that the registered disabled are not effectively protected by their special legislation; the only effective way that has so far been found for giving them jobs is to raise the pressure of demand for labour in the country as a whole.

The evidence, then, is against labelling the long-term unemployed either as work-shy or as unemployable. What are the characteristics of this group? The main characteristic is simply that they have committed the industrially unforgivable sin of growing old. The vast bulk of them are in the age group 50 to 65. This is part of the general ethos of our Society, of course; given half a chance, it will junk everyone over the age of 50, since it is a Society which despises age. Those made redundant at the age of 50, it must be remembered, have still nearly a third of a normal working life to go. It is true that one will find other characteristics among the long-term unemployed as well; if one compares them with the average of employed persons, one will find among them a higher proportion of the unskilled and of persons with some physical or mental disability. But the dominant characteristic is just simply age.

At rates of unemployment higher than $2\frac{1}{2}$ per cent this picture becomes more qualified. Long-term unemployment then begins to become significant in some regions among teenagers just entering the labour force. This has been noticeable in Northern Ireland, for example, through most of the post-war period.

Long-term unemployment, then, consisting as it does neither of the work-shy nor of the unemployable, can be removed by raising the demand for labour. Further, it is hard to see how it can be removed in any other way. Without a higher pressure of demand for labour, special training facilities for some of the long-term unemployed will only serve to get jobs for them at the expense of others. Programmes of this kind can only operate successfully to reduce the total in an economy with a high demand for labour; otherwise such programmes merely serve to shift the unemployment around. All the studies of long-term unemployment emphasise this point.

The final question, therefore, is to ask how big the social benefit would be to those concerned if the number of long-term unemployed was reduced. To put it another way, what is the social cost of 150,000 long-term unemployed? The term 'social cost' is here, as in many other contexts, a euphemism for 'misery'. I think most people who have read the descriptive studies of the life-style of these men would agree that the social cost is high. To quote just one study – that of Mrs Wedderburn on redundant railwaymen:

'The workshop men were not used to being called upon to express their feelings, but it was impossible to speak to them about their experiences without being disturbed by remarks heard over and over again in the first interview, such as: "The whole world has changed; you have a feeling of abandonment – loneliness – you feel isolated."

"Everyone was downhearted and miserable." "You feel ashamed and all that . . . it was a sorry decision."

Some of the men interviewed said their health had not been so good since being made redundant and some had died. Although "there was no evidence that their deaths had been caused by the redundancy", widows commented with great bitterness: "He was never the same, it was the closure that killed him." [18]

Studies of miners declared redundant in the Netherlands have come to the same kind of conclusion, showing a high incidence among them of broken marriages and alcoholism, for example. So one could go on. The classic studies of the effects of long-term unemployment are, of course, those of the 1930s. There is no reason to alter the conclusions then reached about its effects on morale.

The direct social cost, therefore, of the shift in the unemployment target from $1\frac{1}{2}$ to $2\frac{1}{2}$ per cent has been that in any one year around 100,000 people have been shifted into the category of the long-term unemployed; a shift which represents a quantum jump in the unhappiness of their lives and the lives of their families. This is a dissatisfaction of a different order from the dissatisfaction, say, which a consumer may feel because he has to postpone the purchase of a new car from one year to the next. It is major, not minor.

Here then we have a disadvantaged group of a fairly formidable size. They do not come much to public attention. There is no large-scale organisation to represent them; the trade unions represent the employed, not the unemployed. Many of them feel ashamed of their position; Society's normal assumption will be that if they cannot get a job after a year there must be something wrong with them. Some social problems catch the attention of politicians and the media, and others do not – in much the same way as some diseases catch the attention of medical research, and others do not.

OTHER SOCIAL COSTS

That is not the end of the story of the social costs of higher unemployment. There are indirect social costs as well.

The number of registered unemployed is not the measure of all those who would like jobs. There is a fairly large army of people who join the labour force when unemployment falls, and leave it when unemployment rises, but who do not register as unemployed. At the present level of unemployment, there are probably at least another ½ million people who would like a job if a suitable one offered itself. Their dissatisfaction at not having a job is presumably not great, but they clearly prefer working to not working – otherwise they would not take a job when the pressure of demand is high and when, consequently, work is available near to where they live. So there is a gain in the satisfaction of their lives when they are at work. It is presumably a much smaller gain than the gain to the man who has been desperately seeking work for a year; none the less it has to be counted.

A second, and important, category of social costs of higher unemployment arises because unemployment is not an isolated social phenomenon. It tends to have other social concomitants. This is really not surprising; unemployment is an intensely frustrating experience and one might well expect this to appear in actions which are labelled anti-social. A recent study in Liverpool looked at indicators of social malaise for the 40 wards of the city, and looked at the correlations between them. Correlations do not imply causation, of course, but they can indicate useful hypotheses. It is interesting that the highest single correlation found in the study – a correlation of 0·9 – was between unemployment and the crime of assault. It is more plausible to believe that unemployment leads to violence, rather than that violence leads to unemployment. (This matches other evidence – such as the evidence which shows that the incidence of baby-battering is higher in high-unemployment than in low-unemployment regions.) There is a high correlation between unemployment and debt, of course; also a high correlation (0·8) with the crimes of burglary and theft. The authors attempted by various techniques to isolate the 'core' problems, and comment:

'The close inter-linkings within each group point to the ineffectiveness of treating individual social problems in isolation. Certain types of malaise, for example unemployment . . . appear to occupy crucial positions in the problem network and remedial action in any sphere may well be forced to pay particular attention to these problems if any lasting benefits are to ensue.'[19]

To take another example, one may legitimately suspect in Northern Ireland that the recruitment of young men into the Provisional I.R.A.

was helped by the fact that there were large numbers who had nothing else to do but to stand on street corners. Policymakers have to be prepared to accept evidence which is less than conclusive; otherwise they would never be able to make up their minds at all. I think the evidence is strong enough for the policymaker reasonably to infer that at any one time a Society with a higher level of unemployment will have more violence, more crimes of theft and burglary, and more children in care than a Society with a lower level. These costs, incidentally, are not just psychic costs – though psychic costs are the important ones here; they are substantial real resource costs as well.

CONCLUSION

The conclusion from this brief for an imaginary Chancellor is as follows. The economic benefits from the general shift in the target rate of unemployment are not demonstrable; it is doubtful whether there were any. In retrospect this is perhaps not surprising. The belief in a beneficial effect from a small change in demand pressure, as measured by unemployment, appears to be an Anglo-Saxon idiosyncrasy; the more robust continental policymakers certainly do not share it. Table 14.1 shows the unemployment target set in successive plans or policy statements in certain other countries. No other country has made a significant upward shift in its unemployment target. Belgium moved its target up slightly, and then brought it down again.

While the economic benefits from the upward shift are highly uncertain, the social costs are clear enough. Some 100,000 people have been added to the numbers of the long-term unemployed – defining them as those unemployed for over a year; these persons are neither work-shy nor unemployable, but are mainly men aged over 50 and persons with some disability. (Having a job is far more important for many disabled people than it is for the ordinary able-bodied person; the disabled person is under a much stronger continuous temptation to feel himself or herself useless.) In addition, there are probably a further $\frac{1}{2}$ million people who would like jobs but do not have them. Further, there is reasonable evidence that unemployment brings in its train other social costs, psychic and monetary, in violence and other crime.

The recommendation to the policymaker must surely be that the

Table 14.1. *Unemployment targets[a] in successive plans or policy statements in various countries*

	Years covered by plan	Unemployment target (%)
Belgium	1962–5	1·0
	1966–70	1·5
	1971–5	1·3
France	1965–70	1·7
	1971–5	1·4
Italy	1965–9	2·9
	1970–5	3·0
Netherlands	1966–70	1·1[b]
	1968–73	1·0
United States	1963–5	4·0[c]
	1970–5	3·8
West Germany	1968–73	0·8
	1971–6	1·0

Source: E. S. Kirschen and Associates, *Economic Policies Compared: West and East*, North-Holland, 1974.

[a] All figures on national definitions. On a United States basis the United Kingdom figure of 2·5 per cent becomes 3·7–3·8 per cent.
[b] The central figure of three given in this plan.
[c] Given in the Economic Report to the President for 1963.

shift in the unemployment target from 1½ per cent to 2½ per cent was a mistake; the promised economic benefits were not delivered and the social costs were substantial. Consequently it would be better to go back to the original figure.

I would like finally to raise two points. First, how is it that an economic establishment consensus has emerged for the higher unemployment figure? Indeed a number of people seem now to wish to push the target figure up even further. It was remarkable how quickly the cry of 'overheating' was raised at the end of 1973, without any allowance being made for the effect – on either the market for goods or the market for labour – of a sharp rise in output after a long period of slack. Without waiting for any adjustment, it was immediately concluded that the level of unemployment was too low. One reason for the support of the higher target figure, I think, is that the doctrine of the desirability of a 'margin of spare capacity' had been so thoroughly absorbed that it is still retained after the evidence for any beneficial effects from the existence of such a margin has disappeared. A second reason is that to many commentators unemployment is just a number – a quantity which can be used for manipulating the economy. The net economic benefit from a higher rate of unemployment may be uncertain – but it may be there – so why not accept a higher unemployment figure, just in case? The concept of social cost is not normally employed in this context. A middle-class economist may indeed find it difficult to make the imaginative leap which is needed to assess that cost; to appreciate how empty life can become for an unskilled worker made redundant at the age of 50.

There is a risk that politicians will discover that they can run the country with 1 million unemployed without committing electoral suicide – since the employed are not particularly concerned with the fate of the unemployed, in much the same way as the developed countries of the world are not particularly concerned with the fate of the developing countries. The essential case against a high-unemployment policy is not that it would be economically or politically catastrophic; it is that it would inflict substantial misery on an already under-privileged minority in exchange for wholly uncertain benefits – of a minor nature if they exist at all – for the majority.

To some extent the choice between a higher unemployment target and a lower unemployment target is representative of a wider choice between different types of Society. The high-unemployment Society discards those who are relatively inefficient in the production of goods; those over 50 may well be slower to adapt to new processes, and the disabled will be less than fully efficient – so neither should be allowed to detract from the full efficiency of the economic machine.

The low-unemployment target Society is concerned less with output and more with the sum total of human satisfactions. It recognises that it is a serious thing for Society to say to anyone that they are useless. It is prepared, if necessary, to pay some cost in loss of efficiency – though it is doubtful in fact whether any such cost is more than miniscule. It treats the reduction of long-term unemployment as an important economic objective in its own right.

NOTES

1 I am grateful to a number of colleagues at the National Institute for helpful comments. I have drawn extensively on material published in the section on 'Spare Capacity' in the *National Institute Economic Review*, November 1973, p. 23 *et seq.*

2 National Economic Development Council, *Growth of the United Kingdom Economy to 1966*, H.M.S.O., 1963.
3 See full references in notes 2, 5 and 6.
4 *Growth of the United Kingdom Economy to 1966*.
5 Department of Economic Affairs, *The National Plan*, Cmnd 2764, H.M.S.O., 1965.
6 Department of Economic Affairs, *The Task Ahead (Economic Assessment to 1972)*, H.M.S.O., 1969.
7 *National Institute Economic Review*, November 1973, p. 24, *et seq.*
8 See M. J. Hill, R. M. Harrison, A. V. Sargeant and V. Talbot, *Men Out of Work: A Study of Unemployment in Three English Towns*, Cambridge University Press, 1973, p. 83.
9 F. W. Paish and J. Hennessy, *Policy for Incomes?* (3rd ed.), Institute of Economic Affairs, 1967.
10 H. G. Johnson and A. R. Nobay (eds), *The Current Inflation*, Macmillan, 1971, p. 85.
11 F. T. Blackaby (ed.), *An Incomes Policy for Britain*, Heinemann, 1972.
12 *I.M.S. Monitor*, July 1973, p. 71 *et seq.*
13 Treasury, *The Determinants of U.K. Imports* by R. D. Rees and P. R. G. Layard, H.M.S.O., 1971. See *National Institute Economic Review*, November 1973, p. 31, for further references.
14 R. A. Cooper and K. Hartley, *Export Performance and the Pressure of Demand: A Study of Firms*, George Allen & Unwin, 1970, pp 35–41.
15 Bill Jordan, *Paupers: the Making of the New Claiming Class*, Routledge and Kegan Paul, 1973.
16 O.E.C.D., Directorate of Manpower and Social Affairs, *The Long-term Unemployed* by Adrian Sinfield, 1968; Hill, Harrison, Sargeant and Talbot, *Men Out of Work*.
17 Ibid., p. 104 *et seq.*
18 Quoted in O.E.C.D., *The Long-term Unemployed*, p. 52.
19 M. Flynn, P. Flynn and N. Mellor, 'Social Malaise Research: A Study in Liverpool', *Social Trends*, 1972.

Summary of the Discussion

G. D. N. WORSWICK

SESSION 1

The theme of the opening session was: 'What ought we to measure?'
What are the concepts which economic theorists consider significant?
We were interested especially in Keynes' concept of involuntary
unemployment which appears in Chapter 2 of *The General Theory of
Employment, Interest and Money*.[1] Lord Kahn gave clear answers to
all the questions, though many of them were unexpected. In the first
place the term 'involuntary' did not originate with Keynes. It is to
be found in Pigou's book, *Unemployment*, of 1914[2] and Dennis
Robertson used the term in 1915.[3] As for its use by Keynes, despite
his closeness to the author when the *General Theory* was being
written, Lord Kahn could not recollect any discussion of Chapter 2.
In 15 years as a college tutor he had never discussed involuntary unemployment with a pupil, nor in 30 years as an examiner had he seen
a question on it or an answer which referred to it. The 'involuntary'
fox seemed to be well and truly shot; the concept was being relegated
to a footnote in the history of economic thought. In the discussion
Lord Kahn indicated that he thought Keynes' concern was primarily
conceptual and not for measurement purposes. It was observed that
in the Keynesian definition the word aggregate appears twice, while
voluntary unemployment was a 'micro' concept. There was a question
about the intermediate case, in which a member of a trade union
voted in support of collective action, one consequence of which was
to bring about his own unemployment. Was that voluntary or involuntary unemployment?

The fivefold classification of unemployment into unemployables,
frictional, seasonal, structural and demand deficiency or cyclical
fared a little better in the discussion. On the face of it the conceptual

boxes were appealing, the more so that they indicated that different remedies might be required according to the box in which the unemployment was found. Unfortunately the breakdown of any total unemployment into these categories would depend on the level of unemployment itself. Before the second world war, for example, farmers laid-off workers in the winter, but after the war they would not do so because of the high level of demand, which meant that workers could easily obtain jobs in the towns. The conclusion appeared to be that, notwithstanding this difficulty, the attempt to divide unemployment into categories of this kind was not wholly futile.

Dr Fisher's paper included an account of the recently developing micro theory of job search, which he considered not as an alternative explanation of unemployment but as being complementary to Keynesian analysis. Some scepticism was expressed concerning the alleged advantages of specialisation in search which might lead a man deliberately to give up a job or to remain unemployed. On the one hand it was asked whether a potential employer, confronted by an unemployed salesman seeking a job, would not ask himself why the candidate had failed to sell himself so far. On the other hand, academic economists seemed to be able to move from one post to another without an intervening period of unemployment; some might even seem to be using the present job as a launching pad for the next one. It was true that if a man had lost his job the existence of earnings-related benefits, for example, might enable him to be more discriminating and to lengthen the average duration of unemployment. But it might still be asked whether such unemployment could be said to be voluntary.

In introducing his paper, Professor Hines said that his criticism was directed not at Fisher so much as at the Phelps volume on the micro-economics of unemployment.[4] Fisher, in reply, said that he did not think that the main issue was whether search was undertaken off the job or on the job, but rather, once a man was displaced for whatever reason, did it pay him to select a job immediately or to take his time? From this point of view, duration, age, skill, sex, race, industry and location were the factors to be looked at in the measurement of unemployment. Even so, said Professor Hines, Fisher's theory still required that there should be a positive relationship between the voluntary quit rate and the level of unemployment, as well as with duration, whereas his own empirical work found the relationship in both cases to be negative.

SESSION 2

What is it that we do measure? The paper describing how British unemployment statistics are collected and presented was written by Mr Roger Thatcher, C.B.E., Chief Statistician of the Department of Employment. In his introductory remarks he drew attention to a study of the characteristics of the unemployed which was due to be published in the *Department of Employment Gazette* on the following day and he outlined some of the main results. Members of the conference seized the opportunity to ply Mr Thatcher with questions of all sorts concerning the nature and significance of official unemployment statistics, which he answered with a patience and thoroughness which was much appreciated.

Much of the discussion centred round the question whether unemployment statistics changed their meaning after the introduction of earnings-related benefits and redundancy payments in the mid-1960s. Mr Thatcher pointed out that there were two dimensions to this question: one concerned the rates of flow on to and off the register within a given period; the second concerned the numbers on the register at any point of time and the time spent on the register (duration). As regards the use of unfilled vacancies as an alternative indicator of the pressure of demand for labour, Mr Thatcher thought that the Department's campaign to raise the degree of notification of vacancies had probably not so far had a strong effect upon the reliability of vacancies as an economic indicator, but he expected them to become less reliable in the future.

Mr Harris' paper discussed both the theory and the practice of the E.E.C. Statistical Office in the harmonisation of unemployment statistics in member countries. It was asked whether standardisation was necessary so long as one knew where the differences in methods of collection and measurement lay. Professor Elkan argued that this was especially important, since his experience of many developing countries had led him to appreciate how fortunate we were in Britain in having accurate statistics which were collected in the course of administration; it was important not to sacrifice this accuracy in the interests of international standardisation. Against this it was argued that the administrative process did not always throw up answers to all questions which one might wish to ask and that special surveys would still be needed. But it was also pointed out that there are real dangers in surveys in the international context, where there are differences in both institutions and language. Even where these differences are not present it had been found, in the United States studies for example, that quite small differences in the wording of survey questions could lead to apparently large differences in the answers. Even differences in the briefing of interviewers before putting the *same* question could lead to divergent answers. The question was also raised of the limitations of unemployment data obtained for particular geographical entities when there are large movements of migrant workers across frontiers. This might well affect any trade-off between different levels of 'unemployment' and other policy objectives. This point came up again in the discussion of Professor Wiles' paper, where it was remarked that unemployment in a country such as Yugoslavia would be very much affected by migration. It was suggested that the estimate for the figure for the Soviet Union, which Professor Wiles had worked out to be comparable in concept to that of countries such as Britain, might be unduly low because he had a rather low figure for the average duration of unemployment (20 days in the Soviet Union as compared with two months in the United States) and this arose because he had excluded from consideration certain classes of 'unemployed' who would be taken into account in the West. A considerable discussion arose on the question of whether, if a subsidy had to be paid to certain individuals, this was best done simply in the form of a cash benefit, or whether it would be preferable in the form of disguised simple employment, for example handing out keys in hotels.

SESSION 3

The relationship between unemployment and unfilled vacancies was the subject of two papers by Professor A. J. Brown (presented in absence) and Mr J. Bowers. Statistical work undertaken in the mid-1960s had suggested the possibility of a stable inverse relationship between U (unemployment) and V (vacancies). Such a stable relationship – should it be confirmed – offered a number of possibilities. It could be used to make estimates of 'frictional and structural' as distinct from 'cyclical' or 'demand deficiency' unemployment in a manner which might be especially fruitful in the context of regional differences. Unfortunately, what appeared initially to be a stable relationship prior to 1966, began to shift outwards. Professor Brown's paper made the suggestion that this phenomenon could be accounted for by a shift from internal to external hoarding of labour.

On the practical plane, the discussion turned once more to the significance of the official figures for notified vacancies. Were not many vacancies, for example, for women clerical workers, mainly dealt with through private employment agencies? How could one tell whether a vacancy should be classed as male or female? Will firms continue to notify vacancies even when they have been having no success in filling them? If figures for private agencies are added might there not be some double counting? On the theoretical plane it was pointed out that, in existing work, it is postulated that there is a stable *UV* relationship prior to 1966, which then shifts or changes. Ought not the reverse procedure to be tried, namely to ask what are the necessary and sufficient conditions for a stable *UV* relationship to exist at all. This approach might mean introducing additional explanatory variables, but it could nevertheless give a better insight into why changes have taken place. The general conclusion appeared to be that existing *UV* analysis is inadequate, but that the data recently made available should allow us to concentrate on flow models of the labour market, which it was thought might produce more enlightenment.

Mr Taylor expounded his ideas concerning labour hoarding and its measurement. He suggested that some of the rise in unemployment after 1966 could be accounted for by a shift from hoarding within firms to the unemployment register. This, it will be noted, was similar to the tentative conclusion of Professor Brown's paper. Among the methodological points raised were:

(i) The use of the Wharton method in determining peaks was essentially a judgement about the level of frictional unemployment, and the increase in this type of unemployment was virtually built into the model from the start.

(ii) In principle it should be possible to make estimates of labour hoarding by industries, but it was not certain that the sum of sectoral hoarding would add up to aggregate hoarding estimated from total output.

(iii) There was some uncertainty concerning the effect of variations in the hours of work upon the results.

The impression left by the discussion was that there was quite a lot of support for Mr Taylor's conclusions, but greater uncertainty concerning the methods he had used to reach them. Although taken in a separate session, Mr Leicester's paper belongs in this group, since it outlined an attempt to analyse job search by means of a model of flows on to and off the unemployment register. The discussion was largely concerned with the elaboration of various points in the model. Some doubts were expressed concerning the functional forms employed, especially that of the probability function, P. The results seem to suggest that in the last two years the probability of finding a job had increased, while successful search had fallen. Leicester replied that this was because of the sharp rise in vacancies, so that the unemployed had a large number of prospects to inspect in any given period. It was asked why it seemed to take so long to search for a job, and it was also pointed out that job-searchers are not always unemployed. It was asked whether the model was simply picking up the well-known statistical association between duration and the level of demand. In conclusion, the author said he himself was sceptical of his results, but he had been surprised that such a preliminary model had seemed so initially successful; this had encouraged him to develop it.

SESSION 4

The three papers in this session addressed themselves primarily to the social aspects of unemployment. All three papers were reporting the results of surveys involving unemployment as one of the variables, and inevitably much of the discussion was concerned with elucidation and points of detail. Two major themes emerged during the session. The first was the question of the existence of dual or multiple labour markets. For example, is there a primary sector of firms which have comprehensive promotion policies for all their employees, with a secondary sector of firms with an attitude of easy come – easy go towards their employees? Could firms be classed into more than two categories based on different attitudes towards some or all of their employees? The second theme was the insistence on the importance of the problem of long-term unemployment. Why does it exist, and what costs and hardships are involved? A point which occurred more than once was the need to associate with survey research of this kind some discussion of the possible policy alternatives designed to mitigate the various types of hardship found.

SESSION 5

The conference was completed by Sam Brittan, with a paper, 'Full Employment Policy: A Reappraisal', and Frank Blackaby, with a paper, 'The Target Rate of Unemployment'. These two papers brought the conference back to unemployment as an economic indicator and to the central questions of economic policy and management. Among the main points discussed were the contribution of trade unions to inflation; the potentialities of a social compact; the 'natural' rate of unemployment; the ability or otherwise to control the level of unemployment by demand management; the extent to which changes in unemployment, and more especially the gradual upward trend in recorded unemployment since the 1960s, was real or illusory; and the general range of considerations which go to determine the target rate of unemployment.

CONCLUDING REMARKS

One of the striking features of the conference, and especially the discussion in the last two sessions, was how strong is the flow of emotion released by the word unemployment even among professional economists. No doubt this was partly a question of generation, but it did not seem to be entirely so. To caricature the images conjured up before the mind's eye: at one extreme was the man so cushioned by tax rebates, redundancy payments and earnings-related benefits that his unemployment was no more than an extended holiday at the public expense; while at the other extreme we had the vision of a man whose spirit was being slowly crushed by his inability, in a world of increasing specialisation, to find any occupation which would exercise his talents, provide him with a living wage and enable him to retain his self-respect. In the circumstances one might have expected that the conference would attach importance to the distinction between voluntary and involuntary unemployment, and the light which research might throw on the question of measurement. It was puzzling to see the apparent calmness with which the conference accepted the argument that the distinction was unhelpful. At one point certainly it did seem that one speaker was accepting this because in any case he regarded all unemployment as involuntary, while the next speaker was equally happy because he regarded all unemployment as voluntary.

At the time of writing a number of economists are arguing for the need to run the economy for some years with a higher level of unemployment. There are plenty of people engaged in the debate about whether this would or would not be an effective way of slowing down the rise in prices – that is, whether there would be important economic benefits from this move. But what are the social costs? On this we are rather ill-informed. On one of the views on unemployment noted above, the social cost is not very high; on the other view, it is substantial and serious. Surely we should try to find out which is right, or whether the truth lies half-way between. We could do with more survey studies of the unemployed – both registered and unregistered. It is an area which was fairly thoroughly covered in the 1930s, but has been rather neglected since because it has been more or less assumed that the problem of unemployment had virtually disappeared.[5] Perhaps it is not quite appropriate any longer to phrase the question 'How much of unemployment is voluntary, and how much involuntary?' But the general idea behind the question is right; we should be much clearer than we are now about exactly what we are doing – what damage we are inflicting on the one hand and what satisfactions we are increasing on the other – when we adopt policies which lead to higher or lower levels of unemployment.

The reader will judge for himself the quality of the papers presented, but there are three tests which the conference passed with flying colours. Without exception those invited to write papers did so, they did so in time for them to be circulated before the conference and everyone who came to the conference stayed to the end.

NOTES

1 J. M. Keynes, *The General Theory of Employment, Interest and Money,* Macmillan, 1936.

2 A. C. Pigou, *Unemployment*, Williams and Norgate, 1914.
3 D. H. Robertson, *A Study of Industrial Fluctuation*, P. S. King, 1915.
4 E. S. Phelps (ed.), *Micro-economic Foundations of Employment and Inflation Theory*, Norton, 1970.
5 Survey information is becoming available for Great Britain in the small-scale General Household Surveys, and the results of the larger E.E.C. Labour Force Survey held in 1973 will be available in the future. Meanwhile the results of a survey based on interviews with a sample of nearly 1,500 unemployed workers has been published as W. W. Daniel, *A National Survey of the Unemployed*, Political and Economic Planning, 1974.

List of Works Cited

I. OFFICIAL PUBLICATIONS

(a) *United Kingdom*
Command Papers:
National Insurance Bill, Part II: Unemployment Explanatory Memorandum, Cd 5991, H.M.S.O., 1911.
Unemployment Memorandum, Certain Proposals Relating to, Cmd 3331, H.M.S.O., 1929.
Social Insurance and Allied Services, Cmd 6404, H.M.S.O., 1942.
Employment Policy, Cmd 6527, H.M.S.O., 1944.
The National Plan, Cmnd 2764, H.M.S.O., 1965.
Unemployment Statistics: Report of an Inter-Departmental Working Party, Cmnd 5157, H.M.S.O., 1972.
Report of the Committee on the Abuse of Social Security Benefits, Cmnd 5228, H.M.S.O., 1973.
Central Statistical Office: *Duration of Unemployment on the Register of Wholly Unemployed* by R. F. Fowler, H.M.S.O., 1968.
Department of Economic Affairs: *The Task Ahead (Economic Assessment to 1972)*, H.M.S.O., 1969.
Department of Employment [and Productivity]:
Labour Costs in Great Britain in 1964, H.M.S.O., 1968.
British Labour Statistics: Historical Abstract, 1886–1968, H.M.S.O., 1971.
Effects of the Redundancy Payments Act: A Survey carried out in 1969 for the Department of Employment by S. R. Parker *et al.*, H.M.S.O., 1971.
People and Jobs: A Modern Employment Service, H.M.S.O., 1971.
Gazette (monthly) [formerly *Ministry of Labour Gazette*].
Greater London Council: *Annual Abstract of Greater London Statistics*.
Department of Health and Social Security:
Supplementary Benefits Handbook, H.M.S.O., 1971.
Two-Parent Families: A Study of their Resources and Needs in 1968, 1969 and 1970 by J. R. Howe, H.M.S.O., 1971.
House of Commons: *Hansard* (weekly).
National Economic Development Office [formerly Council]:
Growth of the United Kingdom Economy to 1966, H.M.S.O., 1963.
Labour Statistics: Report of a Conference held under the General Auspices of the Standing Committee of Statistics Users, N.E.D.O., 1973.

Office of Population Censuses and Surveys:
Census 1971. England and Wales. County Reports: Greater London.
H.M.S.O., 1973.
General Household Survey: Introductory Report, H.M.S.O., 1973.
Treasury:
Effects of the Selective Employment Tax: First Report on the Distributive Trades by W. B. Reddaway, H.M.S.O., 1970.
The Determinants of U.K. Imports by R. D. Rees and P. R. G. Layard, H.M.S.O., 1971.

(b) *United States*
Department of Labor: *Monthly Labor Review.*
President's Committee to Appraise Employment and Unemployment.
Statistics: *Measuring Employment and Unemployment,* U.S. Government Printing Office, 1962.

(c) *International*
Organization for Economic Co-operation and Development:
The Long-term Unemployed by Adrian Sinfield, O.E.C.D., 1968.
Economic Outlook (twice yearly).
United Nations, Economic and Social Council: *An Integrated System of Demographic, Manpower and Social Statistics,* United Nations, 1970.

II. BOOKS, ARTICLES AND OTHER SOURCES

Alchian, A. A. 'Information Costs, Pricing and Resource Unemployment' in Phelps (ed.), *Micro-economic Foundations of Employment and Inflation Theory,* q.v.
Barron, R. D. and Norris, G. M. 'Sexual Divisions and the Dual Labour Market' (paper presented to the British Sociological Association Conference, April 1974).
Becker, G. S. 'A Theory of the Allocation of Time', *Economic Journal,* September 1965.
Beveridge, W. H.:
'Employment Theory and the Facts of Unemployment' (unpublished, 1936).
'An Analysis of Unemployment', *Economica,* November 1936, February and May 1937.
Full Employment in a Free Society, George Allen & Unwin, 1944.
Blackaby, F. T. (ed.) *An Incomes Policy for Britain,* Heinemann, 1972.
Bluestone, B. 'The Tripartite Economy: Labor Markets and the Working Poor', *Poverty and Human Resources Abstracts,* July/August 1970.
Bosanquet, N. *Race and Employment in Britain,* Runnymede Trust, 1973.
Bosanquet, N. and Doeringer, P. 'Is There a Dual Labour Market in Great Britain?', *Economic Journal,* June 1973.
Bosanquet, N. and Standing, G. 'Government and Unemployment, 1966-

1970: A Study of Policy and Evidence', *British Journal of Industrial Relations*, July 1972.

Bowers, J. K., Cheshire, P. C. and Webb, A. E. 'The Change in the Relationship between Unemployment and Earnings Increases: A Review of Some Possible Explanations, *National Institute Economic Review*, No. 54, November 1970.

Bowers, J. K., Cheshire, P. C., Webb, A. E. and Weeden, R. 'Some Aspects of Unemployment and the Labour Market, 1966–71', *National Institute Economic Review*, No. 62, November 1972.

Bowers, J. K. and Harkess, D. 'Duration of Unemployment by Age', University of Leeds Discussion Paper, 1974.

Brechling, F. P. R. 'The Relationship between Output and Employment in British Manufacturing Industries', *Review of Economic Studies*, July 1965.

Brittan, S. *Capitalism and the Permissive Society*, Macmillan, 1973.

Brown, A. J.:
'Inflation and the British Economy', *Economic Journal*, September 1958.
The Framework of Regional Economics in the United Kingdom, Cambridge University Press, 1972.

Cairncross, Sir Alec. 'Incomes Policy: Retrospect and Prospect', *The Three Banks Review*, December 1973.

Carter, Michael. *Into Work*, Penguin, 1966.

Castles, S. and Kosack, G. *Immigrant Workers and Class Structure in Western Europe*, Oxford University Press, 1973.

Cheshire, P. C. 'Regional Unemployment Differences in Great Britain' in N.I.E.S.R. *Regional Papers II*, Cambridge University Press, 1973.

Chiplin, B. and Sloane, P. J. 'Real and Money Wages Revisited', *Applied Economics*, December 1973.

Coase, R. H. 'The Nature of the Firm', *Economica*, November 1937.

Cooper, R. A. and Hartley, K. *Export Performance and the Pressure of Demand: A Study of Firms*, George Allen & Unwin, 1970.

Corry, B. A. and Laidler, D. E. W. 'The Phillips Relation: A Theoretical Explanation', *Economica*, May 1967.

Cox, D. R. *Analysis of Binary Data*, Methuen, 1970.

Cripps, F. and Tarling, R. 'An Analysis of the Duration of Male Unemployment in Great Britain, 1932–73', *Economic Journal*, June 1974.

Daniel, W. W. *A National Survey of the Unemployed*, Political and Economic Planning, 1974.

Doeringer, P. B. *Program to Employ the Disadvantaged*, Prentice-Hall, 1969.

Doeringer, P. B. and Piore, M. *Internal Labor Markets and Manpower Analysis*, D. C. Heath, 1971.

Donnison, D. and Eversley, D. (eds) *London: Urban Patterns, Problems and Policies*, Heinemann, 1973.

Dow, J. C. R. and Dicks-Mireaux, L. A. 'The Excess Demand for Labour: A Study of Conditions in Great Britain, 1946–56', *Oxford Economic Papers*, February 1958.

Eagly, R. V. 'Market Power as an Intervening Mechanism in Phillips Curve Analysis', *Economica*, February 1965.

Eversley, D. 'Problems of Social Planning in Inner London' in Donnison and Eversley (eds), *London: Urban Patterns, Problems and Policies*, q.v.

Feldstein, M. 'The Economics of the New Unemployment', *The Public Interest*, Fall 1973.

Ferman, L. A. 'The Irregular Economy: Informal Work Patterns in the Ghetto' (mimeographed, 1967).

Field, Frank. *Unemployment: the Facts*, Child Poverty Action Group, 1975.

Fisher, M. R. *The Economic Analysis of Labour*, Weidenfeld and Nicolson, 1971.

Flynn, M., Flynn, P. and Mellor, N. 'Social Malaise Research: A Study in Liverpool', *Social Trends*, 1972.

Foster, C. and Richardson, R. 'Employment Trends in London in the 1960s and their Relevance to the Future' in Donnison and Eversley (eds), *London: Urban Patterns, Problems and Policies*, q.v.

Friedman, M.:
'The Role of Monetary Policy', *American Economic Review*, March 1968.
The Optimum Quantity of Money and Other Essays, Macmillan, 1969.

Giddens, Anthony. *The Class Structure of the Advanced Societies*, Hutchinson, 1973.

Goldthorpe, John. 'Political Consensus, Social Inequality and Pay Policy', *New Society*, 10th January 1974.

Gordon, D. M. *Theories of Poverty and Underemployment: Orthodox, Radical and Dual Labor Market Perspectives*, D. C. Heath, 1972.

Gordon, R. J. 'The Welfare Cost of Higher Unemployment', *Brookings Papers on Economic Activity*, no. 1, 1973.

Gujarati, D. 'The Behaviour of Unemployment and Unfilled Vacancies: Great Britain, 1958–1971', *Economic Journal*, March 1972.

Hall, R. E. 'Why is the Unemployment Rate so High at Full Employment? *Brookings Papers on Economic Activity*, no. 3, 1970.

Hancock, K. 'Unemployment and Economists in the 1920s', *Economica*, November 1960.

Harris, S. E. (ed.) *The New Economics: Keynes' Influence on Theory and Public Policy*, Knopf, 1947.

Hicks, J. R. *The Theory of Wages* (1st ed.), Macmillan, 1932.

Hill, M. J. 'Unstable Employment in the Histories of Unemployed Men', *I.M.S. Monitor*, December 1974.

Hill, M. J., Harrison, R. M., Sargeant, A. V. and Talbot, V. *Men Out of Work: A Study of Unemployment in Three English Towns*, Cambridge University Press, 1973.

Hines, A. G.:
'The Determinants of the Rate of Change of Money Wage Rates and the Effectiveness of Incomes Policy' in Johnson and Nobay (eds), *The Current Inflation*, q.v.

The Reappraisal of Keynesian Economics, Martin Robertson, 1971.
'The Phillips Curve and the Distribution of Unemployment', *American Economic Review*, March 1972.

Hines, A. G. and Muellbauer, J. 'Wage Inflation and the Sectoral Distribution of Unemployment', Birkbeck Discussion Paper, 1974.

Holt, C. C. 'How Can the Phillips Curve be Moved to Reduce both Inflation and Unemployment?' in Phelps (ed.), *Micro-economic Foundations of Employment and Inflation Theory*, q.v.

Holt, C. C. and David, M. H. 'The Concept of Job Vacancies in a Dynamic Theory of the Labor Market' in National Bureau of Economic Research, *The Measurement and Interpretion of Job Vacancies*, q.v.

House, J. W. and Knight, E. M. *Pit Closure and the Community: Report to the Ministry of Labour*, University of Newcastle, 1967.

Hutt, W. H. *Theory of Idle Resources*, Jonathan Cape, 1939.

Hyman, Richard. *Strikes*, Fontana, 1972.

Industrial Society [formerly Industrial Welfare Society]:
The £.s.d. of Welfare in Industry, 1958.
Costs of Personnel Services and Administration (irregular).

Institute of Manpower Studies. *I.M.S. Monitor* (quarterly).

Johnson, H. G. 'Major Issues in Monetary and Fiscal Policies', *Federal Reserve Bulletin*, November 1964.

Johnson, H. G. and Nobay, A. R. (eds) *The Current Inflation*, Macmillan, 1971.

Jordan, Bill. *Paupers: the Making of the New Claiming Class*, Routledge and Kegan Paul, 1973.

Kaitz, Hyman:
'The Duration of Unemployment', *Proceedings of the American Statistical Association*, 1972.
'Unemployment Issues – Unemployment Flows' (unpublished, 1974).

Kapp, K. W. *Social Costs of Business Enterprise*, Asia Publishing House, 1963.

Kerr, Clark.:
'Labor Markets: Their Character and Consequences', *American Economic Association Papers and Proceedings*, May 1950.
'The Balkanization of Labor Markets' in Massachusetts Institute of Technology, *Labor Mobility and Economic Opportunity*, q.v.

Keynes, J. M.:
A Treatise on Money, Macmillan, 1930 (reprinted as Volumes V and VI of Royal Economic Society edition, q.v.).
Essays in Persuasion, Macmillan, 1931 (reprinted as Volume IX of Royal Economic Society edition, q.v.).
The General Theory of Employment, Interest and Money, Macmillan, 1936 (reprinted as Volume VII of Royal Economic Society edition, q.v.).
'How to Avoid a Slump', *The Times*, 12th, 13th and 14th January 1937.
'The General Theory of Employment', *Quarterly Journal of Economics,*

February 1937 (reprinted in Volume XIV of Royal Economic Society edition, q.v.).

Chairman's address to the National Mutual Life Assurance Society, 24th February 1937.

'Borrowing for Defence', *The Times*, 11th March 1937.

'Relative Movements of Real Wages and Output', *Economic Journal*, March 1939 (reprinted as Appendix 3 to Volume VII of Royal Economic Society edition, q.v.).

'Crisis Finance', *The Times*, 17th and 18th April 1939.

'Will Rearmament Cure Unemployment?', *The Listener*, 1st June 1939.

'Borrowing by the State', *The Times*, 24th and 25th July 1939.

Kirschen, E. S. and Associates. *Economic Policies Compared: West and East*, North-Holland, 1974.

Klein, L. R. 'Some Theoretical Issues in the Measurement of Capacity', *Econometrica*, April 1960.

Klein, L. R. and Summers, R. *The Wharton Index of Capacity Utilization*, University of Pennsylvania, 1966.

Knight, E. M. *Men Leaving Mining, West Cumberland 1966–67: Report to the Ministry of Labour*, University of Newcastle, 1968.

Laidler, D. E. W.:

'A Monetarist Model', University of Manchester Discussion Paper, 1972.

'Simultaneous Fluctuations in Prices and Output', University of Manchester Discussion Paper, 1972.

Leicester, C. 'Vacancies and the Demand for Labour', *I.M.S. Monitor*, October 1973.

Lekachman, R. (ed.) *Keynes' General Theory*, Macmillan, 1964.

Liebow, Elliot. 'No Man Can Live with the Terrible Knowledge that He is Not Needed', *New York Times Magazine*, 5th April 1970.

Lipsey, R. G.:

'The Relation between Unemployment and the Rate of Change of Money Wage Rates in the United Kingdom, 1862–1957: A Further Analysis', *Economica*, February 1960.

'Structural and Deficient-Demand Unemployment Reconsidered' in Ross (ed.), *Employment Policy in the Labor Market*, q.v.

Lipsey, R. G. and Parkin, J. M. 'Incomes Policy: A Re-Appraisal', *Economica*, May 1970.

Lockwood, David. *The Blackcoated Worker*, George Allen & Unwin, 1958.

Lucas, R. E. 'Some International Evidence on Output–Inflation Tradeoffs', *American Economic Review*, June 1973.

McCall, J. J. 'Economics of Information and Job Search', *Quarterly Journal of Economics*, February 1970.

MacKay, D. I. and Reid, G. L. 'Redundancy, Unemployment and Manpower Policy', *Economic Journal*, December 1972.

McKendrick, A. S. 'An Inter-industry Analysis of Labour Hoarding in Britain, 1953–72' *Applied Economics*, June 1975

Marsden, Dennis and Duff, Evan. *Workless*, Penguin, 1975.

Martin, R. and Fryer, R. H. *Redundancy and Paternalist Capitalism*, George Allen & Unwin, 1973.

Massachusetts Institute of Technology. *Labor Mobility and Economic Opportunity*, Chapman and Hall, 1954.

Matthews, R. C. O. 'Why has Britain had Full Employment since the War?', *Economic Journal*, September 1968.

Mortensen, D. T. 'A Theory of Wage and Employment Dynamics' in Phelps (ed.), *Micro-economic Foundations of Employment and Inflation Theory*, q.v.

National Bureau of Economic Research. *The Measurement and Interpretation of Job Vacancies*, Columbia University Press, 1966.

National Institute of Economic and Social Research. *National Institute Economic Review* (quarterly).

O'Cleireacain, C. 'Labour Market Trends in London and the Rest of the South-East', *Urban Studies*, October 1974.

Oi, W. Y. 'Labor as a Quasi-fixed Factor', *Journal of Political Economy*, December 1962.

Okun, A. M. 'Potential GNP: Its Measurement and Significance', *Proceedings of the American Statistical Association (Business and Economic Statistics Section)*, 1962.

Paish, F. W. and Hennessy, J. *Policy for Incomes?* (3rd ed.), Institute of Economic Affairs, 1967.

Patinkin, D. *Money, Interest and Prices: An Integration of Monetary and Value Theory* (2nd ed.), Harper and Row, 1965.

Perlman, R. *Labor Theory*, Wiley, 1969.

Phelps, E. S.:
  'Phillips Curves, Expectations of Inflation and Optimal Unemployment over Time', *Economica*, August 1967.
  (ed.) *Micro-economic Foundations of Employment and Inflation Theory*, Norton, 1970.
  'Money Wage Dynamics and Labor Market Equilibrium' in Phelps (ed.), *Micro-economic Foundations of Employment and Inflation Theory*, q.v.
  'Economic Policy and Unemployment in the 1960s', *The Public Interest*, Winter 1974.

Phillips, D. 'Young and Unemployed in a Northern City' in Weir (ed.), *Men and Work in Modern Britain*, q.v.

Pigou, A. C.:
  Unemployment, Williams and Norgate, 1914.
  The Theory of Unemployment, Macmillan, 1933.
  'Mr J. M. Keynes' General Theory of Employment, Interest and Money', *Economica*, May 1936.

Rawls, John. *A Theory of Justice*, Oxford University Press, 1972.

Reddaway, W. B. *Effects of the Selective Employment Tax. Final Report*, Cambridge University Press, 1973.

Reder, M.:
'The Theory of Occupational Wage Differentials', *American Economic Review*, December 1955.
'The Theory of Frictional Unemployment', *Economica*, February 1969.
Rees, A.:
'Information Networks in Labor Markets', *American Economic Review*, May 1966.
'The Phillips Curve as a Menu for Policy Choice', *Economica*, August 1970.
Robertson, D. H. *A Study of Industrial Fluctuation*, P. S. King, 1915 (reprinted 1948).
Robinson, Joan.:
Essays in the Theory of Employment (2nd ed.), Macmillan, 1947.
Collected Economic Papers, Basil Blackwell, 1973.
Ross, A. M. (ed.) *Employment Policy in the Labor Market*, University of California Press, 1965.
Royal Economic Society. *Collected Writings of John Maynard Keynes*, Macmillan, 1971– .
Sinfield, Adrian.:
'Shortcomings in the Functioning of the Labour Market' (paper presented to an O.E.C.D. Regional Seminar on Youth Unemployment, 1970).
'Poor and Out of Work in Shields: A Summary Report' in Townsend (ed.), *The Concept of Poverty*, q.v.
'Industrial Welfare in the United Kingdom' (report to the United Nations, Department of Economic and Social Affairs, 1970).
'Unemployment Compensation and Employment Security' (paper presented to a Fabian Society Seminar, 1972).
Sonquist, J. A. and Morgan, J. N. *The Detection of Interaction Effects*, University of Michigan Press, 1964.
Sorrentino, Constance. 'Unemployment in the United States and Seven Foreign Countries', *Monthly Labor Review*, September 1970.
Stein, H. *The Fiscal Revolution in America*, University of Chicago Press, 1969.
Stevenson, Olive. *Claimant or Client? A Social Worker's View of the Supplementary Benefits Commission*, George Allen & Unwin, 1973.
Stigler, G. J. 'The Economics of Information', *Journal of Political Economy*, June 1961.
Taylor, J.:
'The Behaviour of Unemployment and Unfilled Vacancies: Great Britain, 1958–71. An Alternative View', *Economic Journal*, December 1972.
Unemployment and Wage Inflation, with Special Reference to Britain and the USA, Longman, 1974.
Taylor, J., Winter, D. and Pearce, D. 'A 19 Industry Quarterly Series of

Capacity Utilisation in the United Kingdom, 1948–1968', *Bulletin of the Oxford University Institute of Economics and Statistics*, May 1970.

Thirlwall, A. P. 'Types of Unemployment, with Special Reference to "Non-Demand-Deficient" Unemployment in the UK', *Scottish Journal of Political Economy*, February 1969.

Thomas, B. M. 'Redundancy among Aircraft Workers: the Fragmentation, of a Work Community' (report to the Social Science Research Council, 1972).

Thompson, E. P. and Yeo, Eileen. *The Unknown Mayhew*, Merlin Press, 1971.

Thurow, L. C. Reply to R. A. Posner, 'Economic Justice and the Economist', in *The Public Interest*, Fall 1973.

Titmuss, R. M. *Commitment to Welfare*, George Allen & Unwin, 1968.

Tobin, J.:
  'Money Wage Rates and Unemployment' in Harris (ed.) *The New Economics*, q.v.
  'Inflation and Unemployment', *American Economic Review*, March 1972.

Townsend, P.:
  (ed.) *The Concept of Poverty*, Heinemann, 1970.
  'The Older Worker in the United Kingdom' in *Elderly People Living in Europe*, International Centre of Social Gerontology, 1972.

Townsend, P. and Bosanquet, N. (eds) *Labour and Inequality*, Fabian Society, 1972.

Triffin, R. *Monopolistic Competition and General Equilibrium Theory*, Harvard University Press, 1940.

Viner, Jacob. 'Mr Keynes on the Causes of Unemployment', *Quarterly Journal of Economics*, November 1936 (reprinted in Lekachman (ed.), *Keynes' General Theory*, q.v.)

Webb, A. R. 'Unemployment, Vacancies and the Rate of Change of Earnings: A Regional Analysis' in N.I.E.S.R. *Regional Papers III*, Cambridge University Press, 1974.

Wedderburn, Dorothy.:
  White Collar Redundancy: A Case Study, Cambridge University Press, 1964.
  Redundancy and the Railwaymen, Cambridge University Press, 1965.
  'Inequality at Work' in Townsend and Bosanquet (eds), *Labour and Inequality*, q.v.
  'Working and Not Working' in Weir (ed.), *Men and Work in Modern Britain*, q.v.

Weeden, R. 'Duration of Unemployment and Labour Turnover' (mimeographed, 1974).

Weir, David (ed.). *Men and Work in Modern Britain*, Fontana, 1973.

Wiles, P. J. 'Note on Soviet Unemployment by US Definitions', *Soviet Studies*, April 1972.

Wood, J. B. *How Much Unemployment?*, Institute of Economic Affairs, 1972.

Index

Alchian, A. A. 43, 47, 49, 77
asset stockpiling 287, 289–90, 291

balance of payments 287, 289–90, 291
Becker, G. S. 38
Beveridge, W. H. 25, 30, 228; curve 68, 77
boom 43–4, 164
Bosanquet, N. 222
Bowers, J. K. 254, 257
Briefs, G. A. 227
bureaucracies 73
business cycle, see trade cycle

Cairncross, Sir Alec 268
capacity utilisation 292
capital stock adjustment 50–1
capitalist economies 55
Censuses of Population 15, 88–9, 140, 158; and the unemployment register 204–5
Cheshire, P. C. 138, 139, 140, 141–2, 210, 211, 255
Coase, R. H. 73
communication networks 73–4
contingency planning 44
Coventry 168–84 passim
Cox, D. R. 196
Cripps, F. 190
cyclical unemployment 22, 25

Daniel, W. W. 233
David, M. H. 194
decision making 35, 36–7, 60
declining industries 223
deficient-demand unemployment 25, 29, 68, 70, 71, 76, 139, 258, 259; and registered unemployment 146, 147, 150, 155, 158–9, 163
demand for labour 40, 114–18; and market imperfections 134–45; and a Phillips curve 60–65; increase in 151–2; fall in 41–3, 152; zero excess 61–3; see also Phillips curve
demand management 77, 261, 263, 269–72, 275–6, 279–80, 284
demand shift 116
depressed areas 223

Depression, the 27–31, 56
Dicks-Mireaux, L. A. 140, 142
disabled workers 223, 230, 297, 301
dismissal 42, 48
Dow, J. C. R. 140, 142
Dunlop, J, G. 32

E.E.C. 95–106
E.E.C. Labour Force Survey 88–9, 104, 105–6
Eagly, R. V. 75
earnings 206; trade off between unemployment and 285
earnings related benefit 112, 172–3, 209, 237, 254, 285
economic policy 279–80; and social structure 241–2; and the unemployment gap 165; implications 76–7
economy: overheating of 271; structural shifts in 118, 123–6, 148, 257
employer search 45–50
employer-worker behaviour model 150–53
employment exchanges 119–20, 209, 284
Eversley, D. 213
expectations 66–7, 287–8

Feldstein, M. 254–5
females 89, 90, 157–8, 235, 239; registered as unemployed 205; UV curve for 129
firm, the, 35, 60; and changes in product demand 48–50; investment by 290–92; search by 45–50
fiscal policy 52–3, 55, 56, 69, 253, 259, 266
Fisher Committee (1973) 255–6
Fisher, M. R. 38
Forbes, A. 190
Foster, C. 213
Fowler, R. F. 91, 190
frictional unemployment 22, 26, 68, 70, 76, 138, 146, 158; and registered unemployment 146, 148, 158, 163–5; upward trend in 159–64, 257
Friedman, M. 54–5, 67, 208, 259, 260, 261

vacancies 49, 109–45, 186–7, 200–202;
actual and predicted changes in
121; duration of 144; rate of 64;
recording of 111, 119–23, 130n,
140–1, 284, 309; simultaneous
existence with unemployment 61–5,
229, 254; trend in rates of 121;
see also UV relationship
Viner, J. 25
voluntary unemployment 14, 22, 23–4,
26, 112, 146; distinguished from
involuntary 26–7, 31, 83, 168–84,
207–8, 258, 311–12; semi-voluntary
254–5
voluntary leaving, *see* quitting

wage rates 40–1, 48; bargaining 267,
288; cuts in 41, 42, 64, 70–1;

wage rates – *cont.*
rigidity of 49; higher 49–50; *see
also* money wages *and* real wages
wage-stop 169, 183, 271–2
wealth 216
Wedderburn, D. 226, 232, 298–9
Weeden, R. 190
welfare 279, 294; costs 69
white collar workers 223, 230, 260
Wilson, Sir Horace 24
withdrawal from labour market 23
Wood, J. 256
work experience 38, 46
work-shy the 182, 243, 275, 295, 296–8
workers' search 37–45

young workers 174, 175, 211, 215, 223,
225, 235, 239, 240